Social Movements in Times of Austerity

Social Movements in Times of Austerity

Bringing Capitalism Back into Protest Analysis

Donatella della Porta

polity

The right of Donatella della Porta to be identified as Author of this Work has been asserted in accordance with the UK Copyright, Designs and Patents Act 1988.

First published in 2015 by Polity Press

Polity Press
65 Bridge Street
Cambridge CB2 1UR, UK

Polity Press
350 Main Street
Malden, MA 02148, USA

ISBN-13: 978-0-7456-8858-9 (hardback)
ISBN-13: 978-0-7456-8859-6 (paperback)

A catalogue record for this book is available from the British Library.

Library of Congress Cataloging-in-Publication Data

Della Porta, Donatella, 1956-
  Social movements in times of austerity : bringing capitalism back into protest analysis / Donatella della Porta.
     pages cm
  Includes bibliographical references and index.
  ISBN 978-0-7456-8858-9 (hardback : alk. paper) – ISBN 978-0-7456-8859-6 (pbk. : alk. paper) 1. Social movements. 2. Protest movements. 3. Democratization. I. Title.
  HM881.D45 2015
  303.48′4–dc23
                       2014043760

Typeset in 10 on 12 pt Sabon
by Toppan Best-set Premedia Limited
Printed and bound in the UK by Clays Ltd, St Ives PLC

For further information on Polity, visit our website: politybooks.com

Contents

Acknowledgements

This book, as many, started with some questions: How does it come about that, while capitalist transformations so clearly nowadays effect massive waves of protests, little reflection in social movement studies is devoted to the social basis for contentious politics? Why, with few exceptions, have issues of class lost relevance in research on social movements? Why is literature on political cleavage more and more focused on elections, and detached from protest?

Looking for (first) answers to those questions, I could fortunately rely on some collective resources. In the stimulating environment of the Centre on Social Movement Studies (Cosmos) at the European University Institute, a growing interest developed, especially among young scholars, for a revisitation of Marxism and post-Marxism. The impression was that some of what I had read and discussed in the 1970s in order to understand the development of capitalism had become again fashionable in the 2010s, even if filtered through much new knowledge and new ways of thinking.

Also, during the last few years, I had collected some empirical data on anti-austerity protests (and protests in times of austerity), which I found useful when addressing my questions. These came from my research project on Mobilizing for Democracy, funded through an Advanced Scholar Grant from the European Research Council; the comparative analysis of anti-corruption sponsored by the European Commission, a research project on 'subterranean politics', coordinated by Mary Kaldor; and the collaborative project 'Caught in the Act of Protest: Contextualizing Contestation' – based on surveys at demonstrations and coordinated by Bert Klandermans and Stefaan Walgrave with funds from ESF and the Research Council of the European University Institute. For their collaboration in these research projects, I thank especially Massimiliano Andretta, Lorenzo Bosi, Lorenzo Mosca, Herbert Reiter and Louisa Parks.

I had the chance to reflect on this empirical evidence while preparing some keynote speeches between 2012 and 2014. As the University of Bergen invited me to give the Stein Rokkan Memorial Lecture, I took the chance to revisit the most Rokkanian concept – cleavage – mapping the introduction to this volume. When preparing the Södertörn Lecture, I looked then at theories and data on the social bases of recent protest, which became the basis for the second chapter. On the cultural dimension of social conflicts – the topic of Chapter 3 – I worked in preparation for a keynote speech at the general conference of the association of the Spanish Social Workers (Consejo del Trabajo Social), who are on the frontline in addressing the consequence of an 'immoral capitalism'. As the Spanish political science association invited me to open their annual conference, I went back to the research on legitimacy crisis and democracy that I use in Chapter 4. For the opening lecture of the Finnish Sociological Association in Rovaniemi, I prepared the first draft of the chapter on democracy in social movements in times of austerity. I'm grateful to those friends who invited me and provided for these very stimulating occasions.

I am also indebted to the colleagues and friends who discussed various versions of those papers during lectures at the London School of Economics (Ralph Miliband Memorial Lecture), Goldsmiths, Oxford University, Cardiff University (Shapiro Memorial Lecture), University of Stockholm, University of Amsterdam (CES Presidential Round Table), University of Iceland (Opening Conference at the Nordic Sociological Association), Charles University in Prague, University of Bucharest, Central European University in Budapest, European University at Saint Petersburg, Max Plank Institute in Cologne, Viadrina University, University of Lypsia, University of Hamburg, University of Osnabruck, University of Konstanz, University of Mainz (ECPR Joint Sessions), Free University of Brussels, University of Lausanne (Conference on the Occasion of the Awarding of a PhD Honoris Causa), University of Istanbul (keynote at the World Conference of the European Communication and Education Research Association), UNED in Madrid, Autonomous University of Barcelona, University of Jyvaskyla, University of Rome III, University of Venice, University of Milan, Bordeaux University (ECPR General Conference) as well as the Humboldt University, Free University, Technical University and Social Science Centre in Berlin, the European University Institute and the Scuola Normale Superiore in Florence.

For useful (but sometimes tough to address) comments I am most grateful to Massimiliano Andretta, Philip Balsiger, Xabier Itcaina, Juan Masullo, Alice Mattoni, Martin Portos, Herbert Reiter, Dieter Rucht, Sidney Tarrow, Manès Weisskkircher. For careful copy-editing, I am, as ever, grateful to Sarah Tarrow, my 'editor-in-chief'.

This investigation into the relations between capitalism and social movements is for me just the beginning of a long-term project that I am very glad to be able to continue at the new PhD and post-doctoral program in Political Science and Sociology at the ancient and prestigious Scuola Normale Superiore in Florence. I thank Fabio Beltram and Mario Citroni for their trust and support.

To Herbert Reiter, who, as usual, discussed with me, challenged me and supported me, this book is dedicated.

1

The Re-emergence of a Class Cleavage? Social Movements in Times of Austerity

On 25 January 2011, four meeting points for protesters are set in four areas of Cairo, including working-class neighbourhoods. Before moving towards the city centres, the marchers travel through narrow residential streets, gathering participants on their way. Marches thus create physical occasions to join, then carry participants to their destination. As a protester puts it, 'You're taken to Tahrir by the demonstration itself as the head of the march guides it there' (El Chazli 2012). *Spontaneous demonstrations follow in the next two days, including confrontations with police. On 28 January, a Friday of Rage is called for, with various demonstrations starting from mosques and churches. While the police assail the protesters with substantial use of teargas, the protesters attack police headquarters as well as the headquarters of the regime party. After that, the camps set up by protesters in Tahrir Square attract more and more people.*

On 15 May 2011, indignant citizens (whom the media called Indignados) *start a permanent occupation of Puerta del Sol in Madrid, building a tent city for hundreds of protesters, but also other infrastructures for thousands of visitors. The mobilization quickly spreads to hundreds of Spanish cities all around the country. In fact, 'the encampments rapidly evolve into "cities within cities"', governed through popular assemblies and committees. The committees are created around practical needs such as cooking, cleaning, communicating and carrying out actions. Decisions are made both by majority rule and consensus. The structure is horizontal, with rotating spokespersons in lieu of leaders. Tens of thousands of citizens are thus experimenting with participatory, direct and inclusive forms of democracy at odds with the dominant logic of political representation. Displaying a thorough mixture of utopianism and pragmatism, the new movement draws up a list of concrete demands, including the removal of corrupt politicians from electoral lists, while pursuing revolutionary goals such as giving 'All power to the People' (Postill 2012). A space is named after Tahir Square.*

In the spring and summer of 2011, on the Spanish example, mobilization against austerity grows in Greece. Beginning on 25 May, the Syntagma Square in Athens becomes a central point for protest: for three days in a row, tens of thousands of people protest in front of the Parliament, following a call circulated on Facebook. The people's assembly asserts that 'any corrupt politician should either be sent home or to jail', and 'their democracy guarantees neither justice nor equality'. On 28 May, the first tents are set up on the Square, while the movement quickly spreads throughout the country. Highly choreographed protests are organized every day at 6pm, but there are also daily assemblies: those who want to speak are given a number, then there is a lottery, and those in possession of the drawn numbers are allowed to speak. The protest peaks with two general strikes on 28 and 29 June, with a convergence of the March in front of the Parliament, where new austerity measures are discussed; in the police charges that follow, 800 protesters are injured (Sergi and Vogiatzoglou 2013).

On 17 September 2011, about a thousand protesters march on Wall Street in New York City, settling in a camp in Zuccotti Park. Also there, 'from these scattered nodes in a small emergent network, a thunderous protest network grew in a matter of weeks, aided by webs of communication technologies deployed by activists and supporters who seized the political opportunities surrounding a severe economic crisis. Soon the city encampments had spread around the United States' (Bennett and Segerberg 2013, 180). *The Occupy Movement uses various platforms to promote the protest: from city or group websites (at least 251), to techno-development sites (about fifty open source and developers' sites), Twitter (almost 900 accounts for a total of more than 11 million followers), Facebook (with almost 500 pages), Livestream (with 244 feeds), meetups (in 2,649 cities), Tumblr (30 accounts), as well as hubs intersecting platforms* (Bennett and Segerberg 2013, 182).

On 15 October 2011, a global day of action called for by the Spanish indignados, *a hundred thousand protesters converge on Rome for a national march. One of the largest, the Roman event was, however, one of the most problematic, as it was disrupted by violent protests and the lack of will or capacity by the police to protect the peaceful demonstrators. The memories are of the brutal policing of the protest against the G8 summits in Genoa in 2001. An important role in anti-austerity protests had been taken in the previous three years by the student movement. In 2011, however, no broad movement had emerged in Italy, in direct imitation of the 15M in Spain: the self-proclaimed 'Italian* indignados' *camping in Piazza San Giovanni in Rome remain few in number. The organization of the Italian mobilization of 15 October became a contentious issue among Italian social movements, with different political groups trying to gain symbolic strength and visibility as the organizers of the protest.*

This book focuses on these major episodes of protests, which will be analysed as an illustration of opposition to austerity measures in the global North, but also of a crisis of political responsibility of the so-called advanced democracies. In recent years, several movements, including those mentioned above, have in fact protested against what they saw as a deterioration of democratic institutions. *Lo llaman democracia y no lo es* – 'They call it democracy, but it is not' – one could read on the poster carried by a member of the Spanish *indignados*, one of the social movements that have recently denounced the corruption of institutional politics, calling for 'Democracia Real Ya'. Beginning with Iceland in 2008, and then forcefully in Egypt, Tunisia, Spain, Greece and Portugal, outrage was raised by the corruption of the political class, with protesters condemning bribes in a concrete sense, as well as the privileges granted to lobbies and the collusion of interests between public institutions and economic (often financial) powers. It was to this corruption – that is, the corruption of democracy – that much of the responsibility for the economic crisis, and the inability to manage it, was attributed. In the years to follow, most recently in Venezuela, Brazil, Russia, Bulgaria and Turkey, citizens took to the streets against what they perceived as a rampant and dangerous degeneration of the state governments, defined as a source of inequality and people's suffering.

These protests have been seen as part of anti-austerity movements, mobilizing in the context of the crisis of neoliberalism. In analysing them, I build on the assumption that, in order to understand their main characteristics in terms of social basis, identity and organizational structures and strategies, we should look at the specific characteristics of the socio-economic, cultural and political context in which these protests developed. While this does not mean to deny that specific national contexts do play a very relevant role in influencing the timing and forms of the protest, I am interested in what follows to single out (some) similarities and to link them to some shifts in neoliberal capitalism and its effects on the society. From the theoretical point of view, the main challenge is to locate protests inside the linkages between the market and the state, capitalism and democracy.

In this introduction, I will first discuss the 'strange disappearance' of debates on capitalism from social movement studies, then bridge social movement studies with cleavage theory. I will close the chapter by presenting the research on which the volume is based, as well as its structure.

Bringing capitalism back into protest analysis?

Social movement studies have recently been criticized for having paid too little attention to long-term structural transformations. Strangely, some valuable exceptions notwithstanding, concerns for the social bases of protest even declined, as socioeconomic claims raised through protest remained stable or even increased. Forcefully, Gabriel Hetland and Jeff Goodwin (2013) have called attention to the strange disappearance of capitalism from social movement studies, pointing at how little note (especially US) scholars have taken of the sources of grievances and, in more general, of the influence of socioeconomic structural development over social movements.

Similarly, a review of studies in political sociology stressed how the narrowing of the focus on the process of collective mobilization has, since the 1980s, diverted attention from the relations between social structures and political participation, as well as collective identities (Walder 2009). In the same direction, Sidney Tarrow pointed at the need 'to connect the long-term rhythms of social change from the classical tradition to the shorter-term dynamics of contentious politics' (Tarrow 2012, 7). These claims did not remain isolated. In fact, recent collections have looked at Marxist approaches to social movements (Barker et al. 2013), or called for bringing capitalism, classes or political economy back into the analysis of recent mobilizations against austerity (Tejerina et al. 2013). Some first research on the 2011 protests points in fact at the grievances neoliberalism and its crisis spread in the Arab countries as well as in Southern Europe (della Porta 2014a). These studies have thus looked at cuts in public spending, as well as deterioration of public services and related growth in inequality and poverty, as sources for grievances, and therefore protests.

In all of these mobilizations, a new class – the social precariat, young, unemployed, or only part-time employed, with no protection, and often well educated – has been singled out as a main actor. Defined as a class-on-the-making, the precariat has been conceptualized by Guy Standing as being composed of people 'who have minimal trust relations with capitalism or the state, making it quite different from the salariat. And it has none of the social contract relationship of the proletariat, whereby labour securities were provided in exchange for subordination and contingent loyalty, the unwritten deal underpinning welfare state' (Standing 2011, 9). Precariat is characterized, that is, by a sum of insecurity on the labour market, on the job (as regulations on hiring and dismissals give little protection to workers), on the work (with weak provisions for accident and illness), on income (with very low pay), all these conditions having effects in terms of accumulation of anger, anomie, anxiety and alienation (Standing 2011, 10 ff.). As he noted, precariat 'is not just a matter of having insecure employment, of being in jobs of limited duration and with minimal labour protection...it is being in a status that offers no sense of career, no sense of secure occupational identity and few, if any, entitlements to the state and enterprise benefits that several generations of those who found themselves as belonging to the industrial proletariat or the salariat had come to expect as their due' (Standing 2011, 24).

In order to analyse recent protests, it is indeed all the more relevant to bring attention to capitalist dynamics back into social movement research. Social movement studies emerged in fact from a critique of economist attempts to derive mobilization from structures: grievances or interests, they claimed, are always present but only occasionally mobilized. Moreover, rather than studying socioeconomic structure, attention focused on political opportunities, both the contingent availability of potential allies (their dispositions and strength) and more stable channels of access of political institutions (mainly functional and territorial divisions of power) (see della Porta and Diani 2006, ch. 7, for a review). The main assumption has been that the presence of mobilizable resources as well as the opening of political opportunities explains collective mobilization and its forms, as rational activists tend to invest in collective action when their effort seems worthwhile.

Broadly tested in cross-national (e.g. Kriesi et al. 1995; della Porta 1995) and cross-time (e.g. Tarrow 1989) perspectives, the main hypotheses of the political opportunity approach seems to hold: protest is, by and large, more frequent and less radical when stable and/or contingent channels of access to institutions by outsiders are open. In fact, even in the face of economic crises and structural weakness of the lower classes, scholars have cited open political opportunities to explain the emergence of protest and even its success (Tarrow 2011).

From several points of view, the recent anti-austerity mobilizations met some of the expectations of social movement scholars, but challenged others. As we will see, in line with expectations derived from the political opportunity approach, those protests react not only to economic crisis (with high unemployment and high numbers of precarious workers) but also to a political situation in which institutions are (and are perceived to be) particularly closed towards citizens' demands, at the same time unwilling and incapable of addressing them in an inclusive way.

Some of the hypotheses developed within social movement studies have however been criticized as too structuralist, and therefore unable to explain agency, a task which needs instead to move from a deterministic into a more processual approach. A first observation is that it is not political opportunities as exogenous structure, but rather the *attribution* of opportunities by activists that affects the propensity to mobilize (McAdam et al. 2001). In addition, not only opportunities but also *threats* can push towards mobilization (Goldstone and Tilly 2001).

From the theoretical point of view, we can observe, moreover, that these movements reacted to something more than a 'threat'. Rather, they developed within and addressed social and political crises that social movement studies have not given enough attention in their theorization: not just contingent opportunities and threats, but what one could call, with Habermas (1976), a crisis of legitimacy. In contrast to those addressed by Habermas, this legitimacy crisis develops in a new social formation that is very different from the organized, state regulated, Fordist, advanced level of mature capitalism to which he referred. It is, I will suggest, a legitimacy crisis of/in a late neoliberal system which takes the form of a crisis of responsibility. This has an effect on some of the specific characteristics of anti-austerity protests, especially on their political claims, frames and organizational forms.

Changing political conditions are indeed related to some specific developments in capitalism, which are strictly tied to political processes. In order to understand today's movements in times of socioeconomic challenges, we clearly need to bring capitalism back into the analysis. The main questions I want to address in this work are, therefore: Which form of capitalism do the mentioned movements face? and How is it brought back into the analysis? Capitalism can be defined – following the Oxford dictionaries – as 'an economic and political system in which a country's trade and industry are controlled by private owners for profit, rather than by the state'.[1] In Wolfgang Streeck's conceptualization, it is 'a social order built on a promise of boundless collective progress – as measured by the size of its money economy – coming about as a side-product of independent maximization of individual utility, prosperity, and profit' (2014, 53). If capitalism is, according to Marxism, one of a set of modes of production, defined on the basis of the relations between the owners of the conditions of production and the producers, then the specific forms exploitation takes during the evolution of capitalism must be expected to have an effect on producers' mobilization (Barker 2013).

Addressing the impact of capitalism on social movements would require, first of all, looking at the ways in which the debate about capitalism developed in other subfields of the social sciences, but also bridging those reflections with discussions of some open issues in social movement studies on concepts such as grievances, interests, classes and identities. This would imply taking into account three temporalities of capitalism: its long-term changes, the middle-term alternation of growth and crisis, and the short-term dynamics of specific critical junctures. In particular, I will focus on neoliberal capitalism, understood as a form of economic liberalism which emphasize free trade, open market and the role of the private sector versus the public one. Within this form, I will look at moments of expansion and decline, reflecting on their effects on social movements.

One should handle the challenge of bringing structures into focus, without losing the attention to mobilizing resources political mediation that has been an important contribution of social movement studies. We can start by observing that the reflection on capitalism had not totally disappeared from social movement studies. If there was indeed a general silence, there were important exceptions. Paradoxically, however, these very exceptions might have been among the reasons for declining attention to capitalism in the field of social movement studies, rather than pushing forward the reflection on the structural basis of conflicts.

A first exception to the capitalism-blind research on social movements has been the definition of collective action repertoires as driven by capitalism and state formation. In Tilly's (1978) analysis, the shift from a local, paternalistic and ad-hoc repertoire of protest to one characterized by nationalization, professionalization, and modularity has been explained by the centralization of economic and political power at the national level. However, his attention was focused on these big historical transformations rather than on the evolution in capitalism or the swinging move between capitalist growth and crisis.

A second exception is research on new social movements, insofar as it paid attention to class development. This was done by concentrating, for example in Hanspeter Kriesi's work (Kriesi et al. 1995), on the emergence of new middle classes as social bases for new social movements. In particular, sociocultural workers were described as the most likely to join new social movements given their prioritization of autonomy but also, given identification with their constituencies, their propensity towards an egalitarian distribution of resources (Kriesi 1998). Looking at big societal transformations, other literature on social movements was also attracted by the potential shift from material to immaterial (or cultural) production to structure their emergence and characteristics (Touraine 1981; Melucci 1989). Fordism was therefore seen as bringing about a pacification of the class cleavage that left space for the emergence of a new type of claim, based not on socioeconomic grievances but on post-materialist values. Very relevant in singling out the characteristics of the emerging movements at the time, this stream of research nevertheless risked 'freezing' the image of new social movements as new middle-class phenomena.

A third exception is more recent research in European political science about specific forms of populism emerging as a result of a new division between the winners and the losers of globalization. When studies moved beyond Fordism and into the evolution of globalized capitalism, they put special attention on the rise of right-wing populism and its electoral expression. Kriesi and others (Kriesi et al. 2008; 2012) have thus described the emergence of a new cleavage between the winners and losers of globalization, with the latter often opposing its cultural dimension through xenophobic and anti-immigrant claims, converging in exclusive forms of nationalism. However, these analyses focused on the right-wing exclusivist reaction of the losers and are not yet fully extended to the type of culturally inclusive losers that mobilized against neoliberalism in 2011 and beyond (but see Hutter 2012; Hutter 2014).

A fourth exception is represented by research on anti-austerity mobilizations developed especially in the global South. Focusing on so-called anti-austerity riots, this work looked at the way in which the debt-crisis and subsequent IMF's imposed conditionalities had brought about a shift from developmentalism – relying on state intervention – to neoliberalism, with its emphasis on cuts in welfare, which spread grievances and therefore mobilization (see, e.g. Walton and Seddon 1994). With some detachment from mainstream social movement studies, however, this literature did not refer much to the mechanisms intervening between discontent and protest that had driven much of social movement studies in the global North.

While all these streams in the social movement literature offer useful contributions, a full understanding of recent waves of protest would require us to go beyond mainstream social movement studies, attempting some cross-fertilization especially with the disciplinary fields of political economy and democratic theory. First, the research should take into account the shifting movements and countermovements between market liberalization and social protection that have characterized much of capitalist history (Polanyi 1957). Second, the analysis must be sensitive to the national variants of global economy: integration in a world economy does not in fact mean equal conditions – or even convergence – in all countries, but rather the division of the world into hegemonic power and dependent economy (Wallerstein 1990). Additionally, capitalism is far from stable: crises of various types (inflation and stagnation, production and distribution) emerge frequently, changing the conditions for political participation as anti-systemic movements produce adaptation in capitalism (Arrighi et al. 1989). Kondratieff's A-upturns with expanding profits (as the one from 1945 to 1970) are followed by his B downturns (Wallerstein 2010). While in expanding phases, capitalists might find it more convenient to make concessions to labour than to risk blocks in production, during recession the margins of negotiation shrinks. Finally, much research in political economy has focused attention on the existing varieties of capitalism, contrasting the liberal market economy (characterized by the prevalence of market relations) with the coordinated market economy (allowing for more consensual relations among enterprises and between the government and social partners) (Hall and Soskice 2001) – or, in more recent debates, on the varieties of capitalism that emerge even within a common neoliberal wave (Bohle and Greskovits 2013).

The effects of these changing conditions on the development of social movements, affecting both their strength and their characteristics, can be expected to be complex. While research on strikes had traditionally emphasized the structural strength of labour in moments of economic growth, protests also emerge in reaction to threats. The degree of inclusion and exclusion changes, together with the degree of social aggregation versus fragmentation of the excluded. Additionally, some main processes, singled out in social movement studies, effect the transformation of structures into action. First, a pivotal role is played by political opportunities – at least in part in an autonomous way from the economic ones: the New Deal, for instance, meant an opening of political opportunities in moments of socioeconomic crisis (Tarrow 2011). Reactions to grievances are also far from automatic as far as the conditions for mobilization are concerned: instead, they require the framing of responsibility through mechanisms of politicization and growth in generality (della Porta 2014a). Citizens must feel the effects of macroeconomic and political crises on their everyday lives – as the legitimacy crisis fuels a motivational crisis (Habermas 1976). Finally, mobilization resources must be available in order to start protesting, even if they often grow during the protest itself (della Porta 2014a). The transfer of interests into collective action is in fact constrained by internal competition as well as ruling ideas, which also effect the shift from economic into political action. So, the movements are fields of arguments, in which conservative and radical elements are mixed (Barker 2013).

Recognizing the role of agency, some debates have developed on the characteristics of those actors that challenge capitalism, in its various forms. Social movements may in fact form in order to react to these threats, but they will have different characteristics as compared to those emerging in times of abundance. In Kerbo's analysis (1982), *movements of crisis* are sparked by unemployment, food shortages, and dislocations, when everyday life is challenged during threatening political and social crises. Their participants are, at least in the early stages, mainly the victims of the requested changes, and protests tend to be more spontaneous, more often involving violent outbursts. *Movements of affluence*, in contrast, are to be found in relatively good times; they are often formed mainly by conscience members, and they are better organized and less likely to use violence (Kerbo 1982, 654). In general, while movements of affluence (and opportunities) are expected to be stronger, larger, longer-lasting, pragmatic, optimistic, and more often successful, movements of crisis (and threats) are expected to be weaker, smaller, shorter, radical, pessimistic, and more often unsuccessful (della Porta 2013b).

Opposing the stereotype of a conjure against free market, Karl Polanyi (1957) described those forces that resisted economic liberalism as disorganized. In contrast with this view of spontaneity, however, much research on the (organized) labour movement stresses instead its role in defence of the principle of social integration (for a synthesis, della Porta 2013a, ch. 2). Faced with economic crises, such as the great depression between the two wars, it was mobilization from below that pushed for a reversal of the dominant economic paradigm, from liberalism to interventionist Keynesianism.

According to the scholars of the so-called world-systems approach, it was indeed the task of anti-systemic movements to resist greedy capitalism, opposing the logic of the system. As Immanuel Wallerstein noted, 'to be antisystemic is to argue that neither liberty nor equality is possible under the existing system and that both are possible only in a transformed world' (Wallerstein 1990, 36). The concept of anti-systemic movements builds upon an analytic perspective about 'the world-system of historical capitalism' that gave rise to them, as 'class and status consciousness were the two key concepts that justified these movements' (Arrighi et al. 1989, 1).

While recognizing the role of some movements in challenging capitalist development, however, both Polanyi's and the world-systems approach said little about the ways in which context shapes the emergence and forms of those movements. This is instead a central focus of social movement studies, which have stressed the role of resource mobilization in order to pass from structure to action. In fact, protests require, and at the same time produce, relational dynamics among social and political groups (della Porta 2014a). Against the assumption that protest emerged spontaneously in the metropolis because of fast modernization and uprooting, research on crisis and protests in the global South has in fact addressed the need for resources of collective mobilization, pointing at the presence of organizational coalitions made of self-help groups, Christian based communities, human rights organizations, environmentalists, and so on (e.g. Walton 1998).

In addition, research on the recent wave of anti-austerity protests in the Northern part of the globe points also at the role of organizations, by looking at the genealogy of these movements in previous protest waves taking place at the national and transnational levels. Practices of direct democracy through general assemblies at *acampadas* aim at building broad movements, overcoming perceived sectorialization and fragmentation of the past. While innovative ideas flow from Cairo to New York, national developments in collective action also play a role. In particular, in the Arab Spring as well as among the *indignados*, the horizontal construction of coalitions is a reaction to the perceived problems of the organizational networking of previous movements – from labour to the Global Justice Movement (GJM) of the first half of the 2000s, especially once mobilization declined – but also of the failures of first attempts to react to the crisis in the second half of the 2000s. However, it also adopts and adapts some organizational innovations towards participatory and deliberative democratic models that had developed in previous movements (Polletta 2002; della Porta 2013a).

As I will argue in what follows, the concept of political cleavages can be usefully integrated in a relational vision of social movements, considered as actors in complex webs of interactions, in view of combining attention to structures and to agency.

Social movements and political cleavages

Linking capitalist transformations to citizens' agency is a main theoretical challenge for social movement studies. As I will argue, the concept of cleavages, as main social conflicts which are culturally and politically structured (Lipset and Rokkan 1967; also Kriesi 1998), could help in investigating the relations between structural conditions and social movements. In general, social movements have played a very important role in the structuration and politicization of conflicts: the labour movement helped in 'freezing' the class cleavage, while new social movements have been said to emerge from growing (electoral and other) volatility. As attention to social movements rapidly increased in sociology and political science, attention to class instead declined steadily. This might help to explain the strange silence from social movement studies on the social bases of conflicts. Its potential usefulness notwithstanding, we can agree that, with few exceptions, 'cleavage theory occupies a central place in literature on conventional political participation, but is remarkably absent in literature on unconventional political participation' (Damen 2013, 944). In fact, 'current research on cleavage politics focuses almost exclusively on the electoral arena' (Hutter 2014, ix).

No doubt, social movement studies developed, as mentioned, in a period of rejection of conceptions of the dominance of the economic sphere, with a shift to the autonomy of the political or the social domains. Considering grievances, strains, cleavages, and the like as always present, social movement studies concentrated on explaining the passage from structure to action, as the title of one of the first influential volumes in the field indicated (Klandermans et al. 1988). On the other side, research on cleavages – much influenced by Stein Rokkan (1999) – focused on their effects on electoral and party politics, disregarding the role of social movements. Moreover, while much of the social science literature on cleavages focuses on the class divide, when the latter is referred to in social movement studies it is instead to highlight its pacification. In fact, as mentioned, focusing on the environmental or women's movements, research noted that these 'new social movements' indeed arose especially when and where the old cleavages had faded away, leaving spaces for new ones to emerge (e.g. Kriesi et al. 1995). Especially but not only in the United States, moreover, any concepts with a Marxist flavour tended to slip away from mainstream sociology and political science.

As I will argue in what follows, there is much to gain from bringing reflection on cleavages back into social movement studies. This is all the more true in a moment in which deteriorating socioeconomic conditions have brought classes back into focus. In order to attempt this bridging, I will first discuss the concept of cleavages, then briefly look at how it has occasionally entered social movement studies, developing an analysis of the ways in which reasoning in terms of cleavages can illuminate our vision of current conflicts in our societies.

As is well known, the concept of cleavages was used by Stein Rokkan to describe the main conflict lines in the development of European societies and politics. As he stated:

Two of these cleavages are direct products of what we might call the *National Revolution*: the conflicts between the *central nation-building culture* and the increasing resistance of the ethnically, linguistically or religiously distinct *subject populations* in the province and the periphery; the conflict between the centralizing, standardizing and mobilizing Nation-State and the historically established corporate privilege of the

Church. Two of them are products of *Industrial Revolution*: the conflict between the *landed interests* and the rising class of *industrial entrepreneurs*; the conflict between *owners and employers* on the one side and *tenants, labourers and workers* on the other. (Rokkan 1999, 284)

While Rokkan thus singled out the social groups on which the structuration of political conflicts developed, looking at the class cleavage in particular, Stefano Bartolini and Peter Mair (Bartolini and Mair 1990; Bartolini 2000) contributed to a conceptualization of cleavages as composed of three elements: (a) a sociostructural reference (referred to as 'empirical' element); (b) a cultural element, as informed by 'the set of values and beliefs that provide a sense of identity and role to the empirical elements and reflects a self-awareness of the social group(s) involved'; and (c) an organizational/behavioural element, linked to a set of individual interactions, institutions, and organizations, such as political parties, that structures the cleavage (Bartolini 2000, 17).

The development of cleavages as a politicized divide is therefore a process composed of various twists and steps such as the generation of opposition due to different interests or *Weltanschauung*; the crystallization of opposition lines into a conflict; the rise of alliances of political entrepreneurs engaged in mobilizing support for some policies; the choice of mobilization strategy (community versus purpose specific) and the conflict arena (electoral versus protest). The cleavage itself emerges through processes of politicization, mobilization and democratization in the nation-state: it is, that is, transferred into politics (rather than repressed or depoliticized) by the action of party translators. Their work is all the more important in keeping emotional feelings of solidarity, as the latter tend to be reduced by social heterogeneity and differentiation, the separation of workplace from residence, the reduction of direct contacts with members of the group, and the development of impersonal contacts in the party (Bartolini 2000). The formation of a cleavage then tends to produce a closure of social relations.

Similarly, social movement studies have stressed the importance of certain group characteristics for their capacity to mobilize by the presence of both specific categorical traits and networks between those sharing such traits (Tilly 1978). In synthesis, 'Collective action on the part of particular social groups is in fact facilitated when these groups are: (1) easily identifiable and differentiated in relation to other social groups; (2) endowed, thanks to social networks among their members, with a high level of internal cohesion and with a specific identity' (della Porta and Diani 2006, 37). While the past strength of the class cleavage contributed to the development of a so-called mid-century compromise

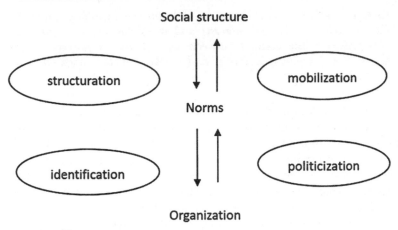

Figure 1.1   Cleavages as processes

between labour and capital, with the growth of welfare states and citizens' rights, new cleavages seemed to emerge.

From the perspective of social movement studies, the link between socioeconomic structure, values and organizations can be seen as characterized by continuous feedback (see Figure 1.1). Within this perspective, I am interested in looking at how social cleavages develop as specific social conditions are linked to a set of values and beliefs that lead to normative choices. Social groups are in fact formed through processes of *structuration* into some special categories, and then of *identification* with specific normative systems. Organizational entrepreneurs develop new codes, often *politicizing* the conflict, by linking grievances and interests to broader visions of collective goods (and bads). The framing of the conflicts then contributes to *mobilizing* social groups (or keeping them mobilized) that aim at changing social structures.

As I will discuss in more depth in each chapter, the so-called processual turn in social movement studies moved attention from static variables to the causal mechanisms and processes connecting them (McAdam et al. 2001). In a similar vein, in my work on political violence (della Porta 2013e) and on democratization from below (della Porta 2014a), I suggested an approach which is, first, *relational*, as it locates social movements within broader fields that see the interactions of various actors, institutional and non-institutional. Not only the very conception of a cleavage is relational as it points at the reciprocity of the conditions of, e.g. capital and labour, but it also connects each conflict within broader fields involving multiple actors and institutions. My approach is, second, *constructivist*, as it takes into account not only the external opportunities and constraints, but also the social elaboration of their experiential reality by the various actors participating in social and political conflicts. Collective identification plays, in particular, a fundamental role as it is around identities that advantages and disadvantages of each path of behaviour and/or situation are assessed. Cognitive mechanisms interact with affective ones in the consolidation of those identities. Third, my approach is *dynamic*, as it recognizes that social movement characteristics develop in intense moments of action, and aims at reconstructing the causal mechanisms that link the macro-system in which conflicts develop; the meso-system formed by the social movement organizations; and the micro-system of the symbolic interactions within the activist networks. Movement activities are not only instrumentally adapting to contextual challenges and existing resources, but they are also emergent as they contribute to transform those resources. Action in fact creates relations, rather than just reflecting them.

In this sense, I will consider capitalism as an important structuring agent, but not one that acts alone. In order to understand the complex interdependence of socioeconomic, cultural and political structures for today's social movements, one has to reflect on the ways in which processes of identification, structuration, politicization and mobilization developed in different periods. As mentioned, the concept of cleavage has entered the analysis of social movements, with reference to the pacification of the old class cleavage and the emergence of a new one. Research on the class bases for new social movements singled out the new middle class, in particular the highly qualified workers in the socio-cultural sector, as the empirical base of a new cleavage, endowed with post-materialist values and structured into sort of archipelagos (Kriesi 1993; Inglehart 1977).

If the new middle classes (especially the sociocultural profession) were considered as the sociostructural element of the cleavage, post-materialist values were identified as its cultural one. As Habermas observed long ago (1987, 392; cit. in Crossley 2002, 160), new conflicts 'no longer flare up in domains of material reproduction; they are no longer channelled through parties and associations; and they can no longer be allayed through compensations. Rather, these new conflicts arise in domains of cultural reproduction, social integration and socialization; they are carried out in sub-institutional – or at least extraparliamentary – forms of protest; and the underlying deficit reflects reification of communicatively structured domains of action that will not respond to the media of money or power.'

Finally, from the organizational point of view, new social movements emerged as networks of networks. Although new parties, such as the

Greens, were founded to represent emerging claims on environmental protection or gender rights, they never reached the structuring capacity of the socialist or the communist party families in the case of the class cleavage (Diani 1995).

Social movement studies have seen recent changes in the social structure as not particularly conducive to mobilization. In short, not only have processes such as de-industrialization and migration 'weakened the structural preconditions that had facilitated the emergence of a class cleavage, particularly in the working-class model of collective action' (della Porta and Diani 2006, 39), but those developments have also jeopardized citizens' rights through poverty, unemployment, and job insecurity. In fact:

> Overall, the size of social groups which lack full access to citizenship and its entitlements has grown, whether because they are migrants (legal or illegal), because they are employed in the hidden economy, or engaged in low-paid work. The sense of general instability has been further reinforced by the growth of individual mobility, principally horizontal: and thus more people tend to change jobs several times in the course of one's life – whether out of choice or out of necessity. The multiplication of roles and of professions and of the related stratifications, and the (re)emergence of ethnicity or gender-based lines of fragmentation within socio-economic groups have made it more difficult to identify specific social categories. (della Porta and Diani 2006, 39)

These weaknesses notwithstanding, strong waves of protest developed in the 1990s and 2000s, first in the global South and then on a worldwide scale, in what was called the Global Justice Movement. These protests had some characteristics that challenged the new social movement paradigm. First of all, from the social point of view, they mobilized coalitions of white- and blue-collar workers, unemployed and students, young and old generations. The need to keep together a heterogeneous social base – as well as the general failures of big ideologies to provide for successful alternative models of social and political organization – fuelled the development of pluralist and tolerant identities, praising internal diversity. This was reflected at the organizational level through the elaboration of a participatory and deliberative model of decision making (della Porta 2009a and 2009b).

Recent anti-austerity protests have to a certain extent further challenged expectations about a decline in collective mobilization. The concept of cleavage can indeed be useful to discuss the extent to which capitalist transformations, in particular neoliberalism and its crisis, have

Table 1.1.   *Cleavage dimensions in temporal evolution*

	Old social Movements	New social movements	Global Justice Movement	Anti-austerity movements
Social basis	Industrial workers	New middle class	Class coalitions	The precariat?
Norms	Class identity with universal norms	Single issue identities	Plural identities	The citizens?
Organization	(Formally) hierarchical	Participated network	Deliberative models	Direct democracy?

contributed to the emergence of a new class (of losers of globalization, or precariat) or the re-emergence of old, formerly pacified, conflicts. As those protests indicated, there is indeed not only an increase, since the 1990s, of contention on socio-economic issues (Hutter 2014, 83, 101–2), but also an attempt to normatively construct some new identities of citizens, while also looking at traditional ones. Rhizomatic and extremely mistrustful of traditional representative democracy, these actors seem also in search for new organizational models, which they often define as direct democracy but whose effectiveness has not yet been proven.

In Table 1.1. I have synthesized the main images present in social movement studies of the main social movements in different phases of capitalist development. They are synthesized around the three dimensions of the cleavage I have singled out above.

I will discuss those issues in what follows, with chapters dedicated to each of the cleavage dimensions I singled out and looking at the mentioned processes of identification, structuration, politicization and mobilization. In particular, I will discuss the question of the potential for an emerging new cleavage that will link all different elements – or rather of less stringent connections between them.

The research

The volume focuses on the relations between structure and agency in today's protests against austerity. In the following chapters, each of the three dimensions of cleavage – social, cultural and organizational – will be addressed in order to investigate the connections between social bases, identity and organization of emerging movements and relate them to the specific evolution of neoliberal capitalism.

The aim is not so much theory testing, but rather theory building, through an attempt to integrate the various streams of social science literature on capitalism and democracy with recent trends within social movement studies. Space is indeed given to a review of different fields of knowledge, which I think could and should be usefully combined in order to address the emerging (analytical, but also social) challenges. From the theoretical point of view, I aim, in an exploratory fashion, at bridging debates in social and political theory, comparative politics, and political economy (which looks at the interplay of capitalism and the political system) with social movement studies. In particular, as Stanley and Goodwin (2013, 946) recently noted, 'political economy offers a range of ideas that are helpful for understanding social movements'. It suggests, in fact, that we look at the actors' material interests – that is, interests linked to their economic and institutional location – as well as at the effects of market mechanisms in terms of distribution of resources and of actors' power, paying attention to the alternation of economic growth and recessions.

In this volume, I focus on protest by progressive, left-wing social movements. While also populist right-wing groups as well as the radical right are of course influenced by the neoliberal developments, mobilizing part of its discontent, I will leave to further research the investigation of reciprocal similarities and differences. For reason of space, but also of conceptual coherence, I think the state of the art justifies a focus on movements that tend to share a left-wing critique against austerity and to belong to similar social movement families (della Porta and Rucht 1996).

Although excluding right-wing protests, my research design includes two comparative foci: cross-time and cross-national. In a cross-time, historical perspective, I will look at the emergence of the anti-austerity movements of the 2010s as rooted in the evolution of the GJM that became visible with the protests against the Millennium Summit of the World Trade Organization in Seattle in 1999 and quickly spread across all continents, peaking in the beginning of the 2000s (della Porta 2007). While this movement also targeted neoliberalism and its misery, it developed before its crisis (which it had indeed predicted). A comparison of the GJM of the early 2000s and the anti-austerity protests ten years later will show some continuity, but also the ways in which the two movements reflect and react to the different stages of neoliberal development. In a cross-national perspective, although aware of national differences, I will look especially for similarities, focusing on the 2011 wave of protest moving from Tunisia and Egypt to Spain, Greece, Italy, the United States and beyond.

In doing this, I will refer as a way of illustration to various pieces of my own research as well as to secondary literature. The primary sources I am using refer mainly to Europe, offering therefore an admittedly selective take on the general questions of the relations between capitalism and movements. Given the internal diversity in the European context, however, even this limited focus allows for some cross-national remarks. Even though I mentioned capitalist diversity, my aim is not a systematic cross-national comparison, but rather the understanding of the ways in which movements are affected by the shift between expansion and crisis of a certain capitalist formation. In this perspective, the empirical data I refer to allow addressing my main concern.

On the GJM, I will summarize some results of the Democracy in Europe and the Mobilization of the Society (DEMOS) project, which has covered six European countries (Italy, Germany, France, Spain, Switzerland and Great Britain, as well as transnational mobilizations). Data come in particular from the analysis of documents of social movement organizations and interviews with their speakers, as well as from surveys with activists (see della Porta 2009a and 2009b for details). The research consisted of an analysis of documents and websites of GJM organizations; semi-structured interviews with movement organizations; surveys of movement activists; and participant observation of movement groups and their experiences with participatory and/or deliberative decision making. In contrast to most social movement research done in the past, we aimed at collecting information on a relatively large number of organizations/groupings per country and on very different organizational models. In the various parts of our research, we combined qualitative in-depth analysis of a few organizations with quantitative analysis of a large number of cases. One of the rationales for enlarging the number of selected cases was the heterogeneity of the GJM, particularly in terms of organizational designs. In order to reflect this heterogeneity, we selected a large number of different groups. I shall refer in particular to the results of an analysis of the websites of 266 social movement organizations (SMOs); the fundamental documents of 244 SMOs; interviews with representatives of 210 SMOs; as well as surveys conducted at European Social Forums (ESF) (della Porta 2009a and 2009b).

The first part of the research focuses on e-democracy as conceived of and implemented in the websites of 266 social movement organizations involved in protest campaigns on global justice. A structured codebook was used in order to collect information on the characteristics that might affect the extent to which online organizations fulfil the democratic potential of the Internet.

The Internet is not only an interesting object of study, but also a rich source for analysing the written production of social movement organizations. Although not relying only upon the Web, a second part of our research analysed the fundamental documents of 244 social movement organizations in order to reconstruct their organizational ideology. The analysis focused on the following organizational documents: (a) the constitution of the organization; (b) a document of fundamental values and/or intent; (c) a formally adopted programme; (d) the 'mission statement'; (e) the 'about us' section of the website; (f) the 'frequently asked questions' section of the website; and (g) equivalent or similar material on the website expressing the 'official' position of the organization as a whole. For the quantitative part of the research, a codebook was prepared in order to analyse general information on the organizational characteristics; membership rules; organizational structures and decision-making methods; relationships with public institutions; identity and conceptions of democracy.

These data were triangulated with the results of a survey of representatives from (whenever possible) the same organizations analysed in the previous parts. Like the document analysis, the semi-structured interviews focused on conceptions of democracy, but shifted attention to the way in which they are addressed by representatives of a sample of social movement organizations belonging to the GJM. The semi-structured questionnaire, administered by phone to key informants covering 210 SMOs, concerned organizational characteristics (name, year of foundation, internal decision making, types of activity, types of campaigns, type of organization, types of members, type of budget and sources of revenue) and relationships with the organizational field (connections with other groups/networks/campaigns of the GJM, interactions with institutions at various territorial levels).

Finally, I will refer to the results of surveys conducted at various editions of the European Social Forum (ESF), a main event of the GJM with meetings and assemblies attended by thousands of activists from thousands of organizations. In particular, a survey of the participants at the 4th European Social Forum in Athens was carried out within the Demos project (della Porta 2009a); similar data had been collected at the 1st ESF in Florence (della Porta et al. 2006) and the 2nd one in Paris (Agrikoliansky and Cardon 2005). Building upon previous experiences, we defined a purposeful sample, selecting participants randomly over the various initiatives, in order to construct a sample that included the various 'souls' of the movement (Andretta et al. 2002). The sample for the survey of the first European Social Forum in Florence in 2002 was similarly constructed (della Porta et al. 2006; see also Fillieule et al. 2004). At the 4th ESF in Athens, we were able to exploit the nature of the event as a long-lasting meeting during which it was possible to find time to complete and return the questionnaires. In consideration of the transnational nature of the event, the questionnaire was translated into all the languages of the countries involved in the project and, additionally, into Greek.

On anti-austerity protests, I present first of all evidences from secondary analyses of original research done on anti-austerity protests in Tunisia, Egypt, Spain, Greece and the United States. I have chosen these countries because they were those in which the most original forms of protest – the camps – were very successful in mobilizing citizens around claims against social inequality and for 'real' democracy. Even though empirical analyses on the topic are still at an initial stage, we already have a range of in depth case studies using an ethnographic approach, as well as some comparative attempts. Research results are in fact starting to accumulate, particularly on the Arab Spring, the Spanish and Greek *indignados*, and the Occupy campaigns, as well as on their successful or failed diffusion (della Porta and Mattoni 2013). With all the caution needed when using secondary sources for comparative analysis (Ritter 2014), I found this research useful – if not yet for theory testing, at least for theory building, which is, as mentioned, a main aim of this volume.

While these were indeed specific forms of mobilization with a focus on neoliberalism and its indignities, I will expand the focus of attention to other countries as well, addressing participation in the most used forms of protest: the demonstration. In fact, in order to look for specific effects of the neoliberal crisis on selected characteristics of demonstrators, I will refer to some results of the surveys carried out by an international consortium coordinated by Bert Klandermans and Stefan Walgrave, within the Contextualizing Contestation project, covering dozens of demonstrations in countries most hit by the financial crisis, such as Spain and Italy, and those which instead seemed less hit, such as the Netherlands, Belgium, Switzerland and Sweden, with the Czech Republic and the UK in between (see www.protestsurvey.eu). In the years of recession, in particular in the 2010s, surveys have indeed been carried out at protest demonstrations by various national teams. Demonstrators were sampled randomly and given a questionnaire to mail back. About 1,000 questionnaires were distributed at each demonstration, with an average return rate of 20 per cent for the Italian case (see della Porta et al. 2013 for more information). A short face-to-face questionnaire was also filled in during the demonstration and used to control for return bias. For each demonstration, we also filled in fact sheets to assess context variations, which included short interviews with both organizers and police (before and after the demonstrations) as well as an analysis of media coverage of the events. Moreover, the interviewers were asked to complete another short survey reporting on such characteristics of the demonstration as number of participants, slogans, weather conditions, and so on, as well as specific questions about responses to the survey. In order to reduce selection bias arising from the tendency of interviewers to select some categories of interviewee rather than others, 'pointers' were asked to assign randomly selected demonstrators to the interviewers (Walgrave et al. 2012). Similar to the one distributed at the ESF, the core questionnaire included questions about socio-demographic variables; mobilization channels and techniques; social embeddedness; instrumental, identity and ideological motives; emotions; conventional and unconventional political behaviour; political attitudes (including political interest, left-right self-placement, political cynicism); and awareness of and identification with protesters elsewhere in the world.[2]

Demonstrations varied within countries as well. Taking the Italian case as an illustration, I will at times compare demonstrations cross-issues, to single out in which ways some of the capitalist developments could be reflected both in demonstrations focusing on social issues, but also in those addressing so-called cultural issues. Some of the demonstrations we surveyed between 2011 and 2013 focused in fact on anti-austerity claims (the Labour Day Protest, Euromayday, a labour strike, the No Monti Day, and the Florence 10+10 demonstrations) and others on different topics, often listed under the 'new social movements' label (the Perugia Assisi March for Peace, the Anti-Mafia Protest, the LGBTQ Pride Parade, and the protest against the Muos in Sicily) (for more information on the demonstrations, see project websites).[3]

On the Italian case, moreover, I have replicated, as much as possible, the mentioned research design we had used in the Demos project when investigating the GJM. Within a broader comparative project, we collected information on all the protests reported in Italy in 2011 in the centre-left newspaper *La Repubblica*, as well as an analysis of documents and websites from social movement organizations (della Porta, Mosca and Parks 2014). After identifying each reported protest event in the national section of *La Repubblica*, we detected a total of 172 separate protest events, and coded them on a structured codebook. These were then used to select a purposeful sample of organizations involved in those protests, whose fundamental documents were analysed using a similar outline to the one developed within the Demos project. In particular, we have analysed the documents of fifty-eight actors that had emerged as most relevant in the mentioned protest event analysis, ranging from trade unions to social centres, from women's groups to environmental organizations, from precarious workers to anti-crisis groups.

This volume

The following chapters will address the dimensions of political cleavages I have just highlighted, as well as the mentioned processes of identification, structuration, politicization, and mobilization. Chapter 2 looks at the social bases of the cleavages, comparing the GJM and anti-austerity movements. First, it discusses some core characteristics of late neoliberalism, which constitute the context in which these protests are embedded. Starting with Karl Polanyi's (1957) analysis of the double movement between free market and social protection, as well as Immanuel Wallerstein's (1990) reflections on world economy and the debate on varieties/diversity of capitalisms, I will then single out some of the specific characteristics of what I will call the crisis of late neoliberalism. As political economists and economic sociologists have suggested, neoliberalism has some similarities, but also some differences if compared with the first wave of liberalism, typical of the 'great transformation'. Theoretical reflections as well as empirical analyses have linked mobilization dynamics in neoliberalism to globalization processes, through the use of such concepts as empire (in Hardt and Negri's work, 2000) or globalization's 'winners and losers' (Kriesi et al. 2012). Confirming results of analyses of anti-austerity protests in the global South, the data on the GJM as well as the anti-austerity protests will show that the social bases of the protest are indeed complex and varied. Research data on participants at demonstrations as well as a secondary analysis of existing research indicate that while the GJM mobilized (even if not exclusively) mainly the middle classes, the profile of those who protested against austerity measures included many of those who are directly affected by the crisis of late neoliberalism, such as workers, in full or part-time positions, as well as the unemployed. Rather than pointing at a return of the traditional basis of the labour movement or the emergence of a new 'precariat' as dominant social group, the research signals the presence of coalitions of various social actors which tend to identify themselves as belonging to the lower classes. Together with students and precarious workers, industrial workers as well as public employees provided a varied social basis to the protests.

Chapter 3 analyses the cultural element of the cleavages, reflecting on the characteristics of the collective identities developing in neoliberalism and its crisis. Reflecting on the first wave of free market ideology, scholars such as Karl Polanyi (1957), Craig Calhoun (1982) and E. P. Thompson (1991) have singled out its immoral dimension, with cynical refusal of values of social protection and solidarity, to which movements responded through appeals to re-establish the social order they perceived as broken. In the same direction, research on agrarian revolts stressed the broad stigmatization of the privatization of common goods through enclosures, as a break in the sets of moral rights and obligations of landowners to ensure help towards subsistence. Focusing on more recent cultural transformations, and putting forward different expectations, social theorists have pointed at liquid identification processes either as hampering (in Zygmunt Bauman's analysis) or fostering (e.g. in Hardt and Negri's theorization) mobilization processes. Empirical research has moreover singled out the exclusionary nationalism developing in right-wing reactions to globalization, but also permanence, on the Left, of post-materialist, libertarian, and cosmopolitan values. After having introduced this debate, I will in this chapter proceed to analyse some identity-related characteristics of the GJM, first, and the anti-austerity movements later on, noting both continuities and discontinuities as linked to the trajectory of neoliberal capitalism. The GJM was in fact characterized by tolerant identities, inclusive of both individual and, especially, associational actors. In comparison with the new social movements of the past, it brought a focus on issues of social justice, bridging it with core concerns from various previous movements (such as women's rights, human rights, peace, or the environment). Social justice as a master frame was located within a global vision and cosmopolitan values. As research results indicate, the anti-austerity movements maintain a focus on social issues with an inclusive vision of civic and political rights. In comparison with the GJM, however, there is more of a focus on a recovery of national sovereignty as well as a moral appeal to the common citizens, rather than to associations, against a corrupt class and a corrupt system – something which had indeed been stressed also in research on anti-austerity protests in the global periphery.

Chapter 4 will link the economic crisis of neoliberalism to a crisis of responsibility, as an additional dimension of the socio-political context in which the movement develops. It starts by identifying the political effects of late neoliberalism in a crisis of legitimacy. In the social sciences as well as in political and social theory, a debate is open on the consequences of this legitimacy crisis on democratic institutions. While some predict a populist backlash, with the spread of antipolitical sentiments, others expect an autonomous development of civil society, through cracks in capitalism (in Holloway's definition) or permanent movement of the multitudes (in Hardt and Negri's reflections). Departing from the mentioned work of Jürgen Habermas (1976) on the legitimacy crisis of Fordist society, and building upon empirical analysis in political economy and democratic theory, I will single out some main political elements of today's crisis. Neoliberal policies of deregulation, liberalization, and privatization reduce the capacity of political institutions to respond to citizens' expectations, while at the same time the growing role of international organizations, of a political and economic nature, diminishes the very sovereignty of some states. If neoliberalism had promised a separation of state and market, the studies of sociologists such as Colin Crouch (2012) as well as economists like Joseph Stiglitz (2012a) point instead at the ways in which political institutions are captured by giant corporations, as well as at the growing collusion between business and politicians. The effects are then visible in a drastic increase of mistrust in institutions of representative democracy – a mistrust which seems indeed shared not only by activists but also by the citizenry at large. Comparing the GJM with the anti-austerity one, we will note a drop in institutional trust, accompanied however by a continuous belief in the need for a return to politics against the market.

Chapter 5 focuses then on the organizational dimension of the cleavages. I will first introduce some main reflections in social movement studies addressing the organizational strategic choices as well as the social, normative, and technological constraints and resources. After having addressed this debate, I will in this chapter present some data on the organizational dimension of both the GJM and the anti-austerity protests. Empirical evidence, based on data on both activists and their organizations, indicate a focus on participatory and deliberative visions of democracy, with embeddedness in rich political and social networks as well as the development of new ones. While in the GJM there was a focus on the associational dimension, the emphasis of anti-austerity protests on direct democracy, prefigured in the occupied parks and squares, represents a new development which, at the same time, reflects and reacts to the mentioned crisis of responsibility of late neoliberalism, which had been noted also in Latin America.

In the concluding chapter, after summarizing the main results of the empirical investigation on the emerging political cleavage, I will discuss some broader implications for social movement studies but also for political economy and broader democracy theory. I will then finish with some reflections on the contributions of the anti-austerity protests in addressing the social and political consequences of late neoliberalism. In particular, I will single out some main effects in the movements' capacity not only to sensitize public opinion, but also to socialize to democratic politics a large number of citizens, restoring dignity to those who have suffered from the indignity produced by neoliberalism. Additionally, the prefiguration of different (participatory and deliberative) forms of democracy can contribute to reflection on the need for another democracy – for what Pierre Rosanvallon (2006) has indeed called counterdemocracy. The question is still open, however, of the ways in which these positive energies and resources can be effective in producing the political changes the movements pursue.

2

Social Structure:
Old Working Class,
New Precariat, or Yet
Something Different?

Tunisia, 17 December 2010. The catalyst of the so-called Jasmine revolution was, in the peripheral region of Sidi Bouzid, the suicide of Mohammad Bouazizi, who had set himself on fire in front of the regional office. As Joseph Pugliese (2013, 7) noted, 'Bouazizi's incendiary act of revolt in the public street of Sidi Bouzid is tinder to the other citizens ground down by the violent practices of the Tunisian state. His sister, Leila Bouazizi, locates his act of self-immolation within larger relations of state power and violence: 'In Sidi Bouzid, those with no connections and no money for bribes are humiliated and insulted and not allowed to live.' Bouazizi's public suicide was so interpreted as an act of revolt against a society in which some members were 'not allowed to live'. In fact, 'His self-immolation inflames a citizenry that is ready to revolt: "The fear had begun to melt away and we were a volcano that was going to explode", says Attia Athmouni, a union leader and official of the opposition Progressive Democratic Party in Sidi Bouzid. "And when Bouazizi burnt himself, we were ready"' (Pugliese 2013, 7).

While there had been other cases (for example, in March and August 2011) of young people immolating themselves in front of government buildings, the new victim had relatives in the progressive party and in the unions who promoted a sit-in in front of the regional government headquarters. An activist thus recalled those moments: 'So on Friday 17 December we gathered in front of the regional government building: hundreds of unionists and activists. We made a sit-in in front of the government building and stopped traffic, until 8 at night … together with the unemployed; and friends of Bouazizi – all throwing oranges and other fruit at the regional government building' (Donker 2012). While the police intervened to repress, young people responded in kind (Ayeb 2011).

Social injustice remained a main frame of the protest. On 22 January 2012, another young person killed himself in Sidi, leaving a note that read: 'no more misery, no more unemployment'. This fuelled other protests, which became stronger after, on the 24th, two demonstrators were killed by police fire in Menzel Bouzaienne, a small town of 5,000 inhabitants. Social claims were central in the mobilization, as 'the Tunisian revolution was started not by the middle class or in the northern urban centres, but by marginalized social groups (the southern mining region workers and the unemployed, particularly graduates) from southern regions, which themselves are suffering from economic, social, and political marginalization. We had to wait till the beginning of January 2011 to see the middle class intervening actively in the revolutionary process' (Ayeb 2011, 468).

The Arab Spring has been depicted as a movement for democratization, but it was also – or even mostly – a movement against a specific form of capitalism, neoliberalism, and the suffering it produced. In Tunisia, as in the revolts that followed in 2011 in the MENA region and elsewhere, issues of social justice were central – as was the overwhelming participation of young people, often unemployed or in precarious positions (della Porta 2014a). The political economy of Tunisia, similarly as the Egyptian one, has been characterized as neoliberal as the decline of the developmental state has left space to austerity policies which have reduced welfare provisions (in terms of public education, assistance, health, housing, jobs, etc.) while a peripheral location within the global economy was expressed in the specialization on few goods and services with high levels of economic dependency from the core. Here, debt crises strengthen the political dependency from core capitalist states as well as international organizations. Bouazizi's extreme act of protest was protesting indeed the increasing precarity of life in peripheral Tunisia – in terms not only of job insecurity, but also of quickly deteriorating welfare provisions and the repression of claims for social justice. Anti-neoliberal claims and calls for social justice became more and more audible in the mobilization that followed. A similar development had, since the 1970s, characterized other peripheral areas.

As the protest moved from the MENA regions to Southern Europe, it pointed at the parallel – although delayed – paths at the semi-periphery of Europe, where the financial crises had followed moments of hope, soon to be disillusioned, in the capacity of free market to solve the structural weaknesses of those national economies. A few months later, as anti-austerity protests spread in the United States, the evidence of the crisis at the core of capitalism became then dramatic. Consumption has been in fact depressed by the excessive concentration of richness in a few hands, as well as by the dynamics of financial fluxes, with the opening of credits to citizens first used as a sort of 'private Keynesianism' solution to keep demand and profits high, followed by a (mainly private) debt crisis (Crouch 2010; Pianta 2012). The crisis in 2008 showed all the fragility of supporting consumption through consumers indebtedness, with the effects of going 'from bubble to bubble' (Wallerstein 2010, 137). Some countries (with traditionally weak economies) were indeed much more hit than others. Also in rich states, however, neoliberalism had the effect of exponentially increasing social inequalities, with a very small percentage of winners and, instead, a pauperization of the working class together with a proletarization of the middle class (Stiglitz 2012a). Under neoliberal capitalism, and especially its crisis, 'growth is lower than ever, unemployment, on cross-country average, higher, the same holds for inequality, wages continue to stagnate, and social benefits are on a steady decline' (Streeck 2014, 49). As we are going to see, these trends are reflected in the social basis of the protest.

In what follows, I will first locate today's movements within a dynamic vision of capitalism, pointing at some important contributions from political economy and economic sociology to social movement studies. Departing from the analyses of the social basis of the protests against neo-liberalism in the periphery at the end of the last millennium, I will then proceed to present empirical evidence on the social bases mobilized in the GJM during the rampant years of neoliberalism, as well as in the anti-austerity protests, during its crisis. While, in different ways, World-System theory and theorization of the Empire expect anti-systemic movements to emerge when exploitation and sufferance increase, social movement studies point at the effects of sociostructural conditions on the grievances but also the resources of the different social groups. As we are going to see, protests under neoliberalism tend increasingly to involve precarious youth, but mostly in coalition with other social groups that have lived a sort of precarization.

Dynamics of capitalism

As mentioned in Chapter 1, capitalism has not totally disappeared from social movement studies, but rather selectively continued to play a role in some areas of analysis, which remained however rather separate from the mainstream. In this part, I will start reviewing some broad shifts in capitalist transformation, as well as its internal diversities. Particular attention will then be paid to some characteristics of the 'second great transformation' – that is, to neoliberalism and its crisis, that I suggest has affected social movement development.

Charles Tilly (1978) has influentially linked social movements to capitalist development (and concentration), particularly within the nation-state. By focusing decision making on the national level, the twin processes of state building and capitalism development have attracted protests at that level, contributing to the creation of national social movements. Economic changes so affected political opportunities and the responses to them (Kousis and Tilly 2005). While state formation is influenced by the mode of production, the latter does not automatically translate into specific institutions; rather, 'the translation from class structure to state organization occurred through struggle' (Tilly 1990, 100). The organization of work generates contentious issues and conditions for struggle. In fact, under precipitating conditions workers activate shared definition of action, which depend on the context as well as previous experiences. Strike waves then leave behind significant changes in industrial relations, especially for those categories that have constructed a reputation of militancy (Tilly and Tilly 1998, 231).

National social movements have historically been prompted by and resisted changes in capitalism, in its continuous move between free market and social protection. Classical works in political economy as well as social history have pointed to the role of collective action by aggrieved groups in promoting social incorporation and resisting de-incorporation (Collier and Collier 2002). As Karl Polanyi influentially noted, analysing the first wave of economic liberalism in what he called the great transformation: 'For a century the dynamics of modern society were governed by a double-movement. The market expanded continuously but this movement was met by a countermovement checking the expansion in definite directions' (1957, 130). In the nineteenth century, the turn towards the free market was in full swing, yet 'simultaneously a countermovement was on foot. This was more than the usual defensive behaviour of a society faced with change: it was a reaction against a dislocation which attacked the fabric of society, and which would have destroyed the very organization of production that market called into being' (Polanyi 1957, 130). Polanyi described this double movement as produced by:

> ...the action of two organizing principles in society, each of them setting itself specific institutional aims, having the support of specific social forces and using its own specific methods. The one was the principle of economic liberalism, aiming at the establishment of a self regulated market, relying on the support of the trading classes, and using laissez-faire and free market trade as its methods; the other was the principle of social protection aiming at the conservation of man and nature as well as productive organization, relying on the varying support of those most immediately affected by the deleterious action of the market – primarily, but not exclusively, the working and the landed classes – and using protective legislation, restrictive associations, and other instruments of intervention as its methods. (Polanyi 1957, 132)

The spectacular failures of the free market after the 'great transformation' were in fact followed by protective countermovements by the landed and worker classes; the great depression between the two wars then reopened the way for social protection. The pressure of the lower classes for incorporation interacted with the so-called Fordist version of capitalism, in which mass production required mass consumption and a related ethic, as well as relatively high wages and state intervention (Barker and Lavalette 2014). While Fordism spread especially after World War II at a time of US hegemonic maturity, by the 1970s a post-Fordist turn had already adapted capitalism to pressures from labour through a progressive dismantling of the welfare state: with a new neoliberal turn, inequalities increased accordingly (Antonio and Bonanno 1996).

While these streams of research addressed the alternation of free market and social protection, looking at these double movements and the return of (neo)liberalism with a view to explaining social movements, one must also consider the internal (cross-national and cross-area) differences within each capitalist turn. In political economy, the social science analyses on world-systems as well as on the diversities of capitalism provide useful specifications in this direction.

In the world-systems perspective, the world is an interdependent system with hierarchical division of labour. Cycles of economic expansion and decline are linked to the cycles of the hegemon's growth and fall, with each hegemonic state advancing a peculiar accumulation system. Accumulation crises introduce the need to adapt to declining profits. So, neoliberalism is a way to address the crisis of the 1970s, with globalized capitalism that limits the state role to regulation of monetary policy and protection of private property. Growth promotion is invoked through international trade, privatization of services, deregulation of business practices, and limits on spending. In this vision, the recent period is marked by frequent crises, as the financialization of capital increases the volatility and vulnerability of the hegemonic order. In Wallerstein's expectation, in a system far from equilibrium, 'small social mobilizations can have very great repercussions' (Wallerstein 2010, 141).

The turn towards neoliberalism happened first in the semi-periphery and in the periphery, where developmental new states had risen during cold-war rivalry, with multilateral sponsorship, developmental assistance, and economic incorporation, as 'developing country governments began to invest in their own economies and regulate them in the interest of planned growth' (Walton 1998, 466). In that time, the developmental state promoted an 'interventionist strategy through mechanisms to support the social wage and ensure the general welfare with central planning, social security, health care, workers' compensation, minimum wage and trade union rights. The developmental state was capitalist and dependent on trade and on aid from Western industrial nations, but it also attempted to husband national capital in a set of policies that included import-substitution industrialization, capital and exchange rate controls, industrial protection, and joint investment ventures' (Walton 1998, 466). In the 1970s, after the debt crisis, the conditionality of structural adjustment programmes implied however severe cuts in public budgets with the consequent loss of access to basic services, and major anti-neoliberal policy protest. This happened, among other places, in Latin America, Asia, and the MENA regions, where developmental states were radically dismantled through several waves of shock therapy in the free market. To remain with the Tunisian example, between 1983 and 1992 the IMF had imposed structural adjustments, with privatization and an end to subsidies as well as price controls, plus lowering of trade barriers. These changes produced increasing unemployment, especially of young people.

In the 1980s, the core capitalist states experienced a similar turn towards the free market, even if with different timing in different models of capitalism. Literature on the varieties of capitalism has in fact pointed at the diversity between an Anglo-Saxon capitalist forms and a European one as located within different models of firms' coordination (Hall and Soskice 2001). While the Anglo-Saxon model trusted to competitive market arrangements the coordination of economic activities, in the coordinated capitalist model in Europe firms relied more on non-market relations to coordinate their activities, with the state policies characterized by support for income interventionism and planning.

The neoliberal turn happened first in the variety of capitalism which seemed already more oriented to trust market self-regulation. The United States and Great Britain, led respectively by Ronald Reagan and Margaret Thatcher, initiated in fact a move towards cuts in the welfare state as justified by an ideology of the free market. As increasing inequalities and the reduction of public intervention risked depressing the demand for goods, low interest rates were used, in a sort of private Keynesianism, to support demands – ultimately fuelling the 2008 financial crisis (Streeck 2014). In fact, in that year, the failure of Lehman Brothers produced such a shock that governments decided to come to the rescue; banks began to introduce this willingness into their calculations. This was followed by increasing government debt.

Faced with US and UK economic decline, coordinated market economies, e.g. in the EU and Japan, seemed to have equal or even superior competitiveness if compared with liberal market economy (Hall and Soskice 2001; Streeck 2010).[4] Given the failure of Clinton's plan for reform and the financialization and deregulation of the US economy, co-ordinated capitalism was expected in fact to offer an alternative to the vagaries of the market self-regulation. Besides its diversity, however, that form of capitalism also moved towards the free market and was hit by the recent financial crisis, showing, indeed, some inherent contradictions of democratic capitalism (Streeck 2014).

This could be seen especially in the EU, where the trend towards welfare retrenchment was aggravated, particularly in the weaker economies, by the European Monetary Union (EMU) which, together with the fiscal crisis, increased inequalities both among and within member states. As Fritz Scharpf (2011) noted, with the abandonment of Keynesian types of intervention, which assigns leading functions to fiscal policies (as governments are supposed to cut taxes and finance expenditures during recession), the monetarist orientation of the EU policies – with the abandonment of full employment as a goal and the dominance of price stability – was responsible fact for the type of crisis which developed in the union.[5] This is all the more the case as the European Central Bank (ECB) is in fact based on monetarist assumptions. After an apparent initial success, 'the political crash programmes, through which unlikely candidate countries had achieved an impressive convergence on the Maastricht criteria, had generally not addressed the underlying structural and institutional differences that had originally caused economic divergences. Once access was achieved, these differences would reassert themselves' (Scharpf 2011, 173). As the problem of the great recession is mainly a lack of aggregate demand, the crisis in Europe has been said to be produced by excessive austerity of the ECB, as 'given the weakness of the economy...deficit fetishism focuses on the wrong problem' (Stiglitz 2012a, 237).

The EMU produced particular problems for countries with below-average growth, as interest rates proved too high for their economies, 'with the consequence that initially weak economic activity was depressed even further by restrictive monetary impulses' (Scharpf 2011). In fact, states had to find solutions without the use of monetary exchange rate strategies. In the so-called GIIPS (Greece, Ireland, Italy, Portugal and Spain), interest rates initially fell to the German level, while the sudden availability of cheap capital-fuelled credit financed domestic demand – with, especially in Ireland and Spain, large investments in housing and consequent price bubbles (Scharpf 2011). On the eve of the crisis, the GIIPS were made particularly vulnerable by severe current-account deficits, dependence on capital inflow, and over-valued real exchange rates. So, in 2007, the monetary union had achieved proximate political purposes, eliminating currency fluctuation and interest rate differentials among member states, but had deprived national representative institutions of their own monetary and exchange rate instruments of macroeconomic intervention (ibid.).

Also in the EU, especially in some member states, neoliberalism was temporarily rescued by the growth of credit markets for the poor and middle classes, and by the spread of derivatives and futures markets among the rich (Crouch 2012; Scharpf 2011). Privatized Keynesianism developed here as well, facilitated by deregulation of the bank system, as families took on debts, until the system started to implode. The rise of external, mainly private indebtedness was not seen as a problem by EU institutions, as the stability pact did not address private debt or differentiate between debt incurred during growth or recession (in fact, both Spain and Ireland were models of fiscal probity) (Scharpf 2011). Since 2008, some effects of the US crisis were in fact felt in the United Kingdom, Germany and Ireland, which had allowed their banks to invest in toxic products (differently, for example, from Spain). The effects of the credit squeeze hit then especially those countries whose economies had relied more on cheap credit. As Scharpf noted (2011), although bankruptcy-cum-devaluation could have been an option for some of these countries given the spectre of sovereign default, surplus countries did not support this solution as they feared difficult political conditions, speculative attacks on the Euro, and losses for their banks, while revaluation of the Euro would have damaged export industries (Scharpf 2011).

When the crisis exploded, the governmental reaction in Europe was based on cuts in public expenditures, even in countries (like Ireland or Spain) in which the public deficit was relatively low. While unemployment increased dramatically (up to one-quarter of the population in Southern European countries, and more than 50 per cent among young people), the crisis of neoliberalism also meant, at the same time, a reduction in available public resources as well as an increase in the number of citizens who need social service support. Accused of low increases in productivity, social services in public hands see cuts in budgets, along with reductions in social workers' salaries and positions in the public sector. Additionally, the very function of social services *qua* public services is challenged. The conception of welfare state moves then towards a residual, charity based one, while the neoliberal credo defines social protection as bad for the economy if paid for by the state: it not only affects the public budget, but is even accused of distorting the functioning of the labour market.[6]

The austerity policies have imposed (or justified) in fact a decline in the share of public spending over which officials and legislators have some discretionary power (Streeck and Mertens 2011, 1). On education, research and development, active labour market, and support for families, the decline is especially high in those states that had once invested more in these areas. Short-term and non-standard forms of employment have increased especially since the 1990s (Saraceno 2005), while the ideology of flexibility spread (Gallino 2007). The concept of precariousness indicates the increasing number of (especially young) citizens characterized by not only the lack of contractual protection on the labour market, but also a growing difficulty in constructing political subjectivities (Mattoni 2012).

While the welfare state under Fordism had represented a decommodification of some goods, defined as public services, neoliberalism brought about the privatization and (re)commodification of once-public goods, as social services are increasingly considered as a commodity to be sold on the market (Graefe 2004). This is the case for health care as for education, for the care of children as of the old or the sick. In parallel to privatization of social services for those who can pay, research has indeed singled out a criminalization of the poor. Public spaces are also privatized in order to keep away those who are considered, once again, as dangerous classes. While in principle there is a legal protection from poverty in the name of human rights, these provisions are usually not binding (e.g. art. 30 of the European Social Charter, Council of Europe 2013, 63; see also Gerds 2013). If in principle nobody can be discriminated against because she is experiencing poverty, de facto the privatization of public services implies discrimination from provisions of even basic goods. While the most urgent functions are increasingly allocated to the third sector, this sector is more and more deprived from public support – in material but also in symbolic resources.

The target of the anti-austerity movements, then, is a crisis of neoliberal capitalism which has been addressed through austerity measures. The evolution of the last thirty years or so has also deeply transformed the social structures. Fordism was said to have created a two-thirds society, with new social movements emerging from the pacification of class conflict, and even the *embourgeoisement* of the working class, with the crisis of the 1970s producing a short but radical wave of protest by the excluded one-third. Today's mobilizations seem instead to reflect the pauperization of the lower classes as well as the proletarianization of the middle classes, with the growth of the excluded in some countries to about two-thirds of the population.

In sum, we can draw from political economy research some preliminary relevant elements for the analysis of social movements in times of austerity. First of all, capitalism has always been transforming itself, through complex and dynamic interactions among different actors. The pendulum between free market and social protection has been accompanied by waves of economic growth and decline. Second, while some changes are global, their specific characteristics vary in different geopolitical areas and within different varieties of relations between the state and the market that for sure affect protest.

These brief references to capitalism developments also lead us to some expectations about the structural bases for the grievances around which citizens of various countries are mobilizing. In what follows, we shall look at their effects on the social bases of those who protest, taking into account that in all the countries where anti-austerity protests spread – not only in Greece and Spain, but also in Tunisia, Egypt and the US – indeed the indicators of social and territorial inequalities are constantly on the rise, the middle class declines, and the number of people defined as poor increases (see Pianta 2012; Stiglitz 2012a; Therborn 2012; Tezanos 2012).

Social movements and social structures

Which are the expected effects of these evolutions of capitalism on social movements and their bases? In Marxist views, capitalism affected directly the mobilization of the oppressed. As capitalist production tended to reduce the power and value of labour, 'the increasing precariousness of working and living conditions induces proletarians to form combinations against the bourgeoisie' (Arrighi et al. 1989, 9), with an enduring crisis of capitalism. While this did not happen, research on the labour movement has, however, addressed in depth the role of socio-economic structures as bases for social conflicts and constraints on their development.

Much scholarship has in fact pointed at the role of the working class in struggling for the civic, political and social rights, which have been incorporated in some conceptions of democracy. According to Rueschemeyer, Stephens and Stephens (1992, 6), 'one would have to examine the structure of class coalitions as well as the relative power of different classes to understand how the balance of class power would affect the possibilities for democracy'.

Attention to the social bases of conflicts remained present in research and thinking on social movement studies, in either a more structuralist or a more dynamic version. First, world-system theory has predicted an important role of anti-systemic movements in the struggle against capitalist exploitation, singling out some success but also some failure. While world-system theory located the anti-systemic movements within a global context, which had however differentiated effects at the periphery, developing a broad and deep research project, recent theorizations on the 'empire' pointed at the global role of emerging multitudes. With more of a focus on the empirical analysis of the social bases of existing movements, some social movement scholars, as mentioned, referred to cleavage theory looking at different stages of post-Fordist societies. After presenting those works, starting from more structural views and moving then to more dynamic ones, I would then suggest some potential bridging among them.

World-systems theory and anti-systemic movements

With a clear focus on structure, the world-systems approach expects capitalist crises to, more or less automatically, fuel an (anti-systemic) movement. The world-systems perspective aimed at coming to terms with the failure of Marx's prediction of a revolution emerging from the crisis of capitalism. According to it, the exploitation of the periphery allowed the hegemon to survive, as state protection and mercantilistic policies 'increasingly transferred world capitalist competition from the realm of relations among enterprises to the realm of relations among the states' (Arrighi et al. 1989, 12). Especially at the core of the capitalist world-system, extra-profits could be invested in granting some benefits to labour.

Crises however still happened at this time. As the system requires constant economic growth, crisis is the situation in which the restitutive mechanisms of the system no longer function well, so that the system will either be fundamentally transformed or disintegrate. According to world-systems theory, in the ascending phase of a hegemonic cycle, the rising state exploits new sets of opportunities, transforming productive advantages into power in commercial and financial areas (Buechler 2000). Growing economic power is then translated into military dominance. In prosperous periods, class conflict is moderated through reforms. Vice-versa, when a state loses its productive advantage, stagnation ensues, resulting in increasing economic and political inequality, and state repression. As the availability of resources diminishes, the scarce investments are oriented to policies that might strengthen national capitalism into crisis, while expenses for welfare are cut (Buechler 2000). In this context, anti-systemic frames are expected to re-emerge when a crisis ensures the persistent presence of and growing pressure by anti-hegemonic movements.

While recognizing transnational effects, world systems theorists still expect increasing protests as exploitation grows. In their prediction, 'When oppression becomes particularly acute, or expectations particularly deceived or the power of the ruling stratum falters, people have risen up in an almost spontaneous manner to cry a halt' (Arrighi et al. 1989, 29). In this approach, resistance to capitalism initially took the form of riots and revolts that rarely made an impact; however, challengers later began to organize in anti-systemic movements. While in the early modern period oppressed peasants did sporadically riot, it was only after 1848 that workers began to create durable organizations and political strategies that represented a 'great innovation in the technology of rebellion' (Buechler 2000, 30). These challenges were to become successful after World War II: social democracy developed in core countries, communism in the semiperiphery and peripheries, national liberation in the periphery. Even when they took state power, however, none was able to end inequality, as their regimes continued to 'function as part of the social division of labour of historical capitalism' (Wallerstein 2004, 71).

The movement of 1968, then, represented a revolt not only against capitalism, but also against the perceived failure of the old anti-systemic movements (for a synthesis, see Schaeffer and Weyer 2013). At the end of the 1960s, new social movements were in fact prompted by 'the tremendous widening and deepening of bureaucratic organizations as a result of the previous wave of antisystemic movements' (Arrighi et al. 1989, 38), and the dissatisfaction with their performance. Direct action was then particularly effective given the highly integrated system of production. This move, however, prompted a new adaptation by capitalism, with centralization of capital in multinational firms, first-world de-industrialization, and third-world industrialization. The debt crisis of large groups of states led them to look for credits at the international level, accepting the cuts in welfare and austerity measures international organizations imposed. Globalization was then also resisted by single-issue, fragmented campaigns that however tended to network into more durable efforts, some of them channelled into International Governmental Organizations (IGOs) or the development machines in the global South, reproducing Western values and patterns of exploitation (Smith and Wiest 2012).

In sum, in this vision, discontent with capitalism is expected to result in the revolt of the oppressed, with different dynamics at the core, the semi-periphery and the periphery. While capitalism changed forms, there has been however no final crisis, with related end of the current capitalist world system, Wallerstein himself expected will happen (Wallerstein 2010). If world-systems theory is influential in pointing at the differences in space within the global cyclical move from free market to social protection and back, it does not, however, focus on how waves of globalization impact on the intensification of relations within and between the various forms of capitalism at the centre, the semi-periphery, and the periphery. This is instead a main aim in the more recent reflections on the novel *Empire*.

Multitudes against the empire?

The Marxist focus on structural transformation as leading to collective action re-emerged in the work of Michael Hardt and Antonio Negri (2000) who, in their *Empire*, single out in the 'multitude' the new anti-capitalist subject, which they see as an emerging global opposition. They define globalization as a condition in which 'the primary factors of production and exchange – money, technology, people and goods – move with increasing ease across national boundaries' (Hardt and Negri 2000, xi). In this sense, the cause for 'the declining of the nation-states and their increasing inability to regulate economic and cultural exchanges is in fact one of the primary symptoms of the coming of the empire' (Hardt and Negri 2000, xii). In their analysis, the empire represents a step forward in the evolution of biopolitical power: it is considered to be a positive development insofar as it puts an end to colonialism and imperialism, but the relations of exploitation it builds are seen as even more brutal than the ones it destroys, with very small minorities in control of enormous wealth, and multitudes living in poverty (Hardt and Negri 2000, 43). Foucault's biopolitical power is here endowed to international organizations such as the UN or IMF, but even more to huge transnational corporations. Communicative production supports an imperial legitimation based not only on military power but also on moral appeal and juridical intervention. The increasing power of corporations and the mechanism of command of the empire replace those of the state.

A move from national to imperial sovereignty implies, in this view, an opening of frontiers but also the closing of the imperial space (Hardt and Negri 2000, 167, 187). Expanding beyond the factory, capitalist exploitation no longer has a place. This also means, however, that 'imperial power can no longer discipline the power of the multitude; it can only impose control over their general social and productive capacities' (Hardt and Negri 2000, 211). The fundamental contradiction of capitalist expansion is thus singled out in the reliance on the outside to realize surplus, as this enters in conflict with the need to internalize the non-capitalist environment (Hardt and Negri 2000, 227). In fact, once civilized, the outside is no longer outside. The world market is considered unified through proletarization and migrations with decolonizing and decentring of production, thus participating in the creation of a disciplinary regime and society. While the hegemonic position of the industrial working class fades away, the proletariat, made up of those exploited by capitalism, increases in number: it 'imposes limits on capital and not only determines the crisis but also dictates the terms and nature of the transformation. The proletariat actually invents the social and productive forms that capital will be forced to adopt in the future' (Hardt and Negri 2000, 268). The spread of precarity – as a modality of work, but also of life – is a relevant condition in the empire, as 'the central characteristic of labour that results from the flexibility and mobility imposed on it in biopolitical production is its precarious nature, that is, its lack of guaranteed contracts, stable schedules, and secure employment, in which work time and life time blend together on the tasks and challenges of informal and changing jobs' (Hardt and Negri 2000, 245).

Here as well, the exploitation in the empire would produce rebellion, but in this case of a global character as the proletariat would now include all those exploited by and subject to capitalist domination (Hardt and Negri 2000, 53). In fact, 'Multitude is thus a concept of applied parallelism, able to grasp the specificity of altermodern struggles, which are characterized by relations of autonomy, equality, and interdependence among vast multiplicities of singularities' (Hardt and Negri 2009, 111). Precarity, although a capitalist control strategy, erodes the normal division between working and nonworking time (Hardt and Negri 2009, 147). As the factory had been for the industrial workers, the metropolis is now the primary locus of biopower; like the factory, it is a place of exploitation, but also a site of rebellion (Hardt and Negri 2009, 258). Similarly, in John Holloway's vision (2010), 'cracking' capitalism can result either from a conscious opting out or from a forced expulsion from capitalist social relations.

While the theoretical reflection around the emergence of a new oppressed class can push forward the debate on the potential social basis for resistance to neoliberalism, the empirical conditions under which the multitudes will rebel are not spelled out. Some indication about how to reintroduce class consciousness as a necessary, and non-automatic, component of class mobilization comes instead if we bridge reflection on structures in a political economy perspective with some main assumptions in social movement studies.

Bridging political economy and social movement studies

Political economy has reflected on several aspects that are important for our understanding of social movements in anti-austerity mobilizations. In particular, it helped in singling out the three mentioned temporalities in capitalism development: first, a long-term temporality refers to general forms of capitalism; second, a middle-term temporality singles out cyclical movements of growth and crisis; third, there is a short-term, contingent temporality within those cyclical shifts. In addition to time, research has also pointed at the spatial dimension of capitalism. As the world-systems approach has suggested, even though capitalist transformations tend to have a worldwide dimension, their specific characteristics vary in the core, the semi-periphery, and the periphery. Even within those broad areas, capitalism emerges as cross-nationally diverse, as far as the dimensions of both social protection and free market are concerned.

These dynamics and varieties of capitalism have an effect on the social structures, first of all affecting the interests of the main classes, and therefore the social bases of contentious politics, which tended to move from the industrial workers of the labour movements to the new middle classes of the new social movements and, nowadays, to cross-class coalitions of the many victims of austerity policies. The world-systems approach noted the development of anti-systemic movements, sometimes successful in challenging capitalism at the core, the semi-periphery, and the periphery. The contemporary capitalist empire had been seen as promoting the rebellion of the multitudes.

While these observations mainly addressed structural characteristics and changes, social movement studies might help to avoid determinism by moving beyond the conception of interest as inherent in a structural position and pointing, instead, at the dynamic way in which structural positions might nurture the development of a social group, which could then become mobilized. In a certain way, we can say that it addresses the Marxist question of the transformation of a class in to a class per se, through a reference to concepts such as grievances, cleavages, and historicity. Bridging these two streams of knowledge could stimulate a reflection, I will develop in the remainder of this chapter, on the transformation of the social basis for progressive movements during the shift from the rampant years to the crisis of neoliberalism.

Modes of production and social cleavages in social movement studies

While the previous analyses focus on the structural characteristics of capitalism as the fundamental condition for the emergence of its opposition, for social movement studies the main concern was with when and how social exploitation was translated into protest. Although rarely concerned with capitalism per se, social movement studies have occasionally looked at the bridging of structures and action. While not a central focus of social movement studies, strains have been considered as important, as 'protesters generally protest against something and we fail to grasp their meaning if we fail to consider what they protest against' (Crossley 2002, 188). Even if much research has demonstrated that grievances are not sufficient for collective action to emerge, nevertheless they are important elements in understanding social movements.

With these caveats in mind, social movement scholars looked, at least sporadically, at the social bases of protest. In the classic theorizations on new social movements, the new social formation of late-modern and post-industrial society produced specific conflicts between administrative rationality and the search for meaning (see Buechler 2013 for a synthesis). The invasion of private life by market and power imposed an instrumental rationality against which social movements developed a search for autonomy and authenticity. For Alberto Melucci (1996), in particular, movements represented a search for collective identities in social life against the instrumental logics of the administrative system and the weakening of traditional collective identities.

Remaining within the analysis of new social movements, Alain Touraine had looked at class action as the 'behavior of an actor guided by cultural orientations and set within social relations defined by an unequal connection with the social control of these orientations' (Touraine 1981, 61). According to him, 'the sociology of social movements cannot be separated from a representation of society as a system of social forces competing for control of a cultural field' (Touraine 1981, 30). The way in which each society functions reflects the struggle between two antagonistic actors who fight for control of cultural concerns which, in turn, determine the type of transforming action that a society performs upon itself (Touraine 1977, 95–6). It is in relation to the concept of *historicity* – defined by the interweaving of a system of knowledge, a type of accumulation, and a cultural model – that different types of societies can be identified, along with the social classes that accompany them. Touraine in fact singled out four types of society, each featuring a distinctive pair of central antagonistic actors: agrarian, mercantile, industrial, and 'programmed'. A particular trait of the latter is the 'production of symbolic goods which model or transform our representation of human nature and the external world' (Touraine 1987, 127). As the control of information constitutes the principal source of social power, the main conflicts are expected to shift from the workplace to areas such as research and development, the elaboration of information, biomedical and technical sciences, and the mass media.

As mentioned, research on the new social movements pointed in fact at the over-representation in them of some specific social groups. In a society in which the traditional social cleavages were supposedly pacified, specific components of the middle class seemed to take the lead in contentious forms of politics. In particular, 'The new middle class, according to these analyses, is constituted from sectors of the population that tend to be employed in the service sector: they are highly educated, yet are not comparable with managers or traditional professionals. As a result of their technical and cultural competence and of their economic-functional position, members of the new middle class are more likely to mobilize in conflicts of the new type' (della Porta and Diani 2006, 55). Protest politics was therefore said to be, like interest group politics, an additional resource for those endowed with rich material and cultural capital, contributing to increase political inequality rather than redressing it.

Besides class, generations also proved a useful concept for identifying the characteristics of the mobilizing basis for social movements. Attention to the social bases of protest was in fact occasionally revived by research on biographical availability (often related to young age) as well as the cultural resources coming from higher levels of education – while results on the class or occupational bases have been less conclusive (for a synthesis, Corrigal-Brown 2013). Especially, the spread of education has been said to increase the role of social movements as agents of change from below, as in fact, 'Participation in social movements demands some degree of awareness, imagination, moral sensitivity and concern with public issues, with the ability to generalize from personal or local experience. All these are positively correlated with the level of education. The educational revolution which accompanies the spread of capitalism and democracy extends the pool of potential members of social movements' (Sztompka 1993, 280). In sum, research on social movements and participation identified a life-course effect, with young adults the most prone to protest politics, then a declining trend, but also the effects of (persistent or discontinuous) socialization to protest (Fillieule 2013a, 2013b).

However, the effects of indicators of biographical availability (such as age, marriage, parenthood, and occupation) are inconsistent, varying with the type of movement as well as the degree of commitment (Beyerlein and Bergstrand 2013). Moreover, the causal direction of some correlation is unclear – for instance, participation in teaching and other helping professions has been said to increase participation in social movements, but the choice of those occupations may also be a biographical consequence of activism itself (Giugni 2013).

Moving from the expansive phase of neoliberalism to the great recession, empirical research within the cleavage tradition has indeed aimed at singling out the social groups made up of those who are suffering most from the neoliberal economic model and its crisis as a potential base for mobilization.

Some time after the fading of the debate on new social movements, the concept of cleavage re-emerged in social movement studies in order to address the effects of economic and political globalization. In a broad research project, Hanspeter Kriesi and his collaborators (2008; 2012) singled out as a political consequence of (neoliberal) globalization the formation of a cleavage between winners (those who have an exit option) and losers (those with no exit option). With the erosion of protected property rights and increasing cultural diversity, a cultural competition adds up to economic and political ones. In this analysis, the new cleavage singles out the losers and winners of globalization: 'the likely winners of globalization include entrepreneurs and qualified employees in sectors open to international competition, as well as cosmopolitan citizens. Losers of globalization, by contrast, include entrepreneurs and qualified employees in traditionally protected sectors, all unqualified employees, and citizens who strongly identify themselves with their national community' (Kriesi et al. 2008, 8).

A cultural and an economic dimension intersect around an integration–demarcation divide, whereby losers oppose and winners support increased global competition. This innovation is seen as being facilitated by the pacification of traditional cleavages around class and religion, high levels of economic development, increasing immigration, and electoral volatility. Initially mobilized on the right, the Weltanschauung of the losers is dominated by a cultural demarcation, often expressed as exclusivist nationalism. While the political space remains two-dimensional, the meaning of the dominant cleavages is expected to be transformed, with the strengthening of conflicts on pro-market versus pro-state issues, and enhanced opposition to cosmopolitan liberalism (Kriesi et al. 2008). The analysis of the positions of the well educated versus the less educated and of sociocultural specialists versus managers, and versus unskilled workers, shows in particular that if education has liberating effects in terms of tolerance and openness, the less educated tend instead to develop xenophobic cultural positions, as cultural closeness becomes a common denominator for a socially fragmented stratum (Kriesi et al. 2012, 17).

If the mobilization on the right of the losers of globalization seemed a major phenomenon, often with relevant electoral repercussions, in the 2000s the critique of globalization (especially in its neoliberalist form) developed on the left as well, in this case more within contentious politics (della Porta 2007). Social movement studies have however considered at the difficulties of transforming structural conflicts into action – or, we can say, social bases into cleavages. Charles Tilly influentially pointed at the need to add to 'category', as similar structural position, 'net-ness', as the presence of dense ties within a certain population. Much social movement research has indeed looked at mobilizable networks, considering individuals as embedded in personal as well as associational nets. Embeddedness in these networks facilitates recruitment and help maintaining commitment (della Porta and Diani 2006, 117–21). While for the industrial workers, the proximity in the fabric as well as in popular neighbour increased the capacity to mobilize, unemployed or precarious people, the poor and the marginal, even when highly hit by economic crises, are rarely embedded in mobilizable networks. Mobilization processes might therefore be long and complex, as those reticula need to be constructed in action.

The question then is, how does it happen that individuals and groups characterized by low 'cat-net-ness' are mobilized? The anti-austerity protests in the global South, addressed in the next paragraph, constituted an important step in emerging mobilization processes, that we will see to some extent reflected later on at the core of capitalism. As shown in particular by research on Latin America, while it is true that those who suffered for increasing poverty and inequalities did indeed mobilize, they needed however to overcome several thresholds, those who were on the losing side of neoliberalism slowly building up cross-class coalition.

Anti-austerity protest in the periphery

Some reflections on the relations between changing social structures and protest can be found in research on social movements against austerity in the periphery, especially in Latin America. Reactions to austerity measures in other parts of the world are particularly relevant to keep in mind when analysing protests today. Counterbalancing the tendency in social movement studies to focus on opportunities, even if admitting threats, their analysis brings attention back to the role of structural conditions as producing grievances and then protest. They also suggest that specific characteristics of the capitalist developments, as well as their conjunctural crises, can be expected to play a role that is worth investigating, on the type of actors who are expected to mobilize.

Somehow detached from studies on social movements in the North, works on the global South have in fact stressed the importance of economic strains in prompting protest. Research on the South has analysed the mobilizations against various waves of austerity policies, paying attention to changing structural conditions. Since the 1980s, social movements in the global South have emerged as responses to extreme dispossession and poverty produced by neoliberalism (Motta and Nilsen 2011). As mentioned, mobilization reflected specific class relations. While in more advanced capitalist states labour movements had brought about a decline in liberal capitalism after the great depression, national liberation movements had fuelled an expansion of the Westphalian system through the participation of popular classes in national liberation movements, so that anti-colonial nationalism included demands by the subalterns (Wallerstein 1990). This contributed to spread an unstable equilibrium around the developmental project, heralded by the bourgeoisie, with social services selectively provided to the urban working class and urban poor in exchange for quiescence (Walton and Seddon 1994).

The debt crisis of the 1970s and related austerity measures broke the social pact around which developmentalism had developed. Especially since the early 1980s, structural adjustment programmes required cuts in services and subsidies. In urban settings, the middle classes also experienced increasing declassing. Access to housing, health services, and education declined as international organizations promoted market strategies, while the state was restructured as a provider of the fundamental services to capital (Chalcraft 2011, 17).

Resistance, which emerged during these transitions to neoliberalism, was carried out not only by labour but also by groups that had been excluded by developmentalist pacts. Since the early 1980s, protest campaigns for democratization developed as Structural Adjustment Plans (SAPs) weakened co-optation and coercion capacities of states. While austerity pushed people to ask for greater popular sovereignty, impoverished states could no longer support clientelism. Not only in Latin America, but also in Africa, astonishing numbers of popular movements grew even in one-party states (Walton 1998).

While popular parties were co-opted, people expressed their outrage at the abrogation of the social pact of developmentalism, now defended by the subalterns (Chalcraft 2011, 37). Anti-World Bank and anti-IMF protests started in the mid-1970s, continuing well into the 2000s, with actions targeting governmental buildings but also banks and international agency offices (for a summary, see Wood 2013). Compared with the first wave of struggles for incorporation during state-building in the early twentieth century, this new one was characterized by the mobilization of a more plural coalition of collective actors (including identity based ones, while labour focused more on defensive struggles) who were more autonomous from the state and parties, and possessed more decentralized organizational structures (Roberts 2008). Ad-hoc coalitions grew, as protest increases the more frequent are the interactions with international financial institutions (IFIs) (Walton and Ragin 1990). Protests involved working-class groups, often with other actors – especially public sector employees and students, but also neighbourhood, human rights, indigenous, churches, street vendors, pensioners, and debtor associations – targeting especially national government.

Under neoliberalism, growing popular movements emerged as independent from states (while before they had been channelled by them) and with more of a focus on the forms of protest on collective consumption than on labour. Movements reacted then to the disruption of everyday life. Looking at less developed countries, Paul Almeida and Hank Johnston have singled out some of the grievances neoliberalism (and its crisis) brought about, and around which anti-austerity protests mobilized. In general, 'the negative conditions typically associated with austerity measures and neoliberal policies are numerous, but a short list must include the following: rising costs of living, cuts in social services, informalization and fragmentation of national economies, ponderous foreign debts, hyperurbanization and, for many workers, low wages, harsh working conditions, and insecure employment in newly privatized enterprises and export processing zones' (Almeida and Johnston 2006, 3). Neoliberal challenges to previously acquired rights included cuts in urban services such as public transportation, water, electricity, sanitation, public health, housing and food subsidies. Labour also protested against privatization, joined by women and those who mobilized in rural areas for land, water rights, loans, communal land access, and price supports. Comparing five Central American countries (Costa Rica, El Salvador, Guatemala, Honduras and Nicaragua) in the late 1970s and early 1980s, Booth (1991) emphasized the impact of economic deterioration after the agro-export boom of the 1960s as a relevant motivation to mobilize. In fact, 'The grievances caused by declining income or wealth, catastrophes, and political dissatisfaction among would-be competing elites led to protests against public policies' (Booth 1991, 36). After some decline of protest following transition in the 1980s and 1990s, perceived threats to everyday life emerged with increases in oil prices and privatization of public services (health, education, public industries).

Research on political protest in the Third World as a response to the debt crisis indicated a link between the number of structural adjustment agreements (especially IMF pressures), dense urban social networks, and the intensity of protest, mobilizing the urban poor (shantytown dwellers, street vendors, unemployed youth) and the working class affected by cuts in services, subsidies, and salaries (Walton and Ragin 1990). Economic dependency weakened states in economic terms as well as in terms of legitimacy. Boswell and Dixon (1990) also noted that dependency had an effect on rebellion, through short- and long-term negative effects in terms of economic inequality and growth. While growth brought about a spread of unions and associations, dependency gave rise to rebellion by polarizing classes and income.

The protests against neoliberal reforms in Latin America can be seen as at the roots of the GJMs, which developed especially strongly in the region at the turn of the millennium. The location of the first editions of the World Social Forum in Puerto Alegre in Brazil, as well as the large participation of Latin American activists in them testify to this link. Indeed the GJM also grew in Europe; here however in a still expansive phase of neoliberal capitalism. As I will show in what follows, presenting some survey data on the European case, the social bases of the protest tended to reflect, to a certain extent, the growing suffering produced by the crisis of neoliberalism.

The social basis of the (European) Global Justice Movement

A debate on the social bases of protests under neoliberalism as moving beyond the new middle classes had developed already in research on the GJM – which had indeed focused on social issues, denouncing the increasing inequalities (among and within countries) that neoliberalism, then in rampant growth, had brought about. Here, research had pointed at some innovation, but also at continuities with the new social movements of the past.

Social diversity was a much appreciated characteristic of the movement. So, a document produced by the first World Social Forums (WSF) stated: 'we are...social forces from around the world (that) have gathered here at the World Social Forum in Porto Alegre. Unions and NGOs, movements and organizations, intellectuals and artists' (World Social Movements 2002b, par. 1), and 'women and men, farmers, workers, unemployed, professionals, students, blacks and indigenous peoples, coming from the South and from the North' (World Social Movements 2002b, par. 3). The social heterogeneity of the movement was stressed indeed over and over again: 'We are diverse – women and men, adults and youth, indigenous peoples, rural and urban, workers and unemployed, homeless, the elderly, students, migrants, professionals, peoples of every creed, colour and sexual orientation...The expression of this diversity is our strength and the basis of our unity' (World Social Movements 2002a, par. 2). Besides its social diversity, the movement also presented itself as multi-generational. According to activists, the movement 'put together different generations...and this is the great novelty and the great richness because it puts together men and women, who are from 20 to 60 years old, who discuss together against the old leftist parties' logic that separated the men from the women, the young from the old' (focus group, cit. in della Porta 2003, 130).

Research on the activists at the European Social Forum (ESF), in various of its editions (the first in Florence, in 2002; the second in Paris in 2003; the fourth in Athens in 2004), indicated, however, a social background that was indeed to a certain extent similar to the one identified for new social movements. While the gender ratio was balanced, young cohorts dominated. As Andretta and Sommier (2009, 115) summarized, 'Those under 25 represent respectively 47.5 per cent in the first ESF, versus 24.5 per cent of the 2003 sample and 29.3 per cent of the 2006 sample...Those under 40 represent respectively 82.9 per cent, 71 per cent, and 63 per cent.' In fact, the majority of the interviewed ESF activists were less than 40 years old, which represents less than 40 per cent of the European population overall.

The ESF participants were also characterized by very high educational levels. In sum:

> 32.5 per cent of participants had a college or university degree at the first ESF, 69.4 per cent at the second, and 80.3 per cent at the fourth. The ratio of technical or professional qualification was stable during the two first forums, at around 15 per cent; but it dropped considerably at the Athens ESF (4.6 per cent of the sample). The high proportion of persons without diplomas (19 per cent) or with only a high school degree (34 per cent) at the first ESF can be easily explained by the particularity of the sample that was composed more than half by students. (Andretta and Sommier 2009, 115)

As for the social background, students clearly dominated, while workers were underrepresented. According to the data collected through surveys at various ESF editions:

> First, the GJM activists are prevalently students. Despite differences among the different editions – with 54.8 per cent at the first, 23.7 at the second, and 38.3 per cent at the fourth ESF – they are consistently overrepresented in relation to their weight in the European population (only 6.6 per cent). While not of the same proportion, this

over-representation is also found for educators, who were represented more than twice as frequently in Athens than in the general European population (7.6 and 3.8 per cent, respectively). In reverse, the working class is remarkably less present among GJM participants. For example, in Paris and Athens, manual workers were only 2.2 per cent (but 22.3 per cent in overall European statistics). The same is true for retired people (6.5 per cent of the sample but 21.5 per cent of the general European population), as would be expected given the age distribution in the ESF population (Andretta and Sommier 2009, 119).

In sum, 'non-manual workers are clearly over-represented among participants, especially those working for the public or associative sectors' (Andretta and Sommier 2009, 125). Additionally, social background was higher among the professional activists and tended to become even more selective with increasing degrees of professionalization within the forum from one edition to the next (Table 2.1).

While farmers and workers' unions were present at the social forums at various levels, bringing in the claims of their constituencies, research on the World Social Forum (WSF) has confirmed some social selectivity. Although a high 42 per cent of respondents were under twenty-six years old, WSF participants tended to be white and well educated (Institute for Research on World-Systems 2006). As many as 70 per cent of respondents were either students (about one-third) or employed in middle-class occupations (about 15 per cent as professors or teachers), while fewer than 10 per cent were part of the working class or peasantry and only about 3 per cent were unemployed or retired (Smith et al. 2007).[7] Additionally, the number of young people, although not low in absolute terms, is declining from one edition to the next.

In conclusion, while not exclusively a movement of the new middle class, the GJM still saw an under-representation of those very social groups whose interests the movement aimed to defend.

The social bases of movements in the crisis of neoliberalism

If the industrial workers constituted the 'empirical base' of the labour movement and the sociocultural professions that of the new social movements, which were also somehow overrepresented in the GJM, the anti-austerity protests are said to have brought into the street social groups that are either losing or never achieved social protection in the retrenching welfare state. If Fordism was the capitalist form in which the labour movement developed, and post-Fordism the capitalist form of New

Table 2.1.   Type of activists by sociographic variables (Athens, column %)

| | Type of activists | | | |
	Loners	Ordinary	Professional	Total
Gender				
Men	52.5	52.8	60.3	55.3
Women	47.5	47.2	39.7	44.7
Total (N)	141	466	320	927
Cramer's V	N.s.			
Level of Education				
Compulsory	4.4	8.9	8.6	8.1
Post-comp.	54.4	36.3	32.8	37.8
University +	41.2	54.9	58.6	54.1
Total cases	136	463	314	913
Cramer's V	.11***			
Age group				
Up to 29	68.8	45.4	34.9	45.4
30–44	16.3	21.4	27.4	22.7
45–53	7.8	14.3	19.8	15.2
54+	7.1	18.8	17.9	16.7
Total (N)	141	467	318	926
Cramer's V	.16***			
Employment status				
Blue and white collars	10.3	22.5	39.5	26.5
Upper class (professionals, managers, employers)	10.3	13.4	17.4	14.3
Teachers	5.2	9.7	10.5	9.2
Unemployed	3.4	7.5	3.5	5.5
Retired	3.4	9.1	5.0	6.8
Students	67.2	37.8	24.0	37.6
Total (N)	116	373	258	747
Cramer's V	.24***			
Working sector				
Private sector	50.0	33.5	16.6	27.5
Public sector	45.0	55.9	39.8	48.0
Associative sector	5.0	10.6	43.6	24.4
Total (N)	40	236	211	487
Cramer's V	.29***			

Source: Andretta and Sommier, 2009: 120, table 6.3.

Social Movement, neoliberalism and its crisis represent the capitalist environment of today's anti-austerity protests (della Porta 2013a).

The sociography of the camps

The social basis for the protest seems to be changing, in fact. In particular, empirical research has pointed at the precariat – mainly young unemployed or underemployed – as a main base for the recent mobilizations. Looking at anti-austerity protests, several researchers noted the importance of the emergence of a new generation, characterized by a specific condition in the society. From the Arab Spring to the United States, passing through Europe, a main social component of the protests of 2011 and thereafter have been young, often well-educated, unemployed, or precarious workers. With youth unemployment above 50 per cent in many of the countries where protest was stronger, and a large majority of new workers in unprotected or at best weakly protected working positions, it is not surprising that young people do indeed represent a large part of those who protest.

In the various campaigns against austerity, the first people to mobilize have been indeed young people between twenty-five and thirty years old, unemployed and underemployed members of the precariat (Benski and Langman 2013). This is the case for the Greek *indignados* (Sotirakopoulos and Sotiropoulos 2013), but also in the saucepan revolution in Iceland (Juliusson and Helgason 2013) or the J14 protesters occupying Rothschild Boulevard in the Israeli capital (Alimi 2012). In Tunisia, protest was also organized by an unemployed and young people's defence committee, with cooperation of urban and rural unemployed (Sergi and Vogiatzoglou 2013). In the 2000s, unemployed graduates had already organized frequent street demonstrations and other protest activity. Pioneers of the movement for democracy were former student activists who mobilized on the powerful frame of a right to work. In September 2006 there were daily demonstrations with up to 1,000 participants, followed by a de facto recognition by the authorities of activists as mediators on the labour market (della Porta 2014a).

The situation was similar in Egypt, where young activists especially moved towards more grassroots movement organizations, such as the 6 April movement, recalling in its name the date of the repressed textile workers' strike in 2008. Mainly very young, many of the founders had attended the same university: 'Thus, when talking about the initial mobilizers, those who put out the call for action, we are talking about young, educated, well connected activists' (Stork 2011, 93).

In Spain, well educated and on the left (especially the more active participants), the *indignados* tend to be young people out of work, even if qualified and embedded in digital forms of knowledge (Calvo 2013). In fact, here the economic crisis has effects on young people, 'making them unable to fulfil modern expectations of financial independence, controlling one's own life, and the ability to lead a life that is self-sustaining, fulfilling, and productive economically, socially and culturally' (Calvo 2013, 528).

Similarly, in the United States, Occupy is presented as a movement of the marginalized, with more and more insecure and low-paid jobs, precarious housing conditions, and few social entitlements, with a particularly strong presence of recent college graduates who have incurred high debts because of the loans taken to finance education (Langman 2013; Gitlin 2012). A *Guardian* journalist wrote in fact of a defiant new generation, with no money, no future and huge debts: 'Most, I found, were of working class or otherwise modest backgrounds, kids who did exactly what they were told they should, studied, got into college, and now are not just being punished for this, but humiliated – faced with a life of being treated as deadbeats, moral reprobates' (cit. in Graeber 2012, 68).

The precarious youth are however met in the streets by other social groups, especially among those most hit by austerity policies. In fact, anti-austerity protests mobilized coalitions of different groups: young, middle class, members of new classes of cultural workers, unemployed (Benski et al. 2013). Precarious workers often allied with members of the small bourgeoisie and the middle classes, in situations of imminent proletarianization, and with workers with a common experience of suffered injustice and felt outrage.

The building of cross-class coalitions has been considered as particularly relevant in the period leading to the Arab Spring. As Jack Goldstone (2011, 460) summarized, in Egypt and Tunisia, 'a broad cross-class and cross-regional coalition was vital to overthrowing the regime. Islamists and secularists, residents of the capital city and rural towns; workers, students, teachers, lawyers; and defecting soldiers, all contributed to the revolutionary effort.' In particular, 'the unions' role in the Tunisian revolution was paramount. The intermediary grades of the General Union of Tunisian Workers (UGTT) managed to launch the movement, articulating the economic demands of workers and the lower middle class as well as the political demands for democracy of the middle classes and the younger generations' (Khosrokhavar 2012, 216). As reforms pushed for by the World Bank brought about increasing unemployment, protest by the unemployed but also by employed or precarious workers multiplied. Young unemployed coordinated via informal friendship networks, unionists through pre-existing militant networks (Mersal 2011). Protests also mobilized unorganized under-proletariat and youth. Resistance came in fact from the subaltern classes, such as street vendors or unemployed, who called at the same time for integration in a consumption society, but also for freedom. As a Tunisian poet wrote: 'It is the unemployed and the vagabonds, the beggars and the hobos, it is the barefoot, the sons of the scarred women, it is the street vendors, who made the revolution' (Calvo 2013, 232).

In Egypt as in Tunisia, labour protests followed each neoliberal turn in the government's policies. Workers entered very early in the struggle for democracy, as the longest and strongest wave of strikes since the end of World War II started in 2006 and continued well after the end of the Mubarak regime (Bishara 2013). Even if accused of advancing narrow demands, workers constituted important actors in political mobilization, often targeting governing agencies as well as introducing new forms of action. Thus, former labour leaders defected from the official trade union, founding independent unions, while rank-and-file workers, who maintained their membership in the official unions, also engaged in protest. As Beinin (2011, 181) observed:

> Egyptian workers have not received the message that class struggle is unfashionable...Supported by intellectuals and pro-labour NGOs such as the Center for Trade Union and Workers Services (CTUWS) and the coordinating Committee for Trade Union and Workers Rights and Liberties, workers mobilized in response to the privatization, throughout the 1990s, of 190 firms. In the second half of the 1990s, food prices increased, salaries dropped, and a sharp increase in inequality was also met by protests: between 1998 and 2003, workers' protests grew from an average of 25 in the previous ten years, to an average of 118, increasing to 265 in 2004 and 614 in 2007.

Indeed, protests exploded especially after, in 2004, a new government with several Western-educated ministers prompted a new wave of strikes during the privatization of what workers considered as their own firms. Labour and hunger strikes sometimes even won concessions (as in July 2006, after three days of work stoppage). Some of these events developed more politically, targeting the government and its neoliberal policies, as was the case on 6 April 2008 with the repression of the textile workers' strike in Mahalla, a large industrial town in the Delta. The continuous strength of labour conflicts is testified to by demonstrations of tens of thousands on Labour Day 2010, with the support of the 6 April coalition and youth groups (Mackell 2012). Labour protests were also very visible all through the uprisings, with three days of general strikes starting on 8 February.

What activists as well as observers stressed the most, was the extraordinary social diversity in the protesters' backgrounds. *The New York Times* wrote that 'Friday's protest was the largest and most different yet, including young and old, women with Louis Vuitton bags and men in *galabeyas*, factory workers and film stars...The protesters came from every social class' (cit. in Alexander 2011, 9). Similarly, *Al Jazeera* noted that, in the street, there were 'not the 50 or 60 activists that we have been seeing protesting in Egypt for the past five or six years', but rather 'normal Egyptians, older women, younger men, even children' – there were, indeed, 'children, the elderly, the ultra-pious and the slickest cosmopolitans, workers, farmers, professional, intellectuals, artists, long-time activists, complete neophytes to political protest, and representatives of all political persuasion' (Alexander 2011, 10).

Also later on in Europe and the United States, different social groups coalesced in anti-austerity protests. The so-called movements of 2010+ mobilized in fact a new age-cohort of activists (Biekart and Fowler 2013), with the growing educated unemployed in combination with impoverished middle classes (working poor). Research based on surveys indicated that in Greece, as Spain, opposition to austerity policies as well as protest potential (that is, belief that people should protest) increased with the worsening of personal financial situation as well as of economic expectations, especially if combined with vote for a left-wing party (at the Left of Pasok) and belief in the effectiveness of participating on demonstrations (Ruedig and Karyotis 2013, 16). Previous involvement in protest is higher for younger, male, well-educated citizens working in the public sector, members of unions and other associations, with left-wing orientations (Ruedig and Karyotis 2013, 18). However, protest in 2010 was indeed not a middle-class phenomenon, but a mass phenomenon in which people with varying educational backgrounds and from different generations took part (Ruedig and Karyotis 2013, 22). In fact, 30 per cent of Greeks who participated in protest were, although mainly coming from the Left, otherwise representative of different social and generational backgrounds, so that 'anti-austerity protest in Greece constitutes a mass movement' (Ruedig and Karyotis 2013, 23).

Coalitions were formed in particular by workers and users of public services. Social workers and welfare users have been at the forefront, often with common mobilizations in defence of public health or public education. Welfare provisions are in fact core claims of those who protest against privatization of services and commodification of rights, proposing instead a vision of common goods to be defended and controlled by the community. As the crisis of late neoliberalism affects social work in several respects, social workers and users of social services respond through various forms of contentious politics, which at the same time react to and are affected by that crisis. If the workers in social professions had been considered as the main social bases of new social movements in the past, in the protest against austerity social workers have been overwhelmingly present, both as individuals and in organized groups.

Several protests also addressed the increasing sufferance of, and disrespect for, the victims of the crisis and of the austerity policies. These were often collective actions by citizens, resisting their categorization as users or consumers. In many such protests, legitimacy comes from the participation of the affected – for example, los Affectados para la Hypotheca in Spain. While much action in favour of the so-called weak people had in the past been carried out in their name, a strong tendency in recent protests has been their direct participation. Groups of homeless, disabled, migrants, SLA patients or unemployed stress the importance of the participation of the affected, rather than of sympathetic advocacy. While large NGOs have sometimes been criticized for their vertical organization and single-issue approach, as well as the internal competition in the sector for declining public financing (e.g. Council of Europe 2013, 105), emerging social movements working on issues of social protection have called for a participatory and horizontal networking logic (Council of Europe 2013, 107; also Berg-Schlosser 2013).

Similar to these are the protests of workers and users against the measures of so-called rationalization, with the closing of hospitals, kindergartens, unemployment offices and other centres for the provision of social services. Increases in the costs citizens have to pay for services, and cuts in the salary and personnel of those services, have sometimes been targeted in broader campaigns on public schools or public health. Voluntary associations also became to a certain extent indignant vis-à-vis the increased responsibility downloaded on their field of action, with a simultaneous decline in public support, at the material and symbolic levels. Associations of victims of house evictions, as well as associations of people affected by serious diseases have been central in calling for a definition of services as rights rather than commodities.

Some cross-national differences emerge in the mentioned cross-class coalitions. The trade unions mobilized the proletarized public employees or industrial workers who, in Tunisia and Egypt, participated in the mass protests that eventually tore the regimes down. This was only occasionally the case in Greece, where general strikes converged in the occupied Syntagma (Sergi and Vogiatzoglou 2013), or in Portugal (Baumgarten 2013), where the struggles of the precarious workers sometimes met with those of unions. Efforts remained, however parallel, with even fewer occasions for encounters, in Spain or, even more rarely, in the United

States. Especially in the latter, ethnic and racial cleavages were still divisive, and the Occupy movement had difficulty connecting to the struggles of the Chinese population in Chinatown in New York City or to those of the native Indians (Barker 2012). These difficulties have also been linked to the presence of different logics of personalized versus communitarian organizing – the former dominating in Occupy, the latter among people of colour and workers (Juris et al. 2012).

The social basis of protest in Europe

In Europe, in general, the survey data collected by social movement scholars working within the 'Contextualizing contestation' project on marches organized by left-wing social movement organizations, allows us to analyse the sociographic background of participants in anti-austerity protests as well as in other types of protests during the austerity periods, comparing them by countries as well as by types of demonstrations.

In all the covered countries, various age cohorts protested during the crisis: if about one-third of the protesters we surveyed were born up to 1956, about the same proportion was born after 1976. In the countries where austerity hit harder – Italy and Spain – younger people took to the streets more often. The generations born before and in 1956 were more often surveyed in the Czech Republic, Belgium, and the Netherlands; the younger cohorts more often in Italy and Sweden (see Figure 2.1).

Data on protesters at various demonstrations in Italy between 2011 and 2013 give us some more information about those who mobilize in different types of movements in times of austerity, as well as on the

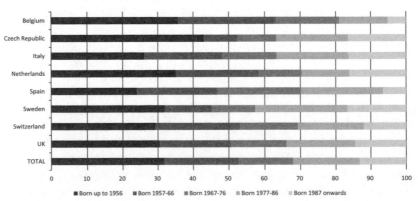

Figure 2.1   Age by country based on surveys at selected marches in EU countries between 2011 and 2013 (%)

specific characteristics of those who protest against austerity policies – as is the case for the three demonstrations on labour issues, the No Monti day and the Florence 10+10 protest on the anniversary of the first European social forum.

First, we notice that 35 per cent of protesters were born after 1977, and were therefore up to about 35 years old at the time of the survey, among which 15 per cent were born in 1987 and after. The remaining participants were distributed as 26 per cent in the age cohort of those born up to 1956, 22 per cent born between 1957 and 1966, and 15 per cent between 1967 and 1976. In this sense, we can talk of a high presence of young people in anti-austerity protests, even if other age groups are present as well. The younger cohort is however more present in protests that do not directly address austerity issues, such as the gay pride movement in Bologna in 2012 (67 per cent born after 1976), the No Muos protest in Sicily (54 per cent born after 1976), and the anti-mafia national demonstration in 2013 (45 per cent born after 1976) (see Figure 2.2). In general, this indicates that a precarious condition, as is related with this age group, does not reduce the propensity to protest in general, but that this group protests less in events against austerity issues and more on gender, environmental, and anti-mafia issues. There is, however, a variation to be noted in the protests on labour issues as well, with Euromayday, which explicitly targets precarity, bringing in many of the youngest cohorts (65 per cent below 35 years old), the Labour Day in Florence the most senior cohorts (86 per cent born before 1967), and the general strike we surveyed in 2011 located in between. In general, it

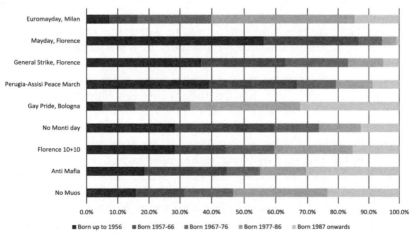

Figure 2.2   Generational variance among participants in various protest demonstrations in Italy in 2011–2013 (%) (No. 1598; Cramer's V = .25***)

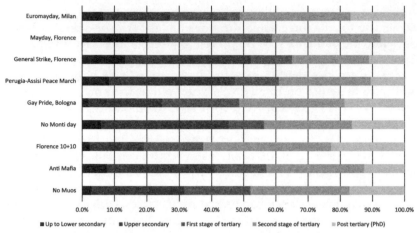

Figure 2.3 Educational variance among participants in various demonstrations in Italy, 2011–2013 (%) (No. 1587; Cramer's V = .16***)

seems that the very precarity of their position on the labour market jeopardizes the participation of young people in mobilizations that are organized on the typical claims of the labour movements.

Remaining with the data on Italy, education is generally high, although somewhat lower for demonstrations on austerity issues (see Figure 2.3). While all demonstrators attended beyond primary school, a low 10 per cent of participants at labour protests have only a lower secondary education. Those with lower levels of education were more frequently represented among the Labour Day marchers in Florence (21 per cent up to lower secondary) – while the opposite is true for the Euromayday paraders, who are much younger but only in 6 per cent of the cases below lower secondary and as many as 17 per cent with post-doctoral studies. The difference between demonstrations is limited, however, as the low value of the correlation coefficient between education and demonstration indicates. At all demonstrations, the most represented group is the one with the second stage of tertiary education (about 30 per cent).

From the point of view of class position, protests, although varying, tend to see the presence of lower rather than higher strata. If we look at the whole sample, almost one-third defines themselves as upper middle class, but over 40 per cent as lower middle class, and about one-fifth as workers. Subjective class location varies by country. The upper middle class were especially highly represented in Switzerland and the Netherlands; lower middle class was a very widespread self-definition in Italy and the Czech Republic; and working class overwhelmingly in Spain

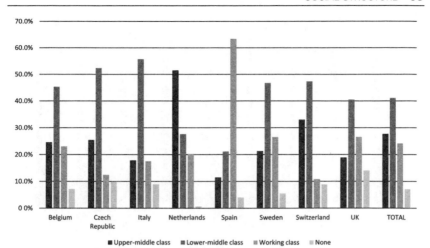

Figure 2.4   Subjective class by country based on surveys at selected marches in EU countries between 2011 and 2013 (%)

(with over 60 per cent) (see Figure 2.4). So, self identification in lower-class positions is higher in those countries where the crisis hits harder.

In the Italian case, in terms of subjective class allocation (Figure 2.5), while one out of five protesters self-locates in the working class (somewhat more for labour protests, with the exception of the Euromayday where working-class self-collocation is rare and there is instead a high presence of lower-class location), reaching about one out of four if we add lower-class self-definition, a majority define themselves as lower-middle-class. Many, especially in demonstrations where young people are particularly present, refute class self-definition altogether, as a precarious position seems to jeopardize even this form of identification. From the point of view of self class location, rather than a middle-class or a working-class dominance (even if the latter is more present in anti-austerity protests), we can therefore speak of a prevalence of those who feel part of the lower classes.

As for job position (see Table 2.2), on the covered European countries less than 40 per cent of protesters in total are employed full-time, about one-quarter are part-time or self-employed, and almost 15 per cent each students and retired people. Only 5 per cent declare being unemployed. The distribution by country is quite homogeneous, with full-time workers, however, more present in the sample in Spain and Belgium, but much less in Switzerland, where part-time workers are more present along with self-employed (the latter much less present in Belgium and Spain). Significantly, the unemployed are more present among Spanish

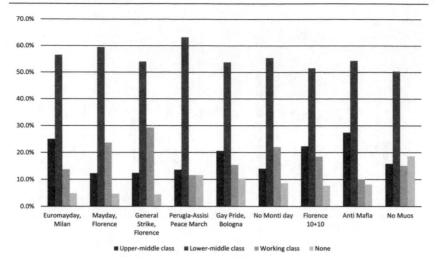

Figure 2.5   Subjective class (self-definition) in various demonstrations in Italy 2011–2013 (%) (No. 1580; Cramer's V .13***)

protesters, as well as in Italy, where the crisis is most felt, as well as in the United Kingdom.

The presence of 'globalization losers' is confirmed in Italy when looking at employment conditions of marchers, as full-time employed reach about half of protesters only in anti-austerity protests (but not in the Euromayday, where full-time workers are less than average, and part-timers more than average), remaining well below in the others (Table 2.3). Hit by cuts in spending for public education and with a perspective or actual experience of precarious job positions, students are overrepresented by far, comprising 14 per cent of protesters (but up to half for the LGTBQ pride and the anti-mafia protest). Also very present at demonstrations are members of another category of losers of austerity policies: retired people (13 per cent of participants), who have seen their pension reduced and suffer most from cuts in public services (especially in public health). While the presence of students and retired people varies by demonstrations (but not so much between anti-austerity and other protests), the unemployed plus part-time employed reach about one fourth of the participants.

Conclusion

Bringing capitalism back into the analysis is an important move if we want to understand changes in the social bases of protest and

Table 2.2. Job position by country based on surveys at selected marches in EU countries between 2011 and 2013 (%)

	Belgium	Czech Republic	Italy	Netherlands	Spain	Sweden	Switzerland	UK	Total
Full-time	50.4	29.1	42.5	32.2	61.6	40.3	24.8	40.5	39.2
Part-time	15.9	2.8	7.7	20.0	5.0	9.4	32.9	9.7	14.5
Self-employed without staff	2.4	11.1	8.2	9.5	3.5	6.1	12.1	11.6	8.4
Student	4.8	16.0	14.6	18.5	9.6	21.5	11.1	14.9	14.2
Un-employed	4.9	4.3	6.3	4.1	10.0	5.5	3.6	6.9	5.5
Retired	17.5	34.9	13.5	10.8	8.9	14.8	12.1	14.1	14.6
Other	4.1	1.7	7.2	4.9	1.3	2.4	3.5	2.4	3.6
Cr. V	.16***								

Table 2.3. Employment condition in various demonstrations in Italy 2011–2013 (%)

	Euro-mayday, Milan	Mayday, Florence	General Strike, Florence	Perugia-Assisi Peace March	Gay Pride, Bologna	No Monti day	Florence 10+10	Anti Mafia	No Muos	Total
Full-time	42.2	47.2	60.1	44.0	37.9	48.1	34.4	36.1	24.1	42.5
Part-time	12.9	7.5	10.6	5.6	7.2	5.4	6.1	7.3	8.8	7.7
Self-employed without staff	9.5	3.8	2.3	7.6	10.3	8.1	10.7	6.8	17.5	8.2
Student	14.7	1.9	5.0	7.6	27.7	10.3	13.0	28.3	21.9	14.6
Un-employed	5.2	2.8	1.4	4.8	5.6	9.2	14.5	2.1	16.1	6.3
Retired	5.2	32.1	14.7	23.2	1.5	10.3	17.6	13.1	4.4	13.5
Other	10.3	4.7	6.0	7.2	9.7	8.6	3.8	6.3	7.3	7.2
Cr. V	.16***									

movements. Political and social theorists have speculated on the effects of the emerging social structures on social conflicts, broadly diverging in their predictions. Empirical research has also provided initial evidence on the emergence of new conflicts, here as well without yet reaching conclusive knowledge on a very dynamic situation.

In this chapter, I have suggested we look at capitalism in a dynamic way, distinguishing three temporalities: a long-term one signalling the transformations of forms of capitalism; a middle-term one singling out moments of growth and crisis; and a short-term, contingent one. In addition to time, the spatial dimension of capitalism is also important, since – as the world-systems approach has pointed out – while capitalist transformations tend to have a global dimension, their timing and characteristics change in the core, semi-periphery, and periphery, as well as in different varieties of capitalism. These dynamics of capitalism have an effect on the social bases of protest, which in the long term moved from the industrial workers for labour movements to the new middle classes for new social movements, but now involves cross-class coalitions of the many victims of austerity policies. As we noticed, anti-austerity protests developed first at the periphery, moving then to the semi-periphery and, finally, at the core of capitalism. In Latin America, as in the MENA region, neoliberal turns have increased inequalities, with dramatic effects on large parts of the population. In the US, similar effects in terms of increasing poverty have been noted. In Europe, while the strongest forms of coordinated capitalism have shown some resilience to the crisis, movements developed especially in the European periphery where the financial crisis of the late years 2000s hit particularly those historically weak economies which had already shown difficulties in adapting to the European Monetary Union.

Concluding, in order to understand the development of social movements in general and anti-austerity protests in particular, we need to consider the dynamics of capitalism, both in terms of the long-term capitalist model and short-term contingency. Referring to Polanyi's double movement, we can state that the anti-austerity movements face the prevalence of free market over social protection in the form of neoliberalism. As in the first movement towards the free market, there is a main focus on liberalization, deregulation, and private property; more specific is instead the financial dominance (versus the commercial one) with attention to shareholders rather than consumers, as well as the development of huge, transnational corporations.

Moreover, looking at more short-term waves, we have to locate protest within the crisis of neoliberalism, with the attempt to increase demand for goods and services through private debt rather than public investments, and then the growing public debts, also linked to the bailing out of banks. In the particular case of the EU, the European Monetary Union had disadvantaged the weak economies with exchange rates that were more profitable for the stronger ones (drugging them with low interest rates), as well as depriving them of the power to devalue the national currencies, which had been an important instrument of economic politics in the past.

Especially, but not only, in the weaker economies, neoliberalism and its crisis brought about increasing social inequalities, as well as the pre-carization of life conditions. Extremely high rates of youth unemploy-ment have been accompanied by new types of labour contracts with very low rate of protection for workers. The closing of factories has added to youth unemployment the unemployment of those once inserted in the protected labour market. Precarization (and often cuts in revenues) even affected the once protected public sector, as well as retired people. If in the 1960s and 1970s, the peak of Fordism was said to have produced the *embourgoisement* of the working class and a larger and larger middle class, neoliberalism and its crisis instead brought about a *proletarization* of the middle classes, as well as general impoverishment.

Two specific concepts – introduced into the debate by scholars par-ticularly interested in political economy, but which are seldom referred to in social movement studies – are the (anti-free market) countermove-ment, as put forward by Polanyi (1957), and the anti-systemic move-ment, in the world-systems tradition. While anti-systemic movements are expected to fight for a radical alternative to capitalism, countermove-ments similar to Polanyi's are more likely to be backward looking, aiming at re-establishing previously existing compromises between free market and social protection. In both traditions, however, the expecta-tion is that those actors whose interests are most affected by capitalism's forms and twists will rebel. Also in recent theorizations on an emerging empire, a link is expected between the specific social structures produced by capitalist development and the mobilization of precarious, mobile multitudes. This seems paralleled by recent observations on the mobiliza-tion by the losers of capitalist globalization, focusing in particular on their exclusivist tendency (Kriesi et al. 2012).

If, with different characteristics, these approaches remind us of the ways in which social conditions affect the willingness to mobilize against socioeconomic settings considered as negative for specific interests, lit-erature on social movements has stressed the complexity of the mobiliza-tion process. Some social groups are easier to mobilize, as they are endowed with symbolic and/or material resources, that are however more likely to be found among 'winners' than among 'losers'. Research on the labour movements of the past as well as on recent campaigns against neoliberalism in Latin America has shown that exploited and marginalized groups also mobilize against their conditions, but that building the necessary resources is a long and complex process. In balance, social movement studies would therefore expect participation in protests not by the most affected, but by coalitions of different social groups that have grievances on which to mobilize as well as resources that support mobilization. Research on the global South has pointed indeed at the mobilization of coalition of public sectors employees as well as workers in the declining industries, of young unemployed, women expelled from the labour market, retired people who see their life quality worsening facing a cut in pensions and in welfare services.

Focusing the analysis on two moments in neoliberal development, I have considered the question of the relations between (capitalist) social structures and mobilized social groups by presenting some data on the sociographic characteristics of participants in the GJM and anti-austerity protests, as two moments in the development of neoliberal capitalism. Following the more structuralist approach, we might expect an increase in participation in contention by those directly affected by the crisis, moving from the former to the latter. Considering the need of resources for participation, however, we might also expect not the total losers, but rather those with grievances, but also specific social and symbolic capital, to mobilize the most. These expectations were indeed, by and large, met in our analysis.

Although stressing social heterogeneity, the GJM was still character- ized by a large presence of the well-educated middle classes, but this had not been the case for participants in anti-neoliberal movements in the periphery. Later on, the traditional bases of the class cleavage – the workers, especially of the industrial sector – are certainly mobilized in the anti-austerity protests. They are, however, not dominant, and they are often part of (sort of) multiclass coalitions, including a large compo- nent of people outside of the protected labour market. According to surveys at demonstrations, young unemployed or precarious workers, with high educational levels, are also very present in the protests – less so however in those on labour issues and they are not alone. They locate themselves on the lower side of the class hierarchy, losers for sure, pre- carious in a broad sense and, to a certain extent, multitudes, even if a main empirical base for a new cleavage did not yet clearly emerge.

If new social movements have been said to react to the pacification of the class cleavage through the development of welfare states, protests against neoliberal capitalism bring instead the language of class back in. In addition, while social movements were said to represent the form of mobilization of new middle classes, reacting to the penetration of the state into the lifeworld, the anti-austerity protests have involved those 'affected' by cuts in public spending and reduced social protection. If new social movements were located in a 'two-thirds society' of broad even if selective inclusion, characterized by the broadening of protection, nowadays they seem to react – from the Arab Spring to Occupy – to the weakening of the once-protected into a one-third society, with large exclusion.

Rather than the emergence of a social class of precariat of young and well-educated but unemployed and underemployed citizens, what we have seen as a social effect of neoliberalism in terms of the bases for protest is a precarization of various positions, with broad cross-generational and cross-class mobilization. This type of mobilization bridges together not only those who were traditionally considered as losers of globalization, but also 'new losers' – or at least, with this self-perception. Young people with high education – considered in previous analysis as 'winners' of globalization, given their high mobility and competitiveness – self identify with the lower classes, as they perceive their present and future as unsecure. Retired people – sometimes said to be able to enjoy declining prices thanks to fixed revenues – define instead themselves as losers, facing a cut in pensions, but also in all those social services (such as those in the public health system) that are particularly needed by the elders. With them, there are the once highly protected workers in large factories or the public sectors, whose conditions also emerge as less and less secure facing draconian financial measures and reduction of state intervention oriented to provision of public services and support to strategic production. In sum, protesters do not belong only to a specific precarious class, but are rather moved by a plural alliance of citizens whose existence is made less and less secure in neoliberalism and, particularly, in its crisis.

This indeed represented a shift – not only vis-à-vis the new social movements of the 1980s and 1990s, but also vis-à-vis the GJM of the beginning of the millennium. While the GJM, at least in the global North, had mobilized in solidarity with the excluded and the poor, denouncing increasing territorial and social inequalities, the social basis of the movement was still skewed towards the highly educated, cosmopolitan members of the new middle classes. Notwithstanding the emphasis on plurality of background, and actual cross-generational participation, together with students, members of the social work professions were over-represented. This changed in the anti-austerity protests, which brought into the streets (and squares) coalitions of those who perceived themselves as the losers of neoliberalism. As in the anti-debt protests in the global periphery, those affected by austerity policies became indeed a large component of those who protested. Especially at the periphery, the degree of impoverishment seems to have been reflected in the large participation of the downtrodden and marginalized social groups; in the semi-periphery, precarized workers and middle classes were more visible; at the core of (disorganized) capitalism, the social bases of the movement seemed more focused on impoverished middle classes (especially indebted former students).

Looking at the diversity of capitalism – beyond the two main capitalist varieties suggested by Hall and Soskice (2001) – can be helpful to explain the dis-homogeneous national spread of the protests. Everywhere, it was especially 'disorganized' capitalism that was targeted – while protests were more limited where the state had kept more control over the market. However, with time, there was a spreading of the neoliberal version, although with some embeddedness, even on the European continent (Bohle and Greskovits 2012). First protests happened in fact in the periphery, among which in Latin America and the MENA region, where developmental pacts had fallen victim to neoliberal doctrine and international conditionalities, but also in the semi-periphery (like in Greece and Spain) and even at the core of capitalism (in the United States).

In sum, the crisis of neoliberalism was reflected in the development of coalition of various social groups that felt particularly hit by austerity policies. These included emerging precarious youth, especially with high levels of education, but also previously protected groups – including blue collars in the big factories, white collars in the public sectors and retired people – that felt less and less secure about their job and life chances.

While I have mainly stressed similarities in trends of mobilization, a more systematic cross-national comparative analysis will, however, be required in order to understand the differences linked to dimensions such as the location at the core, the semi-periphery or the periphery of the world capitalist system; the effects of varieties of capitalism, also in terms of organization of interests and degree of social inequalities; the incidence of the extent and forms of the economic crisis. At the meso level, one should also investigate the specific effects of the neoliberal crisis on the capacity for mobilization of social movement organizations representing different social groups – e.g. of the various precarious types of precarious workers. At the micro-level, moreover, it will be useful to control to which extent individual perceptions of class belonging, grievances, life chances have an impact on the mobilization of various groups.

3

Identification Processes: Class and Culture

*Rome – November 2012. Members of the Comitato 16 Novembre (16 November Committee), made up of citizens affected by very serious and degenerative pathologies, protest against the decision of the so-called Italian technical government, led by Mario Monti and sup-ported by the main centre-left and centre-right parties – Partito Democratico (Democratic Party) and PdL (Partito della Libertà, Freedom Party) – to cancel special funds for those people who need 24-hour per day assistance. As many as seventy very seriously disabled people, including those affected by lateral amyotrophic sclerosis, enter with their relatives in hunger strike and stage sit-ins in front of the Ministry of Economic Affairs. One of them demonstratively takes away the medical machines he needs to use in order to survive, while the group threatens 'extreme and sensational' action. After six days the protest is interrupted as the government agrees to meet the repre-sentatives of the committee. But only to inform them – the minister of social affairs crying in front of the journalists – that unfortunately no money has been made available in the governmental spending review: 'in front of the crisis and the necessity to square the budget, there is nothing to do' (*Repubblica, 5/11/2012). Against what it considers an extreme cruelty, the Comitato 16 Novembre so reacts: 'If you do not respond to our appeal, you will be responsible for what will happen. We do not want charity; we want our rights.' The conflict lasted well into 2013, peaking with the death of one of the protesters, after he had removed some of the medical machines that kept him alive.*

This protest event – similar to others in Spain, Greece and elsewhere – testifies to the degree to which austerity measures are attacking widespread conceptions of humanity, as well as of the dramatic reactions to them. It tells much about the cultural climate in which new identities emerge in times of crisis: as we will see, anti-austerity protesters stress indeed their ethical reasons, although bridging a moral framing with a political one.

In this frame, I will look in particular at identity building. Given a certain sociostructural basis, a step towards the creation of a cleavage is an identification process, with the acquisition of some specific norms and world-views. Regarding the class cleavage, Rokkan in fact noted that 'conflicts between owners and employers have always contained elements of economic bargaining but they have also strong elements of cultural opposition and ideological insulation' (1999, 286). In general, he observed that 'conflicts in the labour market proved much more uniformly divisive' than those linked to other cleavages. Indeed, in research on the labour movement, much attention was paid to how the special concentration of living and working activities facilitated the development of common world-views, as well as the later challenges to 'class consciousness' deriving from the progressive integration of (at least some of) the workers into regulated job positions and the welfare state. New social movement theorists looked then at the emergence of new types of identities, based more on beliefs than on structural positions.

In what follows, I will first introduce some reflections on collective identities in today's society and then assess the nature and extent of the challenge that the actual crisis of neoliberalism presents for the recognition of citizens' rights and for the society in general. Moving from Karl Polanyi's (1957) work on the first wave of economic liberalism, I will suggest that in the neoliberal wave as well, the challenge is not only material but also normative. Neoliberalism, as fanatical defence of the free market, is for the activists an immoral economy. Looking at the recent wave of resistance to the conceptions and practices of neoliberalism, I will focus on the development of a counter-frame to the immoral framing of neoliberal capitalism as, in the definition of the self, the citizens present themselves as indignant in their defence of their dignity. In addressing identification processes, as in the previous chapters, I will in particular compare two waves of protests against neoliberalism: the GJM, in its rampant years, and the anti-austerity protests, during its crisis.

Admitting the difficulties faced when constructing collective identities in a situation of increasing insecurity, social science theory and empirical research points also to the potential for the construction of new definitions of the people, as well as a new critique of capitalism. Following social movement studies, this development can be located within a process, involving changes but also continuities vis-à-vis previous movement frames.

Immoral (neo)liberalism: the challenge

Austerity means cuts in welfare, social services, salaries of social workers – but it also implies the spreading of an ideology, which deeply affects the very idea of social protection. The development of an 'immoral (form of) capitalism' has been indeed a main interpretative counter-narrative in both waves of liberalism.

As Karl Polanyi (1957) observed long ago, the history of capitalism is indeed characterized by a double movement between free market and social protection. Many of the characteristics of the first wave of liberalism that he analysed in his influential *The Great Transformation* hold true, with small transformations, for the neoliberal wave as well.

In Polanyi's view, the justification of liberalism frames gives a positive value to the *dominance of the market over the social*. By critics, free market moves are assimilated to enclosures, as revolutions of the rich against the poor. With enclosures of formerly common land, 'the lords and nobles were upsetting the social order, breaking down ancient law and custom, sometimes by means of violence, often by pressure and intimidation... They were literally robbing the poor of their share of the common' (Polanyi 1957, 35). Similarly, the liberal turn implied a withdrawal of laws and regulations that were meant to assure a modicum of social protection, bringing about also a normative turn, or at least an attempt to impose new values. Liberals shared 'a belief in spontaneous progress' that denied the role of government in economic life. So, 'market economy implies a self-regulating system of markets... it is economy directed by market prices, and nothing but market prices' (Polanyi 1957, 43). Imagining that individuals are moved on the market by economic rather than social concerns, free market economists assumed that 'human beings behave in such a way as to achieve maximum monetary gains' (Polanyi 1957, 68). In this sense, 'self-regulation implies that all production is for sale on the market and that all incomes derive from such sale' (Polanyi 1957, 69). While mercantilism, even if promoting the commercialization of goods, had been opposed to commercializing land and labour, liberalism considered both as commodities, and therefore to be sold on the market. By subordinating 'the substance of society itself to the laws of the market', human society became 'an accessory of the economic system' (Polanyi 1957, 71, 75).

For the great transformation to take place, a *paradigmatic shift away from existing laws and norms* was needed. In England, since the sixteenth century the poor law and the statute of artifice (with yearly wage assessment by public officers, seven years' apprenticeship and so on) defined 'a national organization of labour based on the principles of regulation and paternalism' (Polanyi 1957, 87). Until the end of the eighteenth century, the Speenhamland law stated that a minimum income had to be assured, for example as subsidies in addition to salaries and proportional to the cost of bread. Initially, even laissez-faire doctrine, although fighting against regulations on production, considered the poor law as a help to manufacturers, permitting them to divest themselves from responsibility towards dismissed employees (Polanyi 1957, 137). In contrast, the reform bill of 1832 and poor law amendment of 1834 abolished subsidies – which were accused of reducing productivity – signalling the end of benevolent paternalism.

This represented what some scholars conceptualized as a move towards *amoral capitalism*. Polanyi talked, in particular, of a moral degradation – as 'if workers were physically dehumanized, the owning classes were morally degraded. The traditional unity of a Christian society was giving place to a denial of responsibility on the part of the well-to-do for the conditions of their fellows' (Polanyi 1957, 102). Amoralism was justified by the assumption that progress was linked to pauperism: as, according to liberal thinker Jeremy Bentham, 'in the highest stage of social prosperity, the great mass of the citizens will most probably possess few other resources than their daily labour, and consequently will always be near to indigence' (cited in Polanyi 1957, 117).[8] The poor were not to be helped, as this would have interfered with the labour market: the pathological cases had to be closed in hospitals; the others had to be left to die for the good of progress.

Somewhat coherent with their (blind) faith in economic exploitation was the liberal opposition to voting rights for the non-rich. As Polanyi ironically noted, 'it would have been an act of lunacy to hand over the administration of the New Poor Law with its scientific method of mental torture to the representatives of the self-same people for whom that treatment was designed'. In fact, 'there was not a militant liberal who did not express his conviction that popular democracy was a danger to capitalism' (Polanyi 1957, 224, 226).

In sum, according to immoral liberalism:

> ...while the pauper, for the sake of humanity, should be relieved, the unemployed, for the sake of industry, should not be relieved. That the unemployed was innocent of his fate did not matter: the point was not whether he might or might not have found work had he only really

tried, but that unless he was in danger of famishing with only the abhorred workhouses for an alternative, the wage system would break down, thus throwing society into misery and chaos. That this meant penalizing the innocent was recognized. The perversion of cruelty consisted exactly in emancipating the laborer for the avowed purpose of making the threat of destruction through hunger effective. (Polanyi 1957, 224)

This *cynical* belief, that assessed human beings as selfish, was at the basis of what Polanyi called 'a crusading passion', 'a militant creed', while 'rarely was as much as a reasoned argument on the subject to be found' (Polanyi 1957, 137, 211). In fact, in the nineteenth century, the conception of free market was based upon economic liberalism as 'the organizing principle of a society engaged in creating a market system. Born as a mere penchant for non-bureaucratic methods, it evolved into a veritable faith in man's secular salvation through a self-regulating market. Such fanaticism was the result of the sudden aggravation of the task it found itself committed to: the magnitude of the sufferings that were to be inflicted on innocent persons as well as the vast scope of the interlocking changes involved in the establishment of the new order. The liberal creed assumed its evangelic fervor only in response to the needs of a fully deployed market economy' (Polanyi 1957, 135). As Trevizo (2013, 765) summarized, 'moral economists' stated in general that, as capitalism turns land, forests, natural resources and labour into commodities, 'the cultural change that results exposes peasants to greater forms of human suffering. Cultural shifts unglue the social relations that historically functioned as social insurance.' These changes meant in fact an erosion of patrons' obligations, with consequent outrage at what was perceived as a betrayal of the traditional duties in a moral economy.

From the critique and failure of liberalism, the mentioned move towards social protection brought about an image of a return to a moral economy, based on a specific ethics of capitalism. As Wolfgang Streeck recently noticed, 'in the late 1960s we tried to convince ourselves that we were seeing...a gradual transition to democratic socialism, to be accomplished by politicized trade unions pressured by their rank-and-file and acting in concern with stronger-than-ever Social-Democratic or Eurocommunist political parties' (2014, 45). The Weberian notion speaks of capitalism as 'based, not on a desire to get rich, but on self-discipline, methodical effort, responsible stewardship, sober devotion to a calling and rational organization of life, and dedication to work as an end in itself' (Streeck 2014, 62).

After the interlude of Keynesian economy in what was called a class compromise, free-market ideology in fact came back, with many similarities to its first wave, and some differences. Similar to classical liberalism, Colin Crouch noted, 'the principal tenet of neoliberalism is that optimal outcomes will be achieved if the demand and supply for goods and services are allowed to adjust to each other through the price mechanism, without interference by government or other forces – though subject to the pricing and marketing of oligopolistic corporations' (Crouch 2012, 17). In this wave as well, free market supporters stated that governments do not have to intervene to protect levels of employment, as 'If that demand falls, then workers will become unemployed, and as a result those who remain in work will be unable to increase their wages, for the unemployed will be happy to rejoin the labour market at lower wages. In that way the market will find its equilibrium' (Crouch 2012, 17).

Cynicism, as assumptions and practices of immorality, has been stressed also for neoliberalism – defined by Joseph Stiglitz (2008) as market fundamentalism, characterized by moral depravity. Neoliberalism imposes in fact a moral imperative of competition, bringing an 'ethos of competitiveness at the center of human life' (Amable 2011, 6). As in the first wave, immoral (conceptions and practices of) capitalism – what Streeck (2014, 63) called capitalism's moral decline – developed. Also in this case, as neoliberal ideas came to dominate, 'amorality spreads right across social life' (Crouch 2012, 25). The expected action disposition of rule takers is here as well rational and selfish (Streeck 2011), so that neoliberal thought institutionalizes cynicism and legitimates greed. The most immoral individuals have more chances of success; there is, indeed, expectation of unlimited rewards as, in an imperative of maximization of economic gains, competition wins over solidarity. Elites' interests are thus divorced from interest in system survival (Streeck 2011). Neoliberals preach that 'provided markets are near-perfect, the outcome of a mass of individuals' selfish behaviors will be consistent with overall public welfare' (Streeck 2011, 149). Differently from classic liberalism, where the consumer was presented as most influential for market prices, for neoliberalism the share-holders (and their shares) become the dominant concerns, over investment, customers, employees. A moral crisis ensues as inequalities increase – as 'A political system that amplifies the voice of the wealthy provides ample opportunity for laws and regulations – and the administration of them – to be designed in ways that not only fail to protect the ordinary citizens against the wealthy but also further enrich the wealthy at the expense of the rest of society' (Stiglitz 2012a, xix).

The neoliberal criticism of the welfare state is based upon the primacy of individual responsibility in self-sustenance. The state is allowed to provide insurance, but only in a competitive market, while social benefits are assumed to lessen the costs of immoral behaviour. Cuts in welfare are presented as liberation of individuals from social dependence (Amable 2011). Often cited by proponents of neoliberalism, von Hayek (1967) suggested that private laws should be applied also to the state and public services offered only in competitive markets. In fact, for him, liberty is the first value, above democracy, legitimizing calls to limit popular sovereignty. Similarly supported is Buchanan and Tullock's (1962) statement that economic crisis basically stems from political intervention, so that the role of government is inversely proportional to the strength of moral order. Neoliberalists so propose a misleading vision of a trickle-down economy, based on the assumption that giving money to the top will improve conditions at the bottom (Stiglitz 2012a).

This vision is well synthesized by Allan H. Meltzner (2012) in his *Why Capitalism?*, with his strenuous defence of neoliberalism. In his view, the 2008 crisis is produced indeed not by too much free market, but by not enough of it. While 'costly regulation encourage circumvention' (Meltzner 2012, 12), government activities in the market are considered as intrusive and inefficient as 'well run companies plan for the long term. But governments typically follow the political cycle, a much shorter term' (Meltzner 2012, 14). Even if 'regulation may seek laudable ends', 'as Kant so presciently warned, mankind is endlessly selfish' (Meltzner 2012, 42). As individual preferences are for self-interest, rather than social justice or fairness, the choice of rulers needs to be often enforced by fear. Moreover, elected institutions are expected to overspend in redistribution: as the income of the median voter lies below the mean income, elected politicians are pushed towards redistribution. At the same time, governments are considered to 'have no intrinsic advantage over the private sector in hiring teachers, doctors, nurses, or other professionals, nor any advantage in building schools or hospitals. Rather, they tend to be at a disadvantage, out of lack of expertise, lack of competition, failure to refine their operation, or because they regulate themselves more heavily than the private sector'. While unemployment benefits 'risk the creation of subsidies for leisure', 'much regulation invites corruption, arbitrary decisions, and circumvention' (Meltzner 2012, 49, 61).

In sum, a dominance of the market is based on the assumption that the competition between selfish individuals will bring about economic growth. The effect is that, especially faced with economic decline, 'the struggle for the remaining profit opportunities becoming uglier by the day and turning into asset stripping on a truly gigantic scale...public perceptions of capitalism are now deeply cynical. The capitalist economy being as a matter of course perceived as a world of tricks for further enrichment of the already rich' (Streeck 2014, 64).

The cultural dimension: which identity for which movement?

To which extent these narratives affect the development of collective identities is an open question, which social and political theory as well as social movement studies might help addressing. Identification is a most important component in the formation of a political cleavage. As observed before, the structuration of social conflicts happened via specific cultural processes, through the creation of specific values, norms, and world-views. While the 'old' labour movements had developed strong common visions, embedded in complex ideologies, and new social movements have instead been seen as consolidating and developing new codes, the emergence of collective identities in contemporary societies seems challenged by processes of fragmentation. In what follows, I will first discuss how social fragmentation is expected to impact on identification processes in contemporary sociological reflections on liquid modernity and populism, then looking at how identities have been conceptualized in social movement studies.

Liquid modernity and fragmented societies?

Neoliberalism grew within a specific type of cultural environment. With some pessimism about the capacity of a new collective subject to emerge, Zygmunt Bauman has located in *liquid modernity* the cultural dimension of neoliberalism. This implies insecurity and flexibility, which make collective identities difficult to develop.

In this view, postmodern men and women have 'exchanged a portion of their possibilities of security for a portion of happiness. The discontents of modernity arose from a kind of security that tolerated too little freedom in the pursuit of individual happiness. The discontents of postmodernity arise from a kind of freedom of pleasure-seeking which tolerate too little individual security' (1997, 3). Liquid modernity is so presented as a shift away from the panocticum (based on mutual engagement) towards nomadism. While heavy/solid/condensed/systemic modernity was made of compulsory homogeneity, liquid modernity is said to emphasize momentary impulses. With the end of the illusion of a telos (as a state of perfection to be reached), there is a deregulation and privatization of tasks and duties from collective endowments to individual management. In this view, individualism wins over the collectivity. In a society free of fences, social beings are no longer defined by a fixed place in it (Bauman 2000, 22).

Fordism represented the solid (heavy, immobile) phase of modernity: made of law and routine. Other-directed persons pursued 'fixed-by-others ends in fixed-by-others fashion' (Bauman 2000, 63), and the life of individuals was organized mainly around their role as producers. In liquid modernity, the life of consumers is instead dominated by seduction and volatile desires (Bauman 2000, 76), networks of possibilities rather than long-lasting commitments. With the spread of precarious position, work no longer plays the central role it had in solid modernity and heavy capitalism, characterized by the interdependence of labour and capital (Bauman 2000, 139). Instead, 'Flexibility is the slogan of the "job as we know it", announcing instead the advent of work on short-term contracts, rolling contracts or no contract, positions with no in-built security but with the "until further notice" clause. Working life is saturated with uncertainty' (Bauman 2000, 147). In this vision, at the top of the light/soft capitalism hierarchy are in fact those for whom space matters little, those who can surf. Bauman points therefore at the spreading of insecurity (of position, entitlements, and livelihood), of uncertainty (as to their continuation and future stability), and of unsafety (of one's body, one's self and their extensions: possession, neighbourhood, community) (Bauman 2000, 161). The self-assertion of the individual in fact goes together with a denial of the society: 'To put in a nutshell, "individualization" consists of transforming human "identity" from a "given" into a "task"' (Bauman 2000, 31). So, 'modernity replaces the heteronomic determination of social standing with compulsive, and obligatory self-determination' (Bauman 2000, 32).

As community and corporations no longer offer protection through dense nets of social bonds, the search for substitute targets (such as criminality and terrorism) is a reaction to fear. In the past, the modern state had managed fears through the protection of social state institutions that construct new webs of social bonds (Bauman 2000, 59) or long-term involvement in the Fordist factory; nowadays, a deregulation-cum-individualization develops fears (Bauman 2000, 67). Control of fears is no longer managed by the state, if not in the form of securitarism as defence from new dangerous, redundant, classes (Bauman 2000, 69). While previously citizens' consensus was given in exchange for protection from the vagaries of the market, nowadays 'the specter of special degradation against which the social state swore to insure its citizens has been replaced in the political formula of the "personal safety state" by threats of a pedophile on the loose, a serial killer, an obtrusive beggar, a mugger, stalker, poisoner, terrorist' (Bauman 2000, 15).

In the new context, collective identities are considered as being difficult to develop. Individuals are seen as lukewarm towards common good, common cause, good society: the other side of individualization is the end of citizenship (Bauman 2000, 36). This is however not linked to the colonization of the lifeworld by the state, but rather by its decline, as 'it is no more true that the "public" is set on colonizing the "private"'. The opposite is the case: 'it is the private that colonizes the public spaces' (Bauman 2000, 39), and 'Any true liberation calls today for more, not less, of the "public sphere" and "public power"' (Bauman 2000, 51). This creates vicious circles, as social rights are necessary to keep political rights in place as much as political rights were important in establishing social rights (Bauman 2000, 66). The collapse of confidence is said to bring about fading will to political commitment with endemic instability. A state induced insecurity develops, indeed, with individualization through market flexibility and a broadening sense of relative deprivation, as flexibility precludes the possibility of existential security (Bauman 2007, 14). In this vision, there is nowhere to escape, as 'whatever happens in one place has a bearing on how people in all other places live, hope or expect to live' (Bauman 2007, 6).

A diagnosis of fragmented identities is shared by other scholars, although they are sometimes more optimistic about the potential for collective actors to form in liquid times. According to Michael Hardt and Antonio Negri (2000), the resistance of subjective forces is triggered through 'activities and desires which refuse the dominant order by proposing "lines of flight"' (Hardt and Negri 2000, 48). Disciplinary regimes thus no longer succeed in controlling the values and desires of young people, who no longer dream of getting a job that 'guarantees regular and stable work' (Hardt and Negri 2000, 273). Nomadism disrupts the disciplinary condition, as 'a new nomad horde, a new race of barbarians, will arise to invade or evacuate the Empire' (Hardt and Negri 2000, 213). In this vein, the refusal is visible in various forms of everyday resistance as local struggles 'leap immediately to the global level and attack the imperial constitution in its generality' (Hardt and Negri 2000, 56).

The multitude thus conflicts permanently with the constituted power of the empire through an autonomous and unmediated action, which becomes political as it starts to confront the repressive operation of the empire. Unitarian, centralized, and hierarchical organizational forms are neither possible nor positive, as society is composed of a 'multiplicity of irreducible singularities' (Hardt and Negri 2000, 166). Therefore, the multitude is permanently in the making, assuming rhizomatic forms and leaving no place for political vanguard. Even identity should not aim at consolidation, while there is an emphasis on singularity as always involved in a project of becoming different (Hardt and Negri 2000, 339). During action, singularities are bridged together, establishing what is common and forming a new power oriented to managing the commons. Neither a homogeneous people nor an amorphous mass, the multitude is considered as scattered but united in times of attacks.

In sum, liquid fragmented societies are expected to challenge the development of collective identities, even if, however, there are different views about the capacity for collective mobilization when identities are not consolidated.

Populist logic as search for the people

Beyond the one on the opportunities and constraints on the development of collective identities, a debate is also open on the content of emerging identities. In particular, terms such as populism have emerged to tackle identification processes in times of crisis. First, with their stress on an autonomous new subject, anti-austerity movements have often been defined as populist. Second, a populist reason has been singled out as a need for re-defining the people, particularly strong as previous belongings are challenged.

Populism is a much contested term, as very different movements have been collapsed under its label – including the Russian *narodniki*, the agrarian movements after World War I in Europe, protests for social credit in Alberta, peronism in Argentina. Seeing it as an ideology, McRae (1970) singled out as common to populism elements such as a strong sense of belonging (which can become xenophobia), conspiracy, apolitical thinking, isolationism, social uniformity, reference to a mythical past. In his analysis, sometimes 'under the threat of some kind of modernization, industrialism, call it what you will, a predominantly agricultural segment of society asserts as its charter of action its belief in a community and (usually) a Volk as uniquely virtuous, it is egalitarian and against all and any elite, looks at a mythical past to regenerate the present' (McRae 1970, 168). Defining populism as a syndrome, Wiles (1970) listed as its defining elements moralism, mystical contact between leaders and masses, loose organization and ideology, anti-intellectualism and anti-scientism, anti-establishment and anti-class feelings, racialism, nostalgia, for small cooperatives against big finance, religious beliefs (but against the establishment). Stewart (1970) noted similar social roots, as populism emerges in the periphery in response to problems of modernization and frustration for a lack of channels of access to decision making. Rather than just a discourse emphasizing the role of the people, populism has been defined, especially in Latin America, as reflecting a specific form of electoral politics from above, based on the leader's appeal to inter-class coalition of citizens. This is explained, in comparison with Western

Europe, by the weakness of classes (in particular the working class) as bases of political mobilization (Roberts 2014).

While so defined the concept of populism is quite fit to describe right-wing reactions to the crisis, the research on anti-austerity protests stressed their inclusiveness as well as their refusal of leaders as at odds with mainstream conceptualization of populism. Empirical research pointed however at some innovation in the identification process as compared with previous movements, with a search for a definition of an all-encompassing subject, often defined at the national level, as well as a strong moral call. In this sense, in this emerging phase, anti-austerity movements seem indeed to develop what Ernesto Laclau (2005) has defined as a populist reason. According to him, populism is a political logic: not a type of movement, but the naming, the construction of the people as a way of breaking order and reconstructing it. In fact, he stated, that the democratic subject is formed through the development of relations between heterogeneous subjects, as 'democracy is grounded only on the existence of a democratic subject, whose emergence depends on the horizontal articulation between equivalential demands. An ensemble of equivalential demands articulated by an empty signifier is what constitutes a "people": so the very possibility of democracy depends on the constitution of a democratic people' (Laclau 2005, 171). Recognizing the difficulties in the construction of the people, he points at historical conditions for emergence of popular identities in 'the multiplication of social demands, the heterogeneity of which can be brought to some form of unity only through equivalential political articulation' (Laclau 2005, 229). Challenging somehow both Bauman's pessimistic view of liquid society and Hardt and Negri's optimism about a move towards the self extension of identities, Laclau points instead at the need for political forms of social reaggregation through a populist reason. Nowadays, globalized capitalism brings about a deepening of the logic of identity formation, but the discursive construction of the people requires frontiers.

It is indeed in times of challenges to previous certainties that specific forms of identification develop. The search for a populist reason, as the need for naming the self and for recognition of the self, is fuelled by a crisis that challenges a process of habituation. Habermas has defined norm conformative action as a habitual and unnoticed adherence to shared social norms – distinguishing it from discourse, which instead testifies for reflexivity (for a discussion see Crossley 2002). Communication plays a central role in this process as far as it is 'oriented towards the achievement of mutual understanding and agreement' (Crossley 2002, 155). In a similar vein, Bourdieu's theory of action stresses the ways in which social life transforms individuals, giving rise to habitus as sentiments, moral competences, interest are related to belonging to a group, but also at how all this can change in turbulent times as opinions challenge doxa. A class habitus is so related to the different mix of resources available: economic capital, such as money, property; symbolic capital, such as reputation; cultural capital, such as cultural goods, dispositions and competences; and social capital, as connections that can be used in specific fields. There is an embeddedness of social agents, with embodied competences, but also innovative ones, as actors act strategically and skilfully, not as calculating machines but rather as game players who stick to the rules. The fields are indeed also sites of innovative interactions: 'structures form agents who reproduce structures through their actions and so on' (Crossley 2002, 179, 177). The autonomy of fields is reduced by economic encroachment, but struggles also tend to spread to different fields with different constraints. In this sense, the crisis itself fuels processes of (new) identification. In times of crisis, a dissonance arises between expectation and reality, as a crisis suspends the doxa, made up of undiscussed ideas, and fuels opinions: a universe of discussion or arguments (Bourdieu 1977, 168).

Actual protests can then be interpreted as non-conformative action using discourse and opinions to challenge habitus and doxa. According to empirical analyses, in fact, in today's protests the search for a naming of the self that could put together different groups has indeed produced the spread of definitions of the self as the people, or even more the persons or the citizens. These reflected and challenged the cultural effects of neoliberalism.

The expectation is therefore that times of intense changes might push for similarly intense processes of identity building as old belongings no longer provide solid bases for identification and recognition.

The new spirit of capitalism and its critics

Neoliberalism can be indeed expected to raise specific forms of anti-capitalist criticisms. The bases of justification of capitalism – its spirit in Boltanski and Chiapello's (2005) analysis – changed indeed with neoliberalism, at its peak and in its crisis. In their analysis, they consider the need for capitalism (per se, immoral, pursuing the imperative of an unlimited accumulation of capital) to find a justification, outside of itself, within different discourses (or cities), as 'ideological changes...have accompanied recent transformations in capitalism' (Boltanski and Chiapello 2005, 3). While liberal capitalism justified itself on a combination of new economic propensities (such as avarice or parsimony) and traditional domestic values, and Fordism was based on a faith in rationality and long-term planning, a third – neoliberal – spirit of capitalism stresses flexibility, mobility, networks, and merit.

Luc Boltanski and Eve Chiapello have also noted that capitalism has been transformed by criticism, which forced it to adapt its spirit (or justifying ideology). Criticisms can in fact 'delegitimate previous spirits and strip them of their effectiveness', sometimes pushing capitalism to incorporate some of 'the values in whose name it was criticized' (Boltanski and Chiapello 2005, 28). Distinguishing criticism of inauthenticity, oppression, inequalities and egoism (Boltanski and Chiapello 2005, 37), they have suggested that the first two sources of dissatisfaction have fuelled an artistic critique; the last two a social critique. While Fordism emerged from a social critique to the first spirit of capitalism, indeed shifting towards more attention to inequalities and egoism, the movements of the late 1960s and the 1970s brought about a critique of inauthenticity and oppression, which was then addressed by the third capitalism spirit. In fact:

> the second spirit of capitalism, which emerged at the end of the 1930s crisis and was subject to the critique of mass communist and socialist parties, was constructed in response to critiques denouncing the egoism of private interests and the exploitation of workers. It evinced a modernist enthusiasm for integrated, planned organizations concerned with social justice. Shaped through contacts with the social critique, in return it inspired the compromise between the civic values of the collective and industrial necessities that underlay the establishment of the welfare state. By contrast, it was by opposing a social capitalism planned and supervised by the state – treated as obsolete, cramped and constraining – and leaning on the artistic critique (autonomy and creativity) that the new spirit of capitalism gradually took shape at the end of the crisis of the 1960s and 1970s. Turning its back on the social demands that had dominated the first half of the 1970s, the new spirit was receptive to the critiques of the period that denounced the mechanization of the world. (Boltanski and Chiapello 2005, 201)

Changes in the conditions of labour contributed to a weakening of the social critique – among them, the casualization of employment, with job insecurity; the reduction of constraints by labour law; the segmentation of the wage earning class, with a process of selection and exclusion of unskilled workers towards less protected positions or unemployment; an increase in the intensity of work for the same wage. As they noted, the weakening of the unions testify to the difficulties the social critique encountered at this time, as 'changes in the world of work during this period continued to prompt complaints or indignation. But the institutions traditionally responsible for transforming complaint...into a general condemnation and public protests were widely discredited and/ or paralyzed' (Boltanski and Chiapello 2005, 272). Deunionization was in fact accompanied by repression and criticism. Although unions struggled to adapt to the changing times, they lost legitimacy because of their participation in cutting employment – up to the crisis of the model of the social class itself (Boltanski and Chiapello 2005, 300).

As Boltanski and Chiapello observe, however, since the 1990s, a social critique is again on the rise (Boltanski and Chiapello 2005, 201 ff.), moving from stigmatization of exclusion in the humanitarian movement to its politicization in movements against precarity, along with calls for more intensive controls on the market. At the same time, an artistic criticism develops given an increase in anxiety, and a lack of liberation, as there is no abolition of alienation, but rather increasing commodification.

The two types of criticism can indeed approach each other, as we can see in the GJM, first, and the anti-austerity protests later on. In both, fragmentation is addressed by a positive emphasis on diversity, although with different characteristics: as a tolerant identity bridging a plurality of experiences in the GJM, or rather as the appeal to an all-encompassing people or citizenry suffering from the crisis of neoliberalism in the anti-austerity protests. Linked to this, while the GJM had stressed cosmopolitan visions as the only way to challenge global capitalism, the anti-austerity protests focus attention on the nations, defending national sovereignty facing the also cross-national iniquities imposed by neoliberalism and its crises. A sort of nationalism of the oppressed emerges especially where external conditionalities imposed by the EU or the IMF hit harder. Additionally, while the GJM still showed hope in the political reformability of national and international organizations, this is no longer the case for the anti-austerity protests, which stress more the depth of degeneration of basic ethical principles. We can expect that a moment of crisis of neoliberal capital could facilitate the approaching of different critiques of capitalism, which had appeared as rooted in different social groups.

Identity in social movement studies

Social movement studies can contribute to address the questions related with the strength and content of collective identities in times of neoliberalism, as they contribute to research on identification a relational view, stressing the cognitive and affective mechanisms which intervene in the creation and consolidation of collective identities.

Scholars of the labour movement looked at the relations between structural strains, consciousness thereof, and then mobilization: class *in itself* and class *for itself* have in fact been discussed in the analysis of the making of the working class (Thompson 1991; Calhoun 1982). At the same time, all the challenges in the creation of an identity of the working class were recognized. Class consciousness did gather some attention in Marxist approaches interested in the development of an awareness by the proletariat of itself as a class, with a resulting shift from class *in* itself to class *for* itself (Crossley 2002). In Marx's expectation, industrial workers were the most likely to develop a class consciousness, given the centrality of the conflicts around the factory as well as their particular concentration (Eder 2013). However, the worsening of exploitation and the concentration of capital proved an insufficient condition for the development of such awareness. While Craig Calhoun (1982) noted the difficulty for a class to act as collectivity if there are no communal bonds, Offe and Wiesenthal (1980) pointed at the workers' need to develop a collective identity, on which they can assess the value of collective action. In fact, in the evolution of the labour movement, bonding happened, often at the local level, when relations were dense, corporate (linking groups), and multiplex (with overlapping of different relationships) (Savage 1987). In Antonio Gramsci's view, in order to challenge the hegemonic discourse of the bourgeosie, the workers need indeed a collective intellectual, which, embodied in the party, could develop a counter-cultural consensus in a dispersed social basis (Gramsci 1955; also, Tarrow 2012).

Also in social movement studies, collective identification is expected only if there is awareness of the fact that one's own destiny is in large part linked to material conditions, while the lack of such awareness is defined as false consciousness (Snow and Lessor 2013). In order for a grievance to emerge a specific strain has to be cognitively linked to criticism of the ways in which authorities treat social problems/groups – on the bases of suddenly imposed grievances or assessments of violation of widespread principles (Klandermans 2013b, 5). In general, the responsibility for the unpleasant situation needs to be attributed to a deliberate producer (Klandermans 2013a). Grievances, as feelings of dissatisfaction, resentment, or indignation, in fact originate in material conditions but, in order to mobilize, require psychological processes of comparison with others and cognitive processes producing assessment of procedural injustice (Snow 2013a).

Together with an assessment of one's own interest, there is however also a mobilization of normative concerns. An ethical appeal was often linked with the political one. Some social movement scholars have in fact pointed at a moral dimension of protest. In particular, James Jasper, in his *The Art of Moral Protest* (1997), presented a collective identity as consisting of 'perceptions of group distinctiveness, boundaries and interests for something closer to a community than a category' (Jasper 1997, 86). Identity is in this vision pre-eminently moral as it carries moral obligations, based on moral aspiration such as ontological or economic security, professional ethics, religious beliefs, community allegiances, and political ideologies (Jasper 1997, 140). Action comes in fact 'in fear and moral indignation, not in calculated efforts at personal gain' (Jasper 1997, 3): it is 'their ability to provide a moral voice that makes protest activities so satisfying: to give us an opportunity to plumb our moral sensibilities and convictions, and to articulate and elaborate them' (Jasper 1997, 5). In William Gamson's influential work, injustice frames produce moral shocks that mobilize into collective action (2013; also Gamson, Fireman and Rytina 1982). The centrality of a sense of injustice for workers' rebellion has been noted by historians and linked to the expectation of respect by the authority of corporate collective rights, undermined by spreading of capitalist relations (Tilly and Tilly 1981). Kenneth Tucker (1996, 23) noticed the emergence of a French proletarian public sphere, with radical workers creating an 'equalitarian morality tied to the atelier, in contrast to the atomistic individualism of the bourgeoisie', bridging aesthetic and moral aspects of work. In their advocacy of direct action, they developed the ideal of moral community as linked to active participation.

These processes of identity building through cognitive and affective mechanisms are expected to be especially likely in the presence of double deprivation: at both the individual and group levels. It is not only the cognitive component, but also an emotionally intense sense of injustice that fuels mobilization into action (Klandermans 2013b, 5). In fact, injustice frames are extremely important for mobilization as 'hot cognition', but they require an attribution of responsibility to concrete targets, successfully bridging the abstract and the concrete. As Gamson observed, it is no simple matter to explain 'how the indignities of daily life are sometimes transformed into shared grievances with a focused target of collective action. Different emotions can be stimulated by perceived inequities – cynicism, bemused irony (for example, "Who says life is fair?"), or resignation. But injustice focuses on the righteous anger that puts fire in the belly and iron in the soul' (2013, 607). Exceptional social dislocations are expected to push disadvantaged groups into action, as the loss-averse will accept risks in order to defend their subsistence and everyday routines (see Hosoki 2013; Borland 2013 for a synthesis). In this direction, David Snow and his collaborators (1998) have talked of quotidian disruption, emphasizing the relevance of dislocations that disrupt or threaten routines that had been taken for granted.

Grievances are however still insufficient to long-lasting mobilization. As in labour studies, identity has been a central concept in social movement studies, which have considered it as 'an act of imagination, a trope that stirs people to action by arousing feelings of solidarity with our fellows and, by definition, moral boundaries against other categories' (McGarry and Jasper 2014, 3). Social movements are in fact identity fields: they fuel boundary making processes (Benford 2013) as they simultaneously produce identities, as a shared sense of 'we', and claim recognition (Bernstein and Taylor 2013; Einwohner 2013). Collective identities are 'the shared definition of a group that derives from members' common interests and solidarity' (Taylor 2013, 39). However, they are not fixed, but rather in progress: they change during the evolution of a movement, and they change in interaction with other actors. Social movements are in fact 'discursive communities held together not only by common action and bonds of solidarity but also by identities, symbols, shared identity discourses and practices of everyday life that attribute participants' experiences to particular forms of social injustice' (Taylor 2013, 43).

Group identification therefore supports the development of (individual) social identities (as self-definition in terms of groups) into collective identities (as cognition shared by the members of a group), and then to their politicization, as attribution of blame to an external actor as well as raised awareness of shared grievances (van Stekelenburg 2013; van Stekelenburg et al. 2013). Social movement studies have indeed considered collective identities as an emergent *group process*. In Melucci's influential definition, collective identity is 'an interactively shared definition of the field of opportunities and constraints offered to collective action produced by several individuals that must be considered as a process because it is constructed and negotiated by repeated activation of the relations that link individuals to groups' (1989, 793). A transformation of social identities into *collective* ones emerged as more likely to develop when members are embedded in social networks, which help in drawing boundaries and developing a consciousness of the importance of possessing a certain social identity, which thus acquires saliency and then becomes politicized.

Politicized collective identities, strengthened by common beliefs and lifestyles, offer an instrument to understand the world. They vary, however, in forms and intensity: strong identification can increase internal solidarity but can also isolate from the outside; assimilationist, broad identities are more inclusive, but tend also to have permeable borders (Jasper 2006). In general, ideology, as the articulated system of beliefs, ideas, values that help in making sense of the external reality, is in fact transformed in action (Beck 2013).

In sum, while stressing the potential for identification even in fluid societies social movement scholars present it as linked to an identity work, as identities do not stem directly from social location and structural positions, but they are rather produced through action and agency with some adaptation to social, political and cultural constraints, but also challenges to them. In this vein, social movement scholars have in particular looked at the shift from the (strong) class identity of the labour movement, with an overlapping of social categories and class culture, to so-called new social movements, defined more by beliefs in general values not embedded in a specific social group. New social movement approaches have singled out a colonization of everyday life as challenging previous consolidated identities, and at the same time multiplying existing personal identities and producing a search for collective ones. In Habermas' perspective, while modern patterns of reasoning make discursive democracy possible, this is jeopardized by a colonization of the lifeworld, as the state controls more and more areas of everyday life. Economic colonization also tends to increase as the welfare state declines (Crossley 2002, 166). Scholars such as Alain Touraine (1981) and Alberto Melucci (1989) have in fact described a move from a unitary vision (the movement personage) to more complex, multiple identities. While new social movements also create codes (Melucci 1989), their values are more flexible and fluid. As other sources of identification lose ground, social movements are expected to become new sources of identities, calling for recognition. Moreover, today's societies are said to produce politicization of identities endemically, given increasing networking and multiculturalism (Taylor 2013, 43).

Especially with the GJM, at the beginning of the new millennium, tolerant and plural identities have developed, bridging together different group identities (della Porta 2005). The need to provide new and broad identities has been considered as all the more urgent in times of crisis, although with different views about the capacity of consolidation of new identities. If new social movements had been seen especially as reactions to state intrusion in the society, anti-austerity protests at the periphery and at the core of capitalism have developed within a context of increasing economic colonization of lifeworlds. These specific conditions might be expected to affect identification processes, especially through increasing fragmentation and resistance to it.

Morality and justice frames in anti-austerity protests in the periphery

The immoral cynicism of elites has been often challenged by a call for the restoration of a moral economy. In his *The Moral Economy of the English Crowds in the Eighteenth Century*, E. P. Thompson criticized the economic reductionism of much literature on food riots, stressing that people revolting were rather 'informed by the belief that they were defending traditional rights or customs, and in general that they were supported by the wider consensus of the community' (Thompson 1971, 78). Looking at food riots as very complex forms of direct action, he observed that conflicts between countryside and town were mediated by the regulation of the price of bread, through a sort of political economy of the Corn Laws. While a paternalist model imposed rules on the use of corn and the selling of bread, the growth of intermediaries and the exports of fundamental goods infringed upon this 'moral economy', as free market was based upon a demoralizing theory of trade and consumption. Rather than just reacting to hunger, 'the crowd derived its sense of legitimation…from the paternalist model' (Thompson 1971, 95), claiming that 'since the authorities refused to enforce the laws, they had to enforce them for themselves' (Thompson 1971, 110). In fact, the targets of protests – often including very ritualized hooting or groaning outside the shops – were those singled out as having violated the (previous) laws. While not requiring much organization, these actions relied upon widespread consensus – in particular, a 'consensus to the moral economy of the commonwealth in times of dearth' (Thompson 1971, 126).

A moral framing of protest as countering the amorality of neoliberalism has been noted in research on the anti-austerity protests in the South. As Kenneth Roberts (2008) pointed out in his analysis of 'The Mobilization of Opposition to Economic Liberalization', rather than reflecting fragmentation and depoliticization, these protests expressed a quest for reincorporation. Similarly, analysing anti-austerity riots in Argentina, Auyero (2007) observed that popular protests were produced and influenced in their form by expectation about right behaviour of the others (including politicians) and the self. In a context of widespread misery and uncertainty, rioters constructed a discourse of rights and the value of work, singling out the politicians as those to be blamed.[9]

Research on anti-austerity protest in Latin America has pointed at the movement's use of reformist calls for restoring old rights. Austerity regimes emerged as inherently unstable, with elite factionalism and popular revolt moved not by blind rage, but by a 'collective sense of injustice' (Walton and Ragin 1990, 887), as expressed in slogans such as 'We won't pay the debt – let the ones who stole the money pay.' The reactions to neoliberalism were often described as Polanyi-like calls for social protection.

The rootness of values of social protection has been observed in research on resistance to neoliberalism since the end of the 1990s, with collective demands fuelled by narratives of rooted rights against the open market, seen as a tornado that destroyed previously existing identities. As Heather L. Williams (2001) observes for Mexico, 'market transition, in idealized terms, is a set of policies and processes that decreased government intervention in the economy by freeing most domestic prices, lowering tariffs on imported goods, cutting programmable public spending as a percentage of total economic activity, privatizing industry and credit markets, and eliminating most subsidies...Most importantly, market transitions must be understood as undermining systems of material distribution and systems of clientelistic political control' (Williams 2001, 55). In fact, as social protection policies in Mexico were altered in favour of market oriented ones, contention shifted towards new constituencies and new frames with changes in sites of protest and in the structure of collective demands (Williams 2001, 23). Spaces of protest were formed at the interstices of patron–client relationships, with growing tension between rhetoric of inclusion and practices of exclusion. Lower salaries and blocked consumption fuelled neighbourhood organizations to call for consumption based demands. In the countryside, as well, protests developed over access to land, autonomy and control over production, commodity prices and debt, linked to independent campesino organizations. Especially targeted was the privatization of land, together with lack of services and education and security, repression. Claims of politicians' corruption spread.

The frame of the moral deterioration of the ruling class was bridged with the call for redressing previous conditions. The stigmatization of the loss of lost rights was effective, as it resonated with widespread values – in fact, 'in Mexico, often a considerable part of the public displays solidarity with distributive insurgencies. This is due to a long process and performances that have drawn upon and subverted official doctrines pertaining to citizens' rights and guarantees before the state' (Williams 2001, 70). There was in fact a belief in the state obligation to defend the rights of workers, farmers, and the poor: not only civil rights, but inalienable rights to employment, affordable food, housing, health care, and land. Revolutionary nationalism is in fact still a hegemonic public ideology, which 'precludes an outright denial by officials that protesters' claims are legitimate' (Williams 2001, 71).

The Mexican case shows indeed the deeply rooted beliefs in the duties of the state to provide for a modicum of social protection. Not only in democracies, but also in developmental states, citizens kept expecting that those in power had a moral and political obligation to reduce inequalities. Defensive in character and reformist in orientation, also in Argentina the protesters put forward demands for political commitment to job creation and subsidies and denounced the corruption of politicians and unionists, opaque political processes, and lack of accountability. The so-called *coralito* – the closing down of banks so the customers could not access their bank accounts – produced anger at the heartless IMF among downward middle class as well. Austerity was accused to illegitimately unsettle pre-existing status; 'I was middle class, now I am lower class', stated a protester (Silva 2009, 97). The memory of dictatorship supported protest, as it gave resonance to the feeling that 'we cannot allow this to happen again in Argentina. It already happened to our parents and grandparents...I am going to protest to defend our democracy, freedom, justice and free speech' (Silva 2009, 97). Also later on, in the 1990s, multi-sectoral protests, including also middle classes (teachers, professors, lawyers, doctors, accountants, salespeople, housewives) were based on a loose coordination, sharing Polanyi-style appeals for protection. Despite strong repression, *puebladas* compelled authorities to negotiate. Slogans included 'la nueva fabrica es el barrio' (Silva 2009, 79). On 20 December 2001, twenty-five deaths and the beating of the Madres de Placa de Mayo fuelled a moral shock, accelerating roadblocks, sackings, loathing but also popular assemblies. An activist noted, 'I used to be against roadblocks, but when repression began I went. How to put it, one goes because it's like an instinct, one doesn't think about it. Somewhere a siren wails or young people pass by shouting and you join them...and then you see your neighbor' (Svampa and Pereyra 2003, 126–7).

A moral claim to dignity allows then to allocate systemic responsibility for poverty and sufferance. So, the inhabitant of a Chilean shantytown remembered: 'I used to be ashamed of my poverty, I saw it as a personal failure. A Communist neighbourhood organizer explained to me that I needn't be ashamed, that we all share the same problems' (Schneider 1995, 10). Organizing within the community allowed then, in the words of another activist, to preserve 'a sense of dignity, pride and identification as pobladores' (Schneider 1995, 172). Also in Argentina, organized unemployed workers' movements spread new frames of indignation at those responsible for their pains – as one of them declared, 'the lie that we are responsible for our unemployment, misery and desperation is over...those who govern us and their accomplices are responsible for our desperation; we have lost all, but will never lose our dignity' (Silva 2009, 79). Through coordination with urban self-help groups, demands focused on long-established citizens' rights, including housing, minimum pensions, universal free public education, defence of state banks, moratoria on foreign debt repayment. As hunger and anger combined, mobilization, in the words of an activist, 'helps us emotionally. You have a space where you can express your anger. This is necessary because we are not heard. What we need is a job, one that is dignified' (Williams 2001, 91).

Once again, some of these moral appeals against neoliberalism that developed at the periphery of the world economy spread, through the GJM, to its core. While, however, at the beginning of the 2000s the aggregate demands for goods was kept here high thanks to consumption driven by cheap loans, only towards the end of the decade the financial crisis hit also the global North, with ensuing transformations in the framing of the protests.

Anti-neoliberalism and tolerant identities in the Global Justice Movement

While the labour movement had been characterized by a class (materialist) discourse and the new social movement had been defined as post-materialist, challenging the idea of increasing post-materialism, the GJM addressed social issues as central to its own message. Located in the rampant years of neoliberalism's development, the movement warned about the injustice of increasing inequality as well as its economic inefficiency. Despite the warnings of a potential financial crisis to come, the movement discourse retained some optimistic trust in political reforms that could re-establish social protection. Addressing neoliberal globalization as a worldwide phenomenon, driven mainly by multinational corporations and international organizations, the movement aimed at developing cosmopolitan identities that could incorporate diversity within a tolerant and inclusive vision. While moral frames were certainly used, the political language dominated.

This emerges in particular from the research on the European Social Forum (ESF), that shows frequent reference to a broad political opposition to neoliberalism. So, the activists participating in the Assembly of the Movements of the fourth edition of the ESF in Athens presented themselves: 'We, women and men from social movements across Europe, came to Athens after years of common experiences, fighting against war, neoliberalism, all forms of imperialism, colonialism, racism, discrimination and exploitation, against all the risks of an ecological catastrophe' (Declaration of the Assembly of the Movements of the 4th European Social Forum, Athens, 7 May 2006). In their documents, the activists claimed to have been part of a successful fight against neoliberalism: 'This year has been significant in that a number of social struggles and campaigns have been successful in stopping neoliberal projects such as the proposed European Constitution Treaty, the EU Ports Directive, and the CPE in France' (Declaration 2006). 'Globalization and liberalism' was a main thematic axis at the first European social forum; 'anti-neoliberalism, anti-patriarchy, for a social and democratic Europe of rights' a main one in the second ESF; and the topic of social justice remained central also in the following editions (Haug et al. 2009).

Cosmopolitan frames were needed to face the global nature of the challenge. The targets of this struggle were identified in a number of IGOs, considered as responsible for neoliberal globalization. Again the ESF stated that 'Movements of opposition to neoliberalism are growing and are clashing against the power of trans-national corporations, the G8 and organizations such as the WTO, the IMF and the World Bank, as well the neoliberal policies of the States and the European Union' (Declaration of the Assembly of the Movements of the 4th European Social Forum, Athens, 7 May 2006). At the first ESF in Florence (in 2002), the activists were already rooting their movement in a history of struggles targeting IGOs. As the Call of the European Social Movements stated: 'We have come together from the social and citizens movements from all the regions of Europe, East and West, North and South. We have come together through a long process: the demonstrations of Amsterdam, Seattle, Prague, Nice, Gothenburg, Genoa, Brussels, Barcelona, the big mobilizations against neoliberalism as well as the general strikes for the defence of social rights and all the mobilizations against war, show the will to build another Europe' (cit. in della Porta 2009a).

While critical of existing international institutions, the GJM proposed alternative institutions of world governance (della Porta and Giugni 2009). Without rejecting either the need for a European level of governance or the existence of a European identity (that goes beyond the borders of the EU), it criticized EU policies but asked for 'another Europe': a feminist, ecological, open, supportive, and just Europe. Stressing the internal diversity as an enriching characteristic of their collective identity, the Declaration of the Assembly of the Movements at the third ESF, held in London in 2004, claimed: 'We come from all the campaigns and social movements, "no vox" organizations, trade unions, human rights organizations, international solidarity organizations, anti-war and peace and feminist movements. We come from every region in Europe to gather in London for the third European Social Forum. We are many, and our strength is our diversity.' 'Coming together', 'diversity', 'Another Europe': these are all expressions repeated over and over in the documents of the European Social Forum (della Porta 2009a and 2009d).

While denouncing the attack brought about by neoliberal globalization to previously accepted conceptions of citizens' and human rights, the movement's discourse still stressed hope in the possibility of political changes. Similarly, the previous Assembly of the Movements, held at the third ESF, stated:

We are fighting for another Europe. Our mobilizations bring hope of a Europe where job insecurity and unemployment are not part of the agenda. We are fighting for viable agriculture controlled by the farmers themselves, a farming industry that preserves jobs, and defends the quality of the environment and food products as public assets. We want to open Europe up to the world, with the right to asylum, free movement of people and citizenship for everyone in the country they live in. We demand real social equality between men and women, and equal pay. Our Europe will respect and promote cultural and linguistic diversity and respect the right of peoples to self-determination and allow all the different peoples of Europe to decide upon their futures democratically. We are struggling for another Europe, which is respectful of workers' rights and guarantees a decent salary and a high level of social protection. We are struggling against any laws that establish insecurity through new ways of subcontracting work.

Thus, hopes developed around the aim of networking diversities, bridging once-divided movements. The representatives of the GJM organizations interviewed during the Demos project perceived the movement itself in varied and multiple ways (see della Porta 2009a and 2009b). As Table 3.1 shows, re-aggregating the answers to an open question, its main aims were defined as social by two-thirds of the groups, international by more than one-third; more than half of the groups pointed at new social movement issues, and around one fourth underlined the issue of democracy.

Organizations converged, in fact, in perceiving the movement as a space in which their own specific concerns could find a larger audience. Respondents did focus on some main issues that have converged in mobilizations on global justice. For organizations active on the South of the world, the GJM represented an occasion for developing alternative mechanisms to regulate markets, trade and development (the Italian network Sdebitarsi); promoting 'a vision of the world based upon the dignity of the persons and the respect for human rights' (Amnistia Internacional Spain). They asked for 'worldwide legislation for protection of labor rights according to ILO norm' (the German Kampagne für saubere Kleidung); aiming at eliminating the global inequalities that force people to migrate and fighting against the concept of a fortified Europe (Swiss Solidarité sans Frontières); organizing 'fair trade, in order to promote sustainable development and put at the centre the small producers' (International Fair Trade Association) and calling for 'a change in the rules of international trade' (Altromercato). Issues of peace and human security were considered as main values for the GJM (Stop the War Coalition) and the eradication of poverty and hunger as necessary in order to achieve peace through justice (Caritas Internationalis), as a

Table 3.1. *Perception of movement aims by country, based on interviews with representative SMOs ESF (%)*

Main aims of the movement	Country							
	France	Germany	Italy	Netherlands	Spain	Sweden	UK	Total
Social issues	77.3	71.4	88.2	83.3	58.6	22.2	68.0	67.0
International issues	27.3	33.3	32.4	70.8	37.9	29.6	36.0	37.9
New social movement issues	50.0	47.6	52.9	54.2	65.5	88.9	24.0	55.5
Democracy / free access to information	45.5	9.5	38.2	29.2	27.6	3.7	40.0	28.0
Total	12.1	11.5	18.7	13.2	15.9	14.8	13.7	100.0
(N)	(22)	(21)	(34)	(24)	(29)	(27)	(25)	(182)

Source: della Porta 2009e, 19.

main aim of the GJM was 'to prevent wars, accomplish disarmament, implement international standards' (Friedens- und Zukunftswerkstatt). Ecological groups stressed environmental issues, presenting the movement as seeking 'alternatives to the capitalist system that widens the gap between the rich and the poor and depletes natural resources' (Swiss Les Verts). Traditional concerns for social justice were represented as central by the unions and left-wing parties. Thus, for the International Metalworkers' Federation, the GJM aimed at ensuring 'basic human rights, democracy and social justice, through fighting for an alternative model of globalization which put decent work at the centre of development and trade'. These are not 'single issue' concerns, but clearly what each organization considered as a core topic for the agenda of a complex movement (della Porta 2009a).

Singling out neoliberal globalization as a main target, besides these different emphases, the respondents converged on four main concerns: calls for rights, social justice, democracy from below, and the global nature of the action. First of all, a *language of rights* was used by virtually all groups, with different emphasis on some specific ones. Second, *social issues* were mentioned, in one way or another, by most respondents. Social justice was the most quoted aim. As stressed by the Italian human rights organization Emergency, the GJM aimed at 'Engagement on concrete issues: stating equality among human beings, emphasizing human rights and reduction of differences. These aims can be summarized with the term social justice.' The quest for *another democracy*, built 'from below', is a third bridging theme, always linked with social justice. Especially by the transnational organizations, attention to democracy was framed in terms of the reform of international governmental organizations. Additionally, however, democracy was perceived as the construction of participative and deliberative spaces. The demand for a return of politics against 'the market' was widespread. Finally, a fourth common element was the reference, explicit or implicit, to a *global* dimension, as expressed in the frequent use of words like global, international, or world-wide ('another world is possible').

The Demos data from the document analysis (see Table 3.2) on the basic themes and values mentioned in fundamental documents of social movement organizations involved in the ESF process confirmed in fact the 'bridging' function of such frames as 'alternative globalization' and 'democracy' (about half of the groups mentioned them) as well as 'social justice' (almost two-thirds of our groups), 'global justice', and 'workers' rights' (about half mentioned both) in the development of a critical discourse targeting neoliberalism as a source of injustice and de-democratization. Ecological values also emerged as quite relevant (about half of the groups cited ecology, and the same proportion

Table 3.2.   Basic Values/Themes in documents of SMOs ESF (% yes)

Widespread frames		Little-spread themes	
Social Justice	69	Socialism	8
Another Democracy	52	Communism	3
Another Globalization	50	Anarchism	4
Peace	50	Religious principles	7
Ecology	47		
Human rights	47		
Global justice	45		
Migrant rights	46		
Solidarity with the South	46		
Women's rights	43		

Source: della Porta 2009e, 36.

mentioned sustainability, with much less frequent attention to animal rights). The global South was mentioned by about half of the groups calling for solidarity with third world countries, but half of them also stressed the importance of human rights, and one-third referred to fair trade. References to women's rights and peace were also very present (in half of the groups sampled), and the same is true for migrant rights. The big ideologies of the past were instead less often mentioned by our groups (socialism: 7.8 per cent; communism: 3.3 per cent; anarchism: 3.7 per cent; religious principles: 7 per cent).

Identity is also related with the perception of one's own role. As diversity is presented as a positive characteristic of the GJM, the process of identity building was in fact a tolerant one, with the criticism of neo-liberal capitalism as a master frame. Inclusiveness seemed indeed necessary in order to address the existing fragmentation of the social basis and the weakening of traditional community and associational bonds. The heterogeneity of the movement was highlighted as an innovative feature and an enhancement by comparison to movements of the past (Epstein 2000). The self-definition as a 'movement of movements' emphasized the positive aspects of heterogeneous, multi-faceted identities that reflect social complexity while, as activists often stressed, respecting their 'subjectivity'. There was in fact an identity shift from single-movement identity to multiple, *tolerant identities*, characterized by inclusiveness and positive emphasis upon diversity and cross-fertilization, which helped the movement in dealing with its heterogeneous bases (della Porta 2005), as well as reflecting some individualistic tendency of the new spirit of capitalism. These tolerant identities developed especially around common campaigns on issues perceived as 'concrete' and nurtured by an 'evangelical' search for dialogue – in a focus group with

Florentine activists they pointed indeed at plurality as 'a great novelty and a huge asset, because it brings together men and women, from twenty to sixty, who discuss with each other, opposing the logic of the old Leftist parties of separating women, young people and so on' (in della Porta 2005). The activists from the various generations present in the movement seemed to agree that 'the fine thing about this movement is its *variety* and its capacity to bring together the most varied individuals, on objectives common to them' (in della Porta 2005).

Something seen as a 'kind of epoch making' was the *inclusiveness* of the movement: the fact that 'there really is belonging... yet they're actually not exclusive, that's the novelty'. The common campaigns reflected and promoted overlapping memberships, with simultaneous expression of multiple identities. This is expressed in this quote from a focus group held with Florentine activists:

> G. we are going to the demonstration, what part of the demonstration will we be with? What banner do we parade under?...identity as a social forum is taking roots from the identity viewpoint...those who belong to bigger organizations, according to me they feel belonging to the social forum as something that matters...
>
> B: and try to shift the banner as close as possible...
>
> G: yes, that's true...at the European Social Forum demonstration there was some wonderful dancing around this sort of thing...you wanted to be in four or five places at once...
>
> C: I think it's a kind of sign of the times too...as well as the fact that today you can even experience belonging in a different way...there's no longer political belonging in a strong sense, but you can experience belonging in a different way...(della Porta 2005, 89–93).

It is especially in joint actions that chances emerge for building common values, for being '*contaminated*' or, as one activist says, 'fluidifying' relations. The various organizational solutions adopted are thus often defined in pragmatic fashion as experimentations, efforts to get as close as possible to the participatory model: 'there's a *new willingness to really fluidify*, to confront ideas without wanting to pull this way or that' (3C, 66). Building a common organizational network thus does not rule out other membership – indeed, the co-presence of organizational memberships and identities is seen as enriching, enabling a specific nature to be kept while building common identities. As one activist explains, there is participation '*as long as I can manage to find myself...*' (della Porta 2005).

Concluding, in the GJM the critique of neoliberalism was bridged with a hope for political reform, while plural and tolerant identities emerged as a way to address the perceived heterogeneity of the social basis. Calls for global justice worked as a master frame, bridging social concerns to political solutions.

Morality framing in anti-austerity movements

The anti-austerity protests of 2011 stemmed to a certain extent from the GJM, taking over some of its concerns: not only in terms of the denunciation of neoliberalism but also the stress on a plural identity. As we will see in what follows, there was however a stronger moral framing, as well as more of a reference to all-inclusive identities. If the GJM had indeed presented itself as a movement of movements, an arena for the encounter of minorities, in the anti-austerity protests broader categories such as the people, the citizens, persons, the *indignados*, or the 99% are referred to as collectives resisting the immorality of neoliberalism.

Indignation and occupation

In a similar way as in Latin America, in anti-austerity protests of the 2010s, a *moral call for recognition* has been expressed (della Porta 2013a, b). The framing of neoliberalism as immoral has indeed been linked to a definition of the self, with the appeal to morality as the common basis of a wide, and broadly different, mobilization base. Pointing at the failure of monetarism to achieve promised stability and growth and at the blatant unfairness of people losing their homes while bankers continued to enjoy large bonuses, Joseph Stiglitz noted that 'for the young *indignados* and protesters elsewhere in the world, capitalism is failing to produce what was promised' (2012a, xviii). Calling for recognition of the injustice of their conditions, protesters expressed their indignation against the loss of dignity imposed by authoritarian and democratic regime alike. Invoking 'old rights', they contested the corruption of the political class, in its collusion with the big corporations. Migrating from Latin America to Europe and back to North America, the slogan 'we do not pay for your crisis' targets the increasing (and increasingly arrogant) power of the '1%'.

As Polanyi's countermovement, anti-austerity protests are, to a certain extent, *backward looking*. In their framing there is in fact an appeal to previously better conditions, which badly deteriorated during neoliberal capitalism and, especially, during its crisis. Joseph Stiglitz (2012b) is said to have contributed to naming the Occupy movement in the United States, writing in *Vanity Fair* about the power 'of the 1%, for the 1% and by the 1%', as the 1% controls 40 per cent of the income. According to Noam Chomsky, the Occupy movement was in fact 'the first major public response...to about thirty years of a really quite bitter class war' (2012, 54).

From this point of view, some of the claims of the movements against austerity can be seen as moderate and reformist – a call for the *restoration of old rights*. Some of the movement's proposals appear indeed as quite moderate – a regulation of financial transaction taxes, reversal of rules of corporate governance, that is, 'a shift of the tax code back to something more like what it used to be when the very rich were not essentially exempt from taxes' (Chomsky 2012, 56). In Spain, the *indignados* called for dignity, against the deterioration of the society brought about by neoliberalism. In Spain, Portugal, Greece or Italy, there has been a strong mobilization in defence of the declining welfare state. In the Occupy Wall Street, demands emerged for debt cancellation, full employment, taxation on small financial transactions, a social wage or guaranteed income, universal care centres, paid sick leaves, and higher taxation for the rich – as well as greater political transparency, in particular by getting corporate money out of politics (Taylor et al. 2011, 5). The Italian *indignados* of the Assemblea San Giovanni group stated in particular the need to defend fundamental rights: 'The priorities of any advanced society must be: equality, progress, solidarity, freedom of access to culture, ecological sustainability and development, wellbeing and people's happiness. There are fundamental rights that should be protected in these societies: the right to housing, work, culture, health, education, political participation, free personal development and consumers' rights to access to those goods necessary for a healthy and happy life' (cit. in della Porta et al. 2014).

There are also specific calls for a *reversal* of the legal instruments that neoliberal actors introduced through amendments to then existing laws, which often dated back to the first turn towards social protection after the defeat of the first wave of liberalism in the 1930s. For instance, in the United States, among the claims often put forward by Occupy activists is the abolition of corporate personhood. This was achieved by a constitutional amendment declaring that the 14th amendment should not be used for the purpose of requiring corporations to recognize the right of persons (including the right of speech through donations). In connection with this, posters read, 'Corporations are not people and money is not speech' (Gitlin 2012, 109). One of the few specific calls is for restoring a 1933 law (the Glass–Steagall Act) that had kept commercial banks from mixing with securities trading, until its repeal through a bipartisan vote in 1999, under President Clinton. Activists also called for taxes on financial transactions, and a reestablishment of regulations against usury as ways for protecting citizens from the vagaries of the market.

If claims might appear moderate – to fix the system rather than changing it – there is however a very strong moral appeal spread also through personalized messages. The immorality of the system is denounced, often with reference to its concrete effects on everyday life. As it was observed, 'over and above these collective emotions of shock and rage is also a "moral vision"', which goes beyond consistent pressures to oust leaders and end regimes, and to propagate a social order that embodies a new social contract. It embodies a different utopian politics that delivers a nation from degradation, serves as a barometer of future progress and calls for democratic politics, citizen participation, demands an end to corruption, and seeks a new beginning' (Langman 2013, 515). The moral appeal in movements' discourse is even seen, somehow critically, as avoiding central political issues (e.g. Žižek 2012, 79).

Dignity is a main claim with strong moral tones. With reference to the Arab Spring, the importance of framing has been stressed by Jeffrey C. Alexander, who reminded us that 'Social facts enter into history as meanings, not only to outsiders but to revolutionaries themselves' (2011, 3), observing that 'The Egyptian revolution was a living drama whose political success depended on its cultural power' (Alexander 2011, x). The Egyptian events were in fact framed as aiming at re-establishing a lost dignity. Activists stated, 'This is not a political revolution. This is not a religious revolution. This is an all Egyptians revolution. This is the dignity and freedom revolution' (cit. in Nigam 2012, 7). The uprising was carried out 'In the name of my brother's dignity', as 'It isn't a question of politics, it is a question of dignity' (Nigam 2012, 7). A demand for dignity is in fact said to characterize the Arab Spring: 'Dignity is not a political matter. Dignity is a moral virtue that had now become a political force…a virtue sui generis. The innate humanism operative at the heart of an appeal to "dignity" in effects defines the revolutionary gathering of an inaugural moment for humanity at large' (Dabashi 2012, 127).

Similarly, in Spain the call was to all those who suffered the indignities produced by neoliberalism in its crisis. A YouTube video promoting the 15 May 2011 demonstration stated, 'Because we are more humane. Because we are more decent. Because we are more respectable. Because we are more' (Gerbaudo 2012, 67). Many Spanish *indignados* in fact told their life stories, singling out the effects of the austerity measures on their everyday lives as well as their future perspectives.

In the same vein, in the United States, on wearethe99percent tumblr. com, activists invited citizens to 'let us know who you are. Take a picture of yourself holding a sign that describe your situation...Below that, write "I am the 99 percent"' (Gerbaudo 2012, 27). People wrote there about the deep injustice they suffered: 'I am 20 years old and I can't find a job because I have no experience. I have no experience because I can't find a job. I am the 99%'; 'I am a single mum of four, college student, shelf stocker, I go hungry every day. I am the 99% per cent' (cit. in Gerbaudo 2012, 119). Stories uploaded point in particular at the loss of dignity related with the huge debt crisis, which forced honest people into bankruptcy: 'I lost my house. I went bankrupt. I still am paying over one thousand dollars in student loans for myself and my husband and that's just interest. We will not have children. How could we when we can't even feed ourselves? I am the 99%' (van Gelder et al. 2011, 5); '50,000 dollars per year debt for son's tuition at state university'; and: 'I am a two times felon with no job and I owe over $10,000 in medical bills. I am the 99%'; 'My parents put themselves into debt so that I could get a fancy degree. It cost over 100 grand $ and I have no job prospects. I am the 99%' (in Gerbaudo 2012, 119). Recommending politeness, a website invited readers to write to executives and trustees of big banks about the indignity of their firms' behaviour.

Not only is the system considered immoral, but the *illegality* of the action of the powerful is also denounced. As Stiglitz noted, 'At one level these protesters are asking for so little: for a chance to use their skills, for a right to decent work at decent pay, for a fairer economy and society...but at another level they are asking for a great deal: for a democracy where people, not dollars, matter' (Stiglitz 2012b, 21). In the movement's framing, 'they' are accused of 'having taken our houses through an illegal foreclosure process...taken bailouts from taxpayers with impunity...perpetuated inequality and discrimination in the workplace based on age, the color of one's skin, sex, gender, identity and sexual orientation...continuously sought to strip employees of the right to negotiate for better pay and safer working conditions...have held students hostage with tens of thousands of dollars of debt on education, which is in itself a human right...donated large sums of money to politicians, who are responsible to regulate them' (van Gelder et al. 2011, 37). The *indignados* in the Assemblea San Giovanni in Roma state that 'The will and the aim of the system is the accumulation of wealth, which takes precedence over the efficiency and wellbeing of society. It wastes resources, destroys the planet, creates unemployment and unhappy consumers. The citizens are gears in a machine designed to make a minority entirely unaware of our needs rich. We are anonymous, but without us none of this would exist, it is us that moves the world.'[10] The main target of

Occupy Wall Street was presented as a symbol of 'opportunity-making and opportunity breaking where anything that can be marketed is marketed' (Gitlin 2012, 7).

As for the *self-definition* by protesters, the struggle against the corrupt 1% is conducted in the name of the citizens suffering from the corruption of the political class. In the Arab Spring, the diversity of participants found a composition in a broad self-definition, as the people fighting against the oppressor: a frequently used slogan was 'Our people, our people, come and join us' (El-Ghobashy 2012, 35). And the slogan 'the people want...' spread quickly and easily across the Mediterranean and Nord-African region. If for Mubarak protesters were foreigners, spies, irrational, primitives, outlaws, chaos; for the protesters the regime was barbaric and arrogant, brutal, and Mubarak a modern day Pharaoh, while they themselves were the people, spontaneous and leaderless, young, democratic, Egyptians (Alexander 2011).

Similarly, in Spain, activists identify with all-encompassing definitions of those who resist. The manifesto of one of the most influential organizations of the 15M movement in Spain, Democracia Real Ya, under the title 'We are normal, common people' read:

> We are like you: people who get up every morning to study, work or find a job, people who have family and friends. People who work hard every day to provide a better future for those around us. Some of us consider ourselves progressive, others conservative. Some of us are believers, some not. Some of us have clearly defined ideologies, others are apolitical, but we are all concerned and angry about the political, economic, and social outlook which we see around us: corruption among politicians, businessmen, bankers, leaving us helpless, without a voice. This situation has become normal, a daily suffering, without hope. But if we join forces, we can change it. It's time to change things, time to build a better society *together*. (cit. in Gerbaudo 2012, 82)

In a similar vein, in the United States, the participants in Occupy wrote: 'We are the 99 percent. We are getting kicked out of our homes. We are forced to choose between groceries and rent. We are denied quality medical care. We are suffering from environmental pollution. We are working long hours for little pay and no rights, if we're working at all. We are getting nothing while the other 1 percent is getting everything' (Gerbaudo 2012, 119).

Moreover, in the self-definition, a reference to the nation represents an innovation vis-à-vis previous movements. National flags are indeed used in many of these protests, from the Icelandic flag to the American one. Appeals to the nation increased, in fact, during the protest of 2011.

Pride on national identities emerged during the Arab Spring, contributing to identification processes that gave the nation a positive value. In the words of a protest leader in Egypt, 'we have been a cowardly nation, We have finally to say "no", and this in the name of "Egypt, the land of the Library of Alexandria, of a culture which contributed groundbreaking advances in mathematics, medicine, and science"' (Alexander 2011, 25). Slogans read 'Raise your head high, you're an Egyptian', 'We shall die for Egypt to live', 'Our country has been humiliated so much', 'Wake up, Egypt', 'We are all the Egyptian people' (Alexander 2011, 26–8, 42). As an al-Jazeera journalist observed, 'despite the number of teargas canisters fired at protesters and the number of those who have been beaten and detained...a long dormant patriotism and pride has been awakened' (Alexander 2011, 30). In fact, in Tahrir Square reference to national symbols even increased over time:

> Liberation was a word with several meanings in the square. People arrived demanding free elections, regime change, an end to police brutality, improvement in their economic lot, or all of the above. As the days passed, the discourse was slowly taken over by expressions of patriotism. The people's art in every corner of the square became less visible in a staggering mass of Egyptian flags. The consensus against Mubarak developed into a jubilee of national pride. Following Mubarak's resignation on February 11, Tahrir erupted in joy. 'Hold your head high', chanted hundreds of thousands, 'You are an Egyptian.' (Shokr 2012, 45)

National flags resonated also with the anti-colonialist tradition in Tunisia where, as an activist stated, 'the flag was a symbol we had especially used [when playing] against the French [national team], but now it means that the politicians have no right to wave it, it has come back into the people's hands' (Sergi and Vogiatzoglou 2013, 228).

In the search for unifying symbols, the exclusion of party flags also facilitated the spread of national ones. In Portugal, songs and slogans of the Carnations Revolution also testified to the national rootedness of the protest (Baumgarten 2013). In Greece, the use of flags from the 1821 anti-ottoman revolution and the references to the heroes of independence helped a part of the protesters to locate their struggle within a glorious past. National flags were indeed problematic symbols here. As an activist remembered, 'When I first saw the flag, I was sick, I said this cannot be happening! I flipped out in the beginning, they would even sing the national anthem in front of the parliament...I said, we must be surrounded by nationalist monkeys, fascist chimpanzees!' (Sergi and Vogiatzoglou 2013, 228). Even in this case, however, the activists realized that the people with the flags 'are members of our society, they are part of the people who will revolt when the time will come. At the very end, we were struggling for the same purposes and goals' (Sergi and Vogiatzoglou 2013, 228). So, one of them stated: 'We came to realize that the flag-carrying people were members of the ex-middle class, those whose life had literally been crashed by the crisis. Those people, when looking for a banner of resistance to identify themselves with, opened their closet and what they found inside was the Greek flag. Therefore, they took the Greek flag and came out to the street' (Sergi and Vogiatzoglou 2013, 229).

The use of national flags became inclusive, however, when more of them started to be shown together. Often, protesters waved at the same time Icelandic, Spanish, Italian, Portuguese, Egyptian and/or Tunisian flags. So, in Greece for example, 'the identification with the national symbols was not perceived as an attempt to construct barriers to the neighboring Mediterranean countries, but rather as a symbol of the Greek people participating in a common effort to overthrow neo-liberal policies at the global level' (Sergi and Vogiatzoglou 2013, 229). In Portugal, similarly, there were expressions of solidarity with those who struggled against austerity in other countries – synthesized in slogans such as 'We are all Greeks'; or 'Spain, Ireland, Portugal: our struggle is international'. In this sense, in some countries especially, national symbols came to symbolize solidarity with citizens struggling against austerity policies.

In sum, in the development of populist reasons we cannot really speak of either fearful individuals or of winning multitudes, but rather of a complex search for identifying a new frame that could encompass the large majority – the 99 per cent – of suffering citizens. Calls for social justice reflected attention to deteriorating material conditions but, differently from in right-wing populism, this did not bring about an exclusivist cultural position.

Inclusive identities in European protests

Survey data at demonstrations confirms that, in the movements we are analysing, claims for social justice are framed in an inclusive way. Calls for re-establishment of social rights and references to the people and the nation do not develop into exclusivist claims. Rather, 'materialist' claims against social injustice are bridged with culturally inclusive 'post-materialist' values.

Our data from the surveys in Italy also confirm a bridging of claims for social and cultural integration, as anti-austerity protesters called for

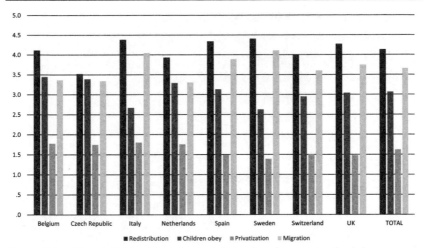

Figure 3.1   Materialist and Post-materialist values by country based on surveys at selected marches in EU countries between 2011 and 2013 (Likert 1–5, means) Legend: ETA (values by country) respectively, .245***; .256***; .167***; .279***

state intervention to reduce inequality *and* for an integration of immigrants. They scored, that is, very high on indicators of both 'materialism' and 'postmaterialism'. In general, even if with some differences, demonstrators strongly support the statement that 'Government should redistribute income from the better off to those who are less well off', and oppose the one that 'Even the most important public services and industries are best left to private enterprise.' On cultural issues, they emerge as anti-authoritarian (on the statement 'Children should be taught to obey authority') and extremely inclusive (on the statement 'People from other countries should be allowed to come to my country and live here permanently if they want to'). There is indeed a very strong agreement on the need for the state to reduce economic injustice and oppose privatization. In most of the covered European countries, protesters strongly support redistribution to the state and resist privatization (Figure 3.1). At the same time, advocacy for migrants' rights testifies to support for cultural inclusivity. Significantly, these values tend to have higher support in the countries more heavily hit by the crisis (Italy and Spain), but also in social-democratic Sweden.

Comparing marches in the Italian case indicates that calls for social protections are more widespread in anti-austerity protests (in particular among participants in the No Monti day, Florence 10 + 10, and labour protests). Participants in the other marches also share however similar

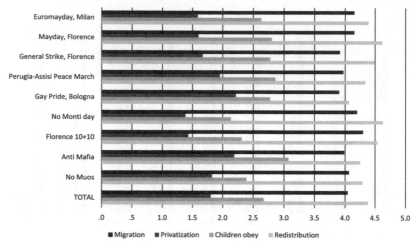

Figure 3.2   Materialist and Post-materialist values of demonstrators at various marches in Italy between 2011 and 2013 (Likert 1–5, means)
Legend: ETA = .144***; .308***; .257***; .207***

positions (Figure 3.2). Moreover, support for state intervention is often combined with inclusive visions on migration issues and anti-authoritarian positions. For this mobilized section of the population, socio-economic and cultural positions converge towards calls for broader social inclusion. Interestingly, these positions tend to be shared by all participants, with just a small decline in the support of the younger cohorts for state redistribution of income from the better off, and opposition to privatization of important services. Subjective class location and job position also have little impact (with only some more orientation towards materialist claims by workers in full-time positions and retired people).

Challenging a view of weak identification, we found that participants tend to identify quite a lot both with each other and with the organizations that called for the protest. In most protest events the identification is more horizontal: higher with the other participants than with the organization (see Figure 3.3). Crossing with age, subjective class position, and job position, we note a slight decline in identification for the younger cohorts and an increase instead for those in full-time positions, or retired.

Feelings of indignation are also confirmed, with frequent expressions of anger and worries. There are, however, strong negative emotions as well. On a scale between 1 (not at all) and 5 (very much), the average score is 4.5 when marchers are asked if they feel angry, and about the same when they are asked if they feel worried (with higher scores, up to

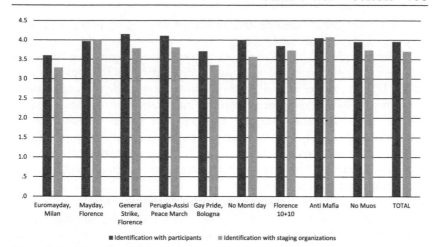

Figure 3.3   Identification with other participants and with staging organizations in various demonstrations in Italy 2011–2013 (Likert 1–5, means)
Legend: ETA = .203***; .229***

4.76, for those who participated in demonstrations on labour issues). Frustration (average 3.8) and fear (3.1) are instead less commonly expressed.

In sum, we find among participants in anti-austerity protests of various types a call for state intervention, linked however with an inclusive conception of citizenship. Even in a liquid society, participants in protests stress feelings of solidarity and collective identities. Moderate in their claims for reforms, sometimes with a reference to long established rights, the activists do express a very strong moral call with broadly encompassing identities.

Conclusion

Cleavages include a cultural dimension: the social background contributes to constitute a cleavage when citizens sharing a certain structural position are embedded in a set of values, norms, ideas on which collective identities are based. Social movement studies have indeed considered the building of collective identities as a central process in the mobilization in collective action. Identities are embedded in the social context, but they are also constructed, continuously changing through time. Strategic dilemmas emerge on the depth and breadth of the collective definition of the self, as well as of the other. Identifying processes are especially relevant for anti-austerity protests developing in times of challenges to a shared doxa.

Collecting identification has always been a challenging but necessary process for emerging movements, as the diversity of individual positions on the labour market as well as social dispersion made mutual recognition difficult. The development of moral indignation into political claims has required time and energies. Especially as social transformations disrupt old identifications, identity works becomes all the more necessary. Social conditions are therefore far from being directly traduced in collective identities, but for sure the contextual conditions in which they develop influence their content.

Recognizing that social scientists are split in their expectation on the capacity of collective identities to raise and, especially, consolidate in liquid societies, I have looked at the specific content of emerging collective identities in social movements targeting neoliberalism. In particular, I have considered what Polanyi (1957) called the continuous double movements between free market and the protection of the society, focusing the attention upon the immoral dimensions of the second 'great transformation': the neoliberal one.

Social movement studies have pointed at the importance of identity building as a process in which social belonging acquires a cognitive, collective dimension and can then become politicized, as responsibility for problems are attributed to a political entity. Looking at movements as identity fields, social movement studies have examined the relationships between some contextual dimensions and the type of collective (often politicized) identity. If community and associational bonds favour the emergence and survival of strong, unitary, and rigid collective identities, we have expected the shift from Fordism, as balancing capitalism and incorporation, to post-Fordism, as a new free market turn, as challenging those types of identity. While some scholars considered liquid society as individualizing, and others thought that identity work could be avoided in the spontaneous mobilization of precariousness, I suggested that different types of collective identities might emerge, reflecting the challenges of neoliberalism to the old ones. As cultural trends spread precarity and insecurity among broad and heterogenous social groups, the identity work of emerging social movements needs to be oriented towards the building of multiple, flexible, tolerant identifications of the self. If neoliberal hostility to state intervention and to discourses and practices of social protection creates feelings of insecurity, emerging protests can work as critical juncture in constructing new collective identities, as populist reasoning – as re-construction of the identity of the people – is needed in times of challenges. The degree of perceived disruption in everyday life, and the perceptions thereof, can indeed lead to expectations that the content of collective and politicized identities will change with the development of the crisis.

Building upon Polanyi's work, I have suggested that neoliberal attacks against societal protection are not only made up of policies that, led by a monetarist economy, promote cuts in public services and allow for the growth of inequalities, even in the most extreme forms. Rather, neoliberalism is also a cynical ideology according to which profits have to be maximized at all costs. Public intervention is stigmatized as an obstacle to the full swing of the free market, and public services in particular as not only increasing budget deficits but also creating distortion of labour markets. Privatization of services is privileged, with only a residual welfare for the poor.

Like liberalism during the first 'great transformation', neoliberalism defies the compassionate discourse of previous capitalist justifications, and any social pact oriented to balance free market and social protection. It represents a paradigmatic shift away from the recognition of a societal solidarity in the name of individual responsibility. In its cynical view, the most selfish sentiments are considered as the most beneficial for a society, where welfare is supposed to trickle down automatically, from the rich to the poor. Since the beginning of the millennium, social movements have stigmatized the neoliberal ideology as unjust and inefficient. Assuming immorality, it produces immorality.

The effects of these cultural transformations on the construction of collective identities are discussed in social theory as well as in social movement studies. Theorizations of a liquid society, with their emphasis on multiple individual identities, changing subjective identification, and soft (or weak) collective identities, stressed the difficulty of the development of a sort of class consciousness of the emerging groups of losers, and others emphasized instead a sort of automatic insubordination of the multitudes. Social movement studies, meanwhile, pushed to look at identification processes as always in progress: they require an identity work, which is relational in nature, with identities fields which are plural and ever-changing.

In Polanyi's double movement, resistance to free market tends to emerge in the society taking specific cultural forms. The labour movement has traditionally denounced the betrayal by the bourgeoisie of the very values of the French revolution: freedom, equality, and solidarity (della Porta 2013a). In the beginning of the 2000s, the GJM denounced the injustice of rampant neoliberalism, bridging various groups and associations around calls for citizen rights and social justice, as once broadly accepted principles which had been betrayed in the capitalism move from social protection to free market. Within cosmopolitan visions, the building of alternative, democratic institutions of global governance was called for. Tolerant identities framed the social diversity of the basis of reference as a richness of the movement.

With Boltanski and Chiapello (2005), we noticed, in fact, an interaction between the dominant spirit of capitalism and its criticism. After the concern for liberty of the new social movement, under neoliberalism social issues are back as source of identification – the social critique of the spirit of capitalism, in Boltanski and Chiapello's language (2005), came back, even if it did not substitute for what they call artistic critique.

Pushing forward the calls for social justice, the anti-austerity protests construct an ethical critique of capitalism. Against the immorality of capitalism, activists elaborate a moral framing through which neoliberalism is stigmatized (Thompson 1971). Sometimes within a reformist frame, the cynicism of the '1%' is denounced, as responsible for the stripping of citizens' most fundamental rights, such as food, housing, and health. The very legal system that had protected the society, granting a modicum of welfare and the reduction of social inequalities, is seen as falling victim to the greed of an unholy alliance of business and politics. While keeping an inclusive stance towards issues of cultural integration, the activists of the anti-austerity protests seem however more concerned than the global justice activists were with the defence of national sovereignty.

In times of changes and challenges, a populist reason, as definition of the constituency, is a central focus of the identity work of recent movements. Here as well, we find telling differences in the comparison of the GJM and anti-austerity mobilization. In fact, even if both stressed inclusivity, the GJM presented itself, within a cosmopolitan vision, as a movement of movements – that is, an alliance of minorities – while anti-austerity protesters defined themselves as a broad majority (up to the 99%) of those suffering for the injustice of neoliberalism and its crisis. If the former referred to a master frame as social justice, articulated through calls for political reforms, the latter rather (morally) appealed to a common sentiment like outrage or indignation (and indeed, hope seemed more present in the movement in the rampant years of neoliberalism and rage in the years of crises). The perception of a lost sovereignty was reflected in, and contrasted by, a proud reference to the nation, symbolized in the use of national flags (even if in an inclusive fashion) rather than the cosmopolitan rainbow flag of the GJM. A moral discourse was opposed to the immorality of neoliberalism, with expression of indignation and call for recognition of lost (citizen but also human) rights. To a certain extent backward looking, the movement reacting to the crisis of neoliberalism called for the restoration of lost rights, denouncing the corruption of democracy. If a moral framing was intertwined with a political one, the balance of the two seems to be changing, with moral discourses increasing in importance when moving from the Arab Spring to Southern Europe and then to the United States.

All in all, processes of identification also developed within anti-austerity protests, with a framing that reflected resonant visions of the crisis as produced by elites' greed, contrasted with the sufferance of the people. Even in fluid society, times of crisis were not times of total individualism, but rather of a different identity work, to a certain extent pointing to an emotional identification more than to a cognitive one. If a moral dimension was of course present in both the GJM and anti-austerity protests, it was bridged with more reformist hopes towards the achievements of 'concrete utopias' in the former, and instead with deep outrage at the indignity of neoliberalism in the latter. As we discussed, the mentioned differences between the global justice and anti-austerity movements are linked to the evolution of neoliberalism.

Also in this chapter, I stressed similarities across movements in the ways in which, even in times of crisis, identity work is performed and a particular framing of the self develops. More systematic comparison is needed in order to understand how some common themes are bridged with traditional social movement cultures at macro and meso levels, as well as on the impact on the cultural dimension of the cleavage of the location in the capitalist world system, capitalist diversities, the intensity of the crisis. Additionally, while my reflections have addressed the mobilized activists in general, a focus needs to be added on the ways in which collective identification processes are affected, at the micro level, by the objective socio-economic condition and the subjective class location.

4

Lo Llaman Democracia Y No Lo Es: A Crisis of Political Responsibility

Italy. Spring 2013. Activists of the centre-left party, the Partito Democratico (PD), symbolically take over several of their party's head-quarters at the local level. Converging on a platform significantly called OccupyPD, they upload to the Web pictures of themselves holding posters that strongly criticize their party's recent choices (and which are quickly broadcasted over the more traditional mass media). In particular, the OccupyPD activists are indignant about the party leadership's management of the election by the Parliament of the President of the Republic: first and foremost, the refusal to vote for the previous President of the PD and highly reputed scholar Stefano Rodotà, candidate of the new Movimento 5 Stelle, a movement party that entered parliament with about one-quarter of the electorate's support. They were also strongly critical of their leader's plan to elect a compromise name agreed upon with Berlusconi's PdL, as well as of the following ambush to the former PD premier Romano Prodi, put forward for president by the party but not voted by at least 101 of its MPs in the secret ballots. Finally, many militants are outraged at the bipartisan re-election of Giorgio Napolitano, who had been the sponsor of the so-called technical government led by Mario Monti and supported by the PD and PdL, and who had been accused of having opposed a possible governmental alliance between PD and Movimento 5 Stelle, instead supporting a PD-PdL agreement. The OccupyPD activists object to this unholy alliance, but also to what they see as a total lack of transparency and internal democracy in their party. They present their protest as a response to 'those who built a party that is made up (as it proved in these days) only of currents and power agreements' while 'we need an open discussion in order to build policies' (interview OPD no. 4). They stigmatize the 'loss of identity' produced by 'an ignorant leadership' (interview OPD, no. 2). After having been mobilized to carry out the primary election for the choice of the party's candidate for premier, they lament having been totally forgotten by their leaders. Faced with the electoral defeat of the PD – which was expected to win the elections and ended up losing three million voters, failing to form the promised 'government for an alternative' – they see the failure of the leaders as mainly linked to their detachment from their basis.

OccupyPD is not the only movement formed within the party: in the same period, hundreds of critical militants in Turin organize a so-called Pallacorda (resonant in the name of the famous Tennis Court Oath during the French revolution) assembly, while the marshal body, traditionally renowned for its loyalty, refuses to protect the party's leadership during the Labour Day march. While many activists ask to 'ResetPD', party circles give collected money to NGOs such as Emergency rather than forwarding them to the party, and once-loyal volunteers at the Feste dell'Unità (the traditional fund-raising fairs of the Communist Party) now renamed Feste democratiche) refuse to cook tortellini until their leaders stop colluding with Berlusconi. In particular, the activists ask for democracy in the party, with space to discuss alternatives and channels to communicate within the party itself.

When the United States activists called for people to Occupy everywhere, they were certainly not thinking of the headquarters of the Italian centre-left party. Parties and movements are indeed often considered as worlds apart. In reality, parties have been relevant players in movement politics, and movements have influenced parties, often through the double militancy of many of their members. OccupyPD testifies to a continuous fluidity at the movement-party border, but also to a blockage in the party's interactions with the society, which started long before the economic crisis, but drastically accelerated with it.

In this chapter, I will address these issues by moving from the concept of legitimacy crisis, singling out the main elements of what I will define as a crisis of responsibility – by which I mean a drastic drop in the capacity of the government to respond to citizens' requests (what Mair, 2009, called responsiveness). Bridging social movement studies with research on institutional trust and democratic theory, I will look at some political effects of the economic crisis in terms of a specific form of legitimacy crisis, as well as citizens' responses to it, with a particular focus on the political meaning of recent anti-austerity protests. Locating movements against neoliberal capitalism within a crisis of responsibility allows us to understand some characteristics of their mobilizations in terms of their adaptation to threats and opportunities. Linking politics to the market, I will look at the political version of neoliberalism – what has been called 'post-democracy' (Crouch 2004). A minimalist version of liberal visions of democracy, post-democracy, while limiting the political intervention of the citizens to electoral politics, leaves instead large power to business to lobby governments and decision makers. An elitist model, it reduces the competence of the state on the market, giving political power to the economic interests of the few (ibid.). The political effect of the weakening of the industrial labour is accompanied, that is, by a conception of politics that denies influence to the Demos and the value of equality. Indeed, politics and governments fall in the hands of privileged elites, as it happened before the development of the democratic state, and the welfare state retrenches. This has, as we will see, a clear effect on the political conceptions and practices of social movements.

Comparing the GJM and the most recent protests against austerity policies, I will note some similarities in the critique of the neoliberal version of representative democracy, but also some differences. In particular, the tensions with political parties that had emerged in the GJM became much more radical in the following waves of protests, characterized by the broad refusal of alliances with political parties and even associations, which were considered as (corrupted) instruments of domination: 'NO les votas', 'Que se vayan todos' – 'Don't vote for them'; 'They have all to go away' were widespread slogans.

If political theory as well as empirical research indicate that a crisis of legitimacy implies declining trust in political institutions, the development towards either rebellion or acquiescence will be, as social movement studies suggest, related with the appropriation (or even creation) of political opportunities.

Lack of responsibility in (late) neoliberalism

Today's movements reflects, first and foremost, very high levels of mistrust given a perceived legitimacy crisis, which, however, has very different characteristics from the one hypothesized by Habermas for advanced capitalism. As mentioned (Chapter 2), today's legitimacy crisis is not driven by excessive state intervention in the market in order to support labour, but rather by state intervention in support for capital and the related stripping off of civic, political and social rights (Sassen 2006).

While in the 1980s governments were accused of spending too much and moved away from the Keynesian economic policies of full employment described as at the basis of a sort of class compromise of advanced Fordist capitalism, post-Fordism brought about a retrenchment of welfare and increased social inequalities. Deregulation, privatization, and liberalization have been the main policy directions justified with the need to re-establish the efficiency of the market. De facto, these interventions did not help competition, but rather supported the concentration of power in the hands of a few huge corporations, with an ensuing economic crisis rooted not in scarcity or inflation, but rather in redistribution (or lack thereof). Since 2008, public debt has increased, not because of investments in social services and support for the weaker social groups, but rather due to huge expenditures of public money to bail out banks and financial institutions from their financially driven crisis as well as by drastic cuts in the taxation on capital. This development in the interactions between the state and the market takes the form of a corruption of representative democracy through the overlapping of economic and political power.

On the output side of the political system, this means an abdication of responsibility by representative institutions in the face of citizens' demands. As Wolfgang Streeck (2011) noted, democratic capitalism has two conflicting principles of regime allocation: marginal productivity and social needs. The crisis of neoliberalism indicates an incapacity to meet them.

Against the neoliberal promises of defending the market from the state, scholars of various disciplines point at the growing intermingling of the two. Already during the first transformation, the proclamation of free market as separation of state and market was an *illusion*. As Polanyi had noted, 'there was nothing natural about laissez-faire; free market could never have come into being merely by allowing things to take their course...laissez-faire itself was enforced by the state' (Polanyi 1957, 139). The 1830s and 1840s saw indeed a growth of administration as 'the road to free market was opened and kept open by an enormous increase in continuous, centrally organized and controlled interventionism' (Polanyi 1957, 140).

Like in liberalism, also in neoliberalism the assumption of a separation between the state and the market is an illusion. Segregation of economy and polity is rarely present, as governments still have to remedy market failure, and even the market needs laws (for example on protection of copyrights, patents, contracts). In fact, as Crouch wrote about neoliberalism, 'in its attempt to reduce certain kinds of government interventions in the economy, it encourages or provides space for a number of mutual interferences between government and private firms, many of which raise serious problems for both the free market and the probity of public institutions' (2012, 93). Rather than competition, in neoliberalism there is a concentration of capital with the development of 'giant firms' that distort the market, as 'a "giant" firm is one that is sufficiently dominant within its markets to be able to influence the terms of those markets by its own action, using its organizational capacity to develop market-dominating strategies' (Crouch 2012, 49). Too big to fail, 'giant firms' play a strong influence in politics, heavily pushing for their interests.

State capacities to ensure citizens' rights are drastically reduced by policies of privatization, liberalization and deregulation, allowing for the concentration of capital, derived from governments' commitment in terms of favourable legislation. In fact, 'true markets have rarely accompanied these privatizations, problems of oligopoly and limited opportunities for competition usually having been important reasons why these activities had ended up in the public domain in the first place' (Crouch 2012, 80). Long contracts related with privatization rather remove services from the market as, through deregulation, unbalanced politics driven by extremes of inequality lead to instability (Stiglitz 2012a).

The states are indeed accused of repealing rights to social protection in order to increase profits and rents for the few privileged. In fact, 'it is not only regulation, but also deregulation, or absence from regulation, that can produce inappropriate relations between firms and governments' (Crouch 2012, 95). Neoliberalism implied in fact the abolition of several laws and regulations oriented to control the economy. Typically, in 1999, in the United States, the Gramm–Leach–Bliley Financial Modernization Act repealed the Glass–Steagall Act of 1933, which had introduced restraints on the banking system; the new law became 'a fundamental part of the neoliberal deregulation programme', as it 'abolished long-standing restraints on the ability of retail banks to use their customers' deposit for high-risk trading activities' (Crouch 2012, 98). In 2005, a creditor-friendly bankruptcy law gave banks more leverage, exactly at the time that subprime mortgages spread, making it impossible for citizens to discharge debts even in cases of bankruptcy (Stiglitz 2012a, 195). In the United States, as business was writing the rules of the game through participation in regulatory agencies (Stiglitz 2012a, 47), inadequate regulation produced enormous losses (Stiglitz 2012a, 60), as well as excess returns as corporate rents given also the dramatic drop of corporate tax revenues as a share of GDP (Stiglitz 2012a, 73).

Neoliberalism was established – and, as Crouch (2012) observed, strangely survived its crisis – especially through the transfer of a large amount of money from corporations to politicians. In fact, liberalization, deregulation, and privatization fuelled corruption, while their advocates had claimed the opposite (Stiglitz 2012a, 176). For instance, 'The deregulation agenda that led to the irresponsible behaviour of financial markets during the 1990s was itself the result of impressive lobbying in the United States Congress and administration by banking interests' (Crouch 2012, 95). Also in the US, after the 2010 decision Citizens United v. Federal Election Commission, in which the Supreme Court recognized corporations' right to donate to parties as protected under free speech provisions, the influence of business could spread even more freely (Stiglitz 2012a, 131). For instance, after Enron, a Texas oil-producing company, had donated generously to the Bush campaign, Congress passed legislation to allow a firm employed by a corporation to audit the accounts of that corporation.

Wild lobbying has indeed been identified by social science research as a cause of social inequality and political delegitimation. Just to give a few examples, according to the IMF, in 2010, US firms had invested $3.2 billion in lobbying (Stiglitz 2012a, 73 ff.), and in the EU parliament there are about 100 lobbyists for business for each one defending consumers' rights (Crouch 2012, 67–8).[11] Collusion has been so widespread that, as Stiglitz noted, 'Virtually all US senators, and most of the representatives of the House, are members of the top 1 percent when they arrive, are kept in office by money from the top 1 percent, and know that if they serve the top 1 percent well they will be rewarded by the top 1 percent when they leave office' (cit. in Graeber 2012, 39). So that, Crouch concluded, 'The Chicago innovation did nothing to resolve the central issue: economic and political power translated into each other' (Crouch 2012, 70). During the crisis, the bailing out of those banks 'too big to fail' confirmed the need neoliberal developments had for complacent governments.

Corruption spreads indeed, on the one hand, as political parties lose their loyal voters, electoral support needs to be obtained through expansive forms of (visible and invisible) campaigns, but also as 'largest firms are not just too big to fail, but also too big to jail' (Streeck 2014, 63). So, not only, already in the 1990s, 'fraud and corruption had reached all-time highs in the US economy', but also, 'what came after 2008 beat everything: rating agencies being paid by the producers of toxic security to award them top grades; offshore shadow banking, money laundering and assistance in large-scale tax evasion being the normal business of the biggest banks with the best addresses; the sale to unsuspecting customers of securities constructed so that other custumers could bet against them; the leading banks worldwide fraudulently fixing interest rates and the gold price' (Streeck 2014, 63).

At the same time as corporations buy political decisions, there are attempts to present the latter as *depoliticized*. For instance, the widespread principal-agent assumption – stating that the principal (the shareholders) want profits and the agents simply have to maximize share value – was promoted by neoliberalists as a leading principle for public policy making. This denied the political nature of public decision making, with negative consequences as 'democracy does not operate like profit, providing a single measurable indicator. It constantly has to be interpreted by politicians, their advisers and other opinion makers…This raises a highly important question: many marketization strategies in public policy try to put issues beyond the range of conflict and debate and beyond the reach of difficult ethical choices. But these attempts must always fail, as it is not possible to put human life on a technocratic automatic pilot' (Crouch 2012, 91–2).

In a similar direction of depoliticization of decision making, there is an emphasis on *independent authorities*, as an instrument to overcome the pressure by the citizens, or even from within political parties. Polanyi had already stigmatized the increasing political power of financial institutions during the Great Transformation: a free market economy requiring a gold standard, under it 'leaders of the financial markets are entrusted, in the nature of things, with the safeguarding of stable exchanges and sound internal credit on which government finance largely depends. The banking administration is thus in the position of obstructing any domestic move in the economic sphere that it happens to dislike' (Polanyi 1957, 229). As for the second 'great transformation', nobel laureate Stiglitz stigmatized the widespread lack of faith in democratic accountability of those who call for independent banks as deeply troubling, as it does not recognize the economic trade-offs of anti-inflation policies and therefore the need for political decisions (Stiglitz 2012a, 254). This is, he noted, even more the case when central banks are captured by the financial sector and still more in the EU, where the European Central Bank (ECB) is supposed to focus only on inflation, with no consideration of growth and employment (Stiglitz 2012a, 250–5).

Even more directly, the space for political decisions has been denied, by politicians of different colours, on the basis of the assumed absolute dominance of the so-called 'logic of the market', especially of international markets. As Streeck observed, after having been saved by the states, 'As we now read in the papers almost every day, "the markets" have begun in unprecedented ways to dictate what presumably sovereign and democratic states may still do for their citizens and what they must refuse them. Moreover the very same ratings agencies that were instrumental in bringing about the disaster of the global money industry are now threatening to downgrade the bonds of the very same states that had to accept a previously unimaginable level of new debt to rescue that industry and the capitalist economy as a whole' (Streeck 2011, 20). In fact, the democratic aim of obtaining the trust of the citizens has now been rhetorically substituted for by the search for the 'trust of the market', which is to be obtained even at the expense of irresponsiveness to citizens' demands.

The responsibility of democratic states vis-à-vis their citizens is then all the more removed as *external conditionalities* impose cuts in public spending, with often dramatic consequences in terms of violations of human rights to food, health and housing. As Streeck (2011, 20) has noted: 'In countries like Greece and Ireland in particular, anything resembling democracy will be effectively suspended for many years as national governments of whatever political color, forced to behave responsibly as defined by international markets and organizations, will have to impose strict austerity on their societies, at the price of becoming increasingly unresponsive to their citizens.' To give just an example, in what Fritz Scharpf defined as a 'pre-emption of democracy', in May 2010 the Commission's economic adjustment programme for Greece postulated that 'the immediate priority is to contain the government's financing needs and reassure markets of the determination of authorities to do whatever it takes to secure medium- and long-term fiscal sustainability' (2011, 184), through increases in VAT and cuts to public sector wages and pensions, social expenditures and public investments. While national governments formally maintain the competence to impose extremely unpopular measures, de facto their sovereignty is denied by the lending institutions. Significantly, the memorandum of understanding establishes the conditionalities countries that accept economic help have to follow, as 'the quarterly disbursements of bilateral financial assistance...are subject to quarterly reviews of conditionality for the duration of the arrangements. The release of the tranches will be based on observance of quantitative performance criteria and a positive evaluation of progress... The authorities commit to consult with the European Commission, the ECB and the IMF on the adoption of policies which are not consistent with this memorandum... Prior to the release of the installments, the authorities shall provide a compliance report on the fulfillment of the conditionality' (Irish and Greek memoranda, cit. in Scharpf 2011, 185). So, all cruelties even if dictated by the commission bureaucracy and the self-interest of other countries, are inflicted by national governments, with heavy consequences in terms of delegitimation.

Democratic responsibility is therefore further reduced by the lack of electoral accountability of those international organizations that impose conditionalities. As Scharpf notes, with excessive deficit procedures as a tough version of stability pacts: 'From the perspective of citizens in Greece, Ireland and Portugal, the European and international agencies imposing the "rescue-cum-retrenchment" programme are not, themselves, supported by democratic legitimacy' (Scharpf 2011, 193). This happened in a situation in which the results of those policies are not encouraging, as debt still increases and interest rates for government bonds are on the rise (Scharpf 2011, 186). While the minuscule EU budget does not allow imbalances to be alleviated, 'EMU friendly economists have always downplayed the fact that the eurozone was not an "optimal current area" ' (Scharpf 2011, 191).

So, decisions shift to places which are more and more untransparent and subtracted to any democratic logic. As popular demands for prosperity and security increase, international fiscal diplomacy makes decisions more and more insulated from popular democratic pressures (Streeck 2011). Polanyi had already noted that, as a free market economy required a gold standard, under it 'leaders of the financial markets are entrusted, in the nature of things, with the safeguarding of stable exchanges and sound internal credit on which government finance largely depends. The banking administration is thus in the position of obstructing any domestic move in the economic sphere that it happens to dislike' (Polanyi 1957, 229). Similarly, in late neoliberal capitalism, 'the arena where it is decided who is to suffer and who is not has become more remote: it has moved to international financial diplomacy and the backrooms of a handful of leading central banks. The governors, claiming to command the higher wisdom of arcane economic theories that only they understand, now tell governments what "structural reforms" they have to impose on their citizens: how wages are to be set and whose pensions are to be cut' (Streeck 2014, 49).

In a vicious circle, as inequalities not only fuel discontent, but also depress economic growth, the unchecked greed of an oligarchy pushes more and more towards the 'plundering of the public', with heavier and heavier cuts in public spending (Streeck 2014, 59–61). At the same time, increasing repression of forms of protest (in particular but not only, of transnational ones) spread as the main, or at least most visible, response to the expression of citizens' dissatisfaction (della Porta and Tarrow 2012). Neoliberalism promotes indeed a minimalist state in terms of social services, but not of surveillance or repression. Moreover, it tends to dismantle neocorporatist assets of negotiation between business and labours, reducing in particular the space for trade unions.

In sum, economic crises have been linked to declining margins of profits to be invested in policies that would accommodate labour's demands. As noted, the separation of state and market is in reality a mystification, as state interventions are needed for increasing profits and rents, through policies of deregulation, liberalization and privatization. Competition is fictitious, as concentration of capital (especially financial capital) into huge corporations is the main force against social protection.

Crisis of legitimacy in neoliberalism: the abdication of responsibility by representative institutions and its discontent

Anti-austerity protests do not oppose just the economic crisis, but also the political crisis with which it is strictly intertwined. They indeed target and reflect a specific type of crisis of political legitimacy which, although it had already been on its way, has peaked with the financial crisis and the ensuing austerity measures that tended to increase the suffering of a large part of the population subject to them. As I am going to suggest, the Habermasian concept of crisis of legitimacy could help indeed when addressing some deep transformation in the relations between citizens and political institutions, locating the debate on the role of institutional trust (and mistrust) within a broader perspective. The specific version of crisis of legitimation in post-democratic neoliberalism I define as a crisis of responsibility: policies of privatization, liberalization and deregulation strip off competences from the state and rights from the citizens. This calls for a re-thinking of political opportunities and constraints for social movements as, on the input side, the traditional potential allies, such as political parties, loose trust and, on the output side, the capacity of governing is drastically reduced by a general weakening of the state.

Legitimacy crisis and institutional trust

Distinguishing social formations as primitive, traditional, capitalist and postcapitalist, Habermas (1976) defined advanced capitalism (organized or state regulated) by a process of concentration in national and then multinational corporations and in the organization of the market for goods, capital and labour. In this vision, state intervention supplementing the market marks the end of liberal capitalism. It is however also a source of tension, as 'recoupling the economic system to the political – which in a way repoliticizes the relations of production – creates an increased need for legitimation' (Habermas 1976, 36).

In this social formation, crises take on peculiar dynamics. First, the economic crisis – as a systemic crisis in the economic system, either in its input of work and capital or its output of consumable values – tends to transform itself and lead to political conflicts. In fact, economic crises mutate into political crises. As the political system produces as output 'sovereignly executed administrative decisions', 'output crises have the form of a rationality crisis in which the administrative system does not succeed in recognizing and fulfilling the imperative received from the economic system' (Habermas 1976, 46). Since the political system requires input of mass loyalty, input crises are instead legitimacy crises in which 'the legitimizing system does not succeed in maintaining the requisite level of mass loyalty while the steering imperatives taken over from the economic system are carried through' (Habermas 1976, 46). The state intervenes here on the basis of pressure by various classes, creating distortion in the labour market.

According to Habermas, in this social formation, attempts to defuse rationality crises produce inflation and crises of public finances, as the state is unable to generate enough revenue to compensate for economic cycles. As the state takes over more services and responsibilities in welfare but also in sustaining social consumption, economic and rationality crises interact at the level of systemic integration and they also spill over into crises of social integration. As state intervention increases the need for legitimation, the state attempts ways of depoliticization, such as appeals to expertise in the administrative system or the distribution of material resources. In addition, 'because the economic crisis has been intercepted and transformed into a systematic overloading of the public budget, it has put off the mantle of a natural fate of society. If governmental crisis management fails, it lags behind programmatic demands that it has placed on itself. The penalty for this failure is withdrawal of legitimation' (Habermas 1976, 69).

Economic and political crises tend to penetrate the lifeworlds of individuals, fuelling motivational crises that result from changes in the system itself, which does not generate a sufficient amount of action motivating meaning (Habermas 1976, 49). A motivation crisis happens, in fact, as the norms and values into which people are socialized are in tension with the imperative of the occupational system, questioning capitalism and the related lost autonomy of the lifeworld. As various parties outbid each other in their promises in order to become more competitive, this also produces a 'politicization of areas of life previously assigned to the private sphere' (Habermas 1976, 72). Traditional values, which were important in supporting the bourgeois society, are weakened in this development. New values emerge which are unfit to reproduce civil and family vocational privatism; as meanings are weakened, they must be replaced by consumable values. As the state politicizes new domains of social life, forms of resistance to them spread (Offe 1985). Social movements then emerge as places to address motivational crises as cultural malaise (Buechler 2000), with calls for the development of public spheres where people can communicate rationally. However, as research on labour sociology has shown, neoliberalism attacked the very bases of the 'mid-century compromise': it reduced the power of the unions, both by changing the structures of production and reducing the protection of workers. In a most pessimistic vision, Streeck (2014, 48 and 54) noted that, as 'trade unions almost disappeared as did strike' – at least in some parts of the world – while, 'even today, after 2008, the old Left remains on the brink of extinction everywhere while a new Left has up to now failed to emerge'.

Citizens' trust in institutions could be considered as an indicator (even if not the only one) of their perceived legitimacy. High mistrust is usually seen as an indicator of a low institutional legitimacy, testifying to reduced loyalty by the citizens to those in government. Democratic theorists have suggested, in fact, that democracies need trustful citizens. This is the case because, symbolically, governments and parliaments have to enjoy legitimacy between one election and the next, but also because, pragmatically, as, e.g., mistrustful citizens tend to pay less taxes. For a long time, deferent citizens were considered to be the most supportive of democratic institutions, as they were ready to recognize their own limitations – according to e.g. Schumpeter (1976) in knowledge and rationality – and to delegate power trustfully to the (political) experts. Since Tocqueville was revisited in the 1980s, social trust (as indicated by associational memberships as well as norms of reciprocity) has been considered conducive to political trust (Newton 2007). The assumption is that people who engage in associations are more likely to meet obligations and also to pressure for better public performances. Only some organizations – tame and unpolitical – were however considered as sources of trust (e.g. Putnam 2000).

Since the 1980s, much research – by scholars such as Samuel Barnes, Max Kaase (Barnes et al. 1979), Russell Dalton (2004), Pippa Norris (2001) – suggested that citizens were becoming more and more critical: they were less supportive of those in power and they used non-conventional forms of political participation for putting pressure on governors (not relying just on elections). What was more, it was not marginal people who were more critical, but rather the younger ones and the most educated. Additionally, those who mistrusted parties and institutions were still interested in politics. As confirmed repeatedly by numerous empirical studies, trust in democracy as a regime based upon electoral accountability is limited by widespread phenomena such as the decline of electoral participation, but also by the deep transformation in the political parties that, giving continuity in time to pre-electoral promises, allowed the implementation of electoral accountability. The drop in the number of party members and, especially, activists (with the related spread of member-less and personalized parties), as well as the weakening of party loyalties (with the increase in electoral volatility and opinion voting) are tangible signs of these transformations (della Porta 2009f).

Nevertheless, theoreticians of a 'participatory revolution' were not so pessimistic about the consequences of a fall in political trust. Rather, they talked of a democratic Phoenix, ready to (re)emerge (Norris 2001). Critical citizens were considered to be better democrats than deferent citizens were, as they tended to choose voice over exit. In fact, together with narratives of increasing 'crisis', some stressed a sort of revival for democracy. Additionally, it can be recalled that social conflicts have been fundamental for the development of democratic rights even when statistics signalled apathetic or trustful citizens (della Porta 2003; 2013a).

The right amount of trust/mistrust in a given democracy is however an open question. Charles Tilly (2007) explained democratization as the integration of networks of trust in the state. In fact, a mechanism of democratization was, according to him, the disintegration of existing segregated networks of trust, given the decline in patrons' ability to offer goods to their clients and consequent withdrawal of clients' trust (Tilly 2007, 4). The creation of publicly recognized associations is seen instead as a sign of trust-network integration in the state. However, Tilly also recognized the democratic dilemma of needing trust but also mistrust to function, as 'contingent consent entails unwillingness to offer rulers, however well elected, blank checks. It implies the threat that if they do not perform in accordance with citizens' expressed collective will, citizens will not only turn them out but also withdraw compliance from such risky government-run activities as military service, jury duty and tax collection' (Tilly 2007, 94).

Two alternative expectations can be derived from this debate. Lack of trust might depress protest, as citizens believe any action is going to be useless. Alternatively, mistrust can fuel protest, as loss of legitimation enrages the public.

Political opportunities in social movement studies

Social movement studies suggest that mistrust in institutions, especially if bridged with confidence in the efficacy of collective action, would bring mobilization, but only if there are perceived opportunities for change.

If we read the mentioned political changes under neoliberalism and in its crisis in terms of chances for protest, there is no doubt that they imply a closing down of political opportunities for social movements. A basic assumption in the political process approach is, in fact, that more democratically accountable institutions tend to be more responsive to movement claims: as Eisinger (1973) had noted comparing US local governments, social movement claims have more opportunity to be heard in governments led by elected administrators (as opposed to governments, made up of public administrators). Additionally, the territorial decentralization of power has been considered as an opportunity for movements (Kriesi et al. 1995), the nation-state as the arena for the development of proper social movements (Tilly 1984) and political parties as very important allies of social movements (Tarrow 1989; della Porta 1995). Nowadays, several indicators point at a general malaise in democratic countries, including both challenges within and without the nation-state.

The closing down of political opportunities seems to happen at different levels of governance. At the national level, procedural legitimation of democracy as a regime based upon electoral accountability is limited by the mentioned decline of electoral participation (visible at all territorial levels), but also by the deep transformation in the main actors of electoral accountability, the political parties. At the transnational level, challenges to democracy on the input side arise from the necessity to adapt conceptions and practices developed at the national level to a reality in which transnational actors and global events have an increasingly large influence. The normative conceptions and empirical implementations of democracy developed in and about the nation-state are not easily applied at the supranational level where political institutions and civil society are concerned. Indeed, 'democracy as we know it within countries does not exist in a Globalized Space. More accurately, to the extent that Globalized Space is marked by conventional democratic procedures, these are ad-hoc, non systematic, irregular and fragile' (Rosenau 1998, 39). Not only do IGOs usually have no electoral accountability, but a transnational conception of citizenship and citizenship rights is hard to develop. The fundamental principles of nation-state democracy – such as territoriality, majority principles and use of coercive power – 'have to be reformulated, if they are to be applied globally' (Archibugi 2003, 7).

In sum, movements in neoliberal post-democracies face a crisis of responsibility of political institutions. Often in tight connections with business, politicians appear to their citizens as increasingly corrupt. While political institutions try to shift legitimation from the input to the output, proposing a vision of depoliticization, economic crises appear as all the more challenging in terms of political consensus. While the attempt to describe decisions as neutral and led by administrative rationality has low empirical resonance, the very economic policies implemented by governments of various colours tend to effectively reduce the competences of the public decision makers, at different levels. As privatization, liberalization and deregulation reduce the instruments in the hands of the states to steer the market and address social inequalities, the more indebted a country, the more heavily the conditionality attached to

international loans formally constrains the capacity of domestic governments to respond to their citizens' demands.

In terms of attribution of political opportunities, this transformation
means the closing down of some of the channels of access from social
movements to the state. More in depth, it means the need of re-thinking
the potential relations between public institutions and social movements,
as gate keepers (such as political parties) tend to lose citizens' trust and
therefore also capacity to channel movements' demands in the political
system and the very competences of the public institutions shrink. As the
politics of neoliberalism developed first in the global South, a new reflection started on the ways in which movements could create political
opportunities that by-pass the mediation of traditional parties and other
institutions that had been important in channelling movements' demands
in the past. As however attribution of opportunities is not just mere
reflection of institutional processes, we can expect that even under threatening conditions opportunities might be perceived as potentially open,
or at least permeable to protest pressures. Opportunities might, that is,
open up during the protest itself. Additionally, different political opportunities might be singled out outside of institutions.

Protests and re-incorporation in Latin America

The opening up of political opportunities as an effect of repeated waves
of protest against neoliberalism is evident in Latin America. In general,
neoliberalism has been seen as producing the de-incorporation of social
groups that had been previously incorporated in the developmental state.
After long struggles, anti-neoliberal protests have then facilitated a new
turn towards (at least some) social protection.

The importance of capitalist development as related with political
transitions emerges from Eduardo Silva's (2009) study on challenging
neoliberalism in Latin America, which singles out a second neoliberal
juncture in the incorporation of the citizens. After neoliberalism destroyed
the populist-corporatist-nationalist incorporation model, Polanyi-like
movements of resistance to commodification developed, with weakened
labour and, instead, alliances with indigenous, human rights, workers',
middle class (especially in public services) and women's movements
showing the capacity to reconstruct associational powers.

Nationalist–populist regimes had provided for the inclusion of popular
sectors and the spread of some conceptions of citizenship rights which
implied the expectation that the state provided for some level of social
protection. Breaking with the liberal free market of the nineteenth
century, they had stated the need for the state to regulate the market,

developing mechanisms to protect individuals, via employment in the public sectors, labour rights, expanded public education, health, housing and subsidies for basic consumption, rural labour and land tenure rights. De-commodification included at least the middle classes and workers' aristocracy, especially in urban areas, with some 'pockets of efficiency' in the provision of social services. The decline of the model between the 1960s and 1980s brought about a polarization between Left and Right, with military coups and attempts to reduce social rights. While several governments were able to buy credits in the 1970s thanks to high liquidity, they had to face a debt crisis in the 1980s, followed by some twin processes of free market liberalization and (procedural) democratization. First waves of reforms imposed with liberalization and privatization of public enterprises; second waves brought about privatization and reduction of social services, pensions, education and health, while labour flex policies pushed labour to the informal sector (Silva 2009).

In her work on indigenous contentious politics, Deborah Yashar (2005) has looked at shifts of citizenship regime. Since the 1950s, democratic and nondemocratic governments had supported a corporatist citizen regime, in which indigenous people had been incorporated as peasants, with recognized civil rights, varied political rights, increasing social rights and class-based interest mediation. Since the 1970s and with even more strength in the 1980s, a neoliberal citizenship regime spread, based on civil and (with some exceptions) political rights but limited social rights and pluralist interest mediation based on the individual.

The relations between neoliberalism and regime types were complex. In fact, against a narrative of the free market as linked to individual freedom and democracy, the brutal regime of Pinochet in Chile represented the original Latin American free market experiment as, between 1975 and 1978, after the coup d'état, the military regime followed the suggestions of the economists of the 'Chicago School' with policies of privatization, liberalization, cuts in services, repression of labour. As Silva (2009) noted, it was not neoliberalism, but rather the reactions to it that pushed Chileans to mobilize for democracy. With the economic crisis in 1982–3, inequalities in fact increased dramatically – with half of the population below the poverty line – while the neoliberal responses to the crisis alienated even the business sector. Protests followed in 1983–4, mobilizing two separate blocs: on the one hand, moderate unions and the Christian democratic party; on the other, radical shantytown organizations (many former formal sector workers) influenced by the communist party. While the latter were anticapitalists, the moderate front was oriented towards a return to Keynesian policies and democracy. During six months of a state of siege in 1985, attempts at moderate accords for democratic transition failed, with violent reactions by the military, especially in the countryside. In 1988, however, the Concertation de partidos por el No defeated Pinochet at the polls, bringing about transition to democracy. The new government showed some commitment to socioeconomic and political inclusion and to social equity as a value, developing centre-left policies and also addressing human rights violations through a Truth and Reconciliation Commission. Poverty then dropped from 40 per cent in 1990 to 14 per cent in 2006 (Silva 2009). So, in this case, neoliberalism grew under dictatorship and a return to some social protection was one of the outcomes of democratization.

This was, however, not always the case, as in other countries in Latin America neoliberalism developed from the defeat of the authoritarian regimes that had provided for some social protection. Democratization and market liberalization then proceeded in parallel, but on an unstable path. Since the 1990s, in fact, anti-neoliberal waves of protests spread in Argentina, Ecuador, Bolivia and Venezuela through a patient building of resources, pressuring for free market reforms and procedural democracy. They were unexpected, as neoliberalism had produced motives to protest through exclusion but also destroyed traditional resources of mobilization. In a continent known for violence, insurrections and coups d'etat, a left-wing mobilization seemed particularly unlikely after the decline of unions and dominance of neoliberal ideology in the 1990s. In fact, 'Market liberalization in the form of decreasing protection against imports for domestic industry, the privatization of public enterprises, the flexibilization of labour codes, falling wages and the growth of the informal sector of labour…decimated organized labour' (Silva 2009, 7).

As Polanyi would have predicted, the free market created tensions that pushed people to search for security. As neoliberal reforms destroyed the national–populist states, massive numbers 'manned barricades, took over haciendas, turned out by tens and hundreds of thousands in mass demonstrations, rioted and suffered death, injury, imprisonment and exile for their cause' (Silva 2009, 6). In Argentina, Ecuador, Bolivia and Venezuela, protesters demanded that the state reclaim a stronger role in economic development and welfare, also calling for punishment of corrupt politicians and for enlarged democracy. While politically isolated in the beginning, these mobilizations were eventually successful in their advocacy for a reincorporation of the poorer groups in the society, creating the political opportunities for the victory of parties and candidates more open to the movement's claims.

The struggles for re-incorporation had a different political structuration than those for the first incorporation. The developmental states had promoted, in fact, a corporatist system with the spreading of labour and peasants' associations, which were monopolistic, state financed and state controlled. They had recognized Indians' freedom from elite control, granting them rights as peasants through the distribution of land, credits and subsidies, often within clientelistic relations. Although they simultaneously promoted their assimilation in a mestizo culture, the generally weak reach of the states at the periphery did allow for substantial degrees of local autonomy from corporatist institutions. The distribution of inviolable communal lands to peasants' communities and cooperatives allowed for the development of territories where governance by traditional authority and cultural traditions in the forms of *ejidos*, as communally owned land and *ayllus*, as kinship groups governed by indigenous authorities, could survive (Yashar 2005). Neoliberalism eroded corporatist citizenship, trying to impose control by reducing the power of corporatist associations and cutting social rights. This brought about a politicization of claims, which went beyond autonomy and social rights. Mobilization in countries such as Ecuador and Bolivia spread through transcommunity networks, which fostered communication and coordination. Unions and churches as well as the state unwittingly provided for these links, as some freedom of association allowed for free spaces to develop. So, 'shifting citizenship regimes fundamentally affected the politicization of ethnic cleavages' (Yashar 2005, 283), as the indigenous people challenged the neoliberal state. In fact, corporatist regimes allowed for some indigenous autonomy as transcommunity networks and political associational spaces provided capacity and opportunity for action. What started as a demand for redressing rights then developed into an alternative view of citizenship, with claims for recognition of indigenous communities as a political unit.

This was the case, for instance, in Ecuador, where a progressive military regime, particularly between 1972 and 1976, had recognized the social and civic rights of peasants as a way for their integration in mestizo culture. It had also left autonomy to indigenous communities, even if especially as class organizations. Indigenous people then reacted to the erosion of the corporatist citizens' regime, using the transcommunity networks favoured by corporatist associations, the church, the Left, rural unions and so on – as well as the political associational space provided by the populist military regime. Since 1979, as austerity policies introduced a neoliberal regime, with a decline in social spending and the blocking of subsidies, indigenous people began to mobilize for social resources, political inclusion and local autonomy.

A similar process of mobilization emerged in Bolivia, where two strong regional movements developed in the Andes and in Amazonia. In 1952, the only social revolution in Latin America had brought about a corporatist regime, which extended citizens' rights, incorporating Indians from the highlands as peasants. The military in power had in fact implemented a deep distribution of land and promoted class-based organizations. Some autonomy was left, however, to local communities as, in many regions, they 'simply inserted union structures into preexisting indigenous community authority systems (or *ayullo* – kinship groups governed by a set of local-level indigenous authorities)' (Yashar 2005, 161), while in other areas, unions and *ayullos* remained in reciprocal conflict. As early as the 1960s and 1970s, however, there was an erosion of the corporatist regime, particularly with the 1974 monetary devaluation and the ensuing 100 per cent increase in prices for essential goods. In the 1980s, the democratic regime embraced neoliberalism, reducing the size and functions of the state. In the 1990s, as the government declared a ninety-day state of siege and renegotiated foreign public debt in exchange for coca eradication, protests developed and were met by a combination of repression (especially strong with the military governments in the 1970s) and clientelism. Given the repression of corporatist structures, organizations then developed along ethnic lines – as this seemed initially easier. Mobilization had indeed relevant political consequences, bringing about the victory of movements' representative, such as Evo Morales and a turn in politics and policies towards, if not socialism, at least more social protection.

Similar dynamics could be found also in anti-austerity protests in Argentina, where the bases for a neoliberal reform of the economy and the society had been already established by the military regime, between 1976 and 1983 (Silva 2009, 57–8). After transition to democracy, in 1984 Menem took power with a neoliberalist programme in 1989. In the mid-1980s, under the influence of the World Bank, Omnibus economic emergency laws expanded executive power, with co-optation of lower parts of the unions. Also in Argentina, through wave after wave of protest, the neoliberal forces were defeated. Since 2003, Nestor Kirchner and then his wife Cristina Fernandez de Kirchner as presidents represented the left of the Peronists, bringing about tough negotiations with IMF, minimal wages, social security, investigation into corruption and consultation with *picketeros*, with long years of sustained GDP growth.

In general, where free market had developed in authoritarian regimes, the struggle for democracy had included claims for social rights. Where economic and political liberalization had proceeded in parallel, freedom was used to mobilize on demands to change the state by increasing social protection. In fact, mobilization was here favoured by the fact that, together with economic neoliberalism, there was also some political liberalization, which allowed for the organizational growth of social movements (Almeida and Johnston 2006, 3). As Paul Almeida (2008) has shown, in El Salvador, where state-led development brought about modernization, proletarization and urbanization, the economic crisis of the 1970s produced protest, which was heavily repressed. In the 1990s, as in other Latin American countries, neoliberal democratization emerged and, in the 2000s, was targeted by a coalition of social groups (Almeida 2008).

In fact, political liberalization allowed for civil society formation and a further push for liberalization through nonviolent protests, sometimes with reverse political liberalization and repression followed by radicalized protest. Competitive elections promoted democratization, as rights granted to parties were extended beyond them and civic society organizations were empowered by electoral allies and increased institutional access. So, 'democratization seems to have a lag effect on mass contention in the region. The cooling off period of diminished social movement activities observed in the early years of democratic transition in the Americas is giving way to intensified protest campaigns against unwanted economic changes' (Almeida and Johnston 2006, 15).[12] Protests indeed multiplied, on claims of salary increase and defence of the environment, with territorial rooting and horizontal organizational networks (Svampa 2005).

In sum, in Latin America either democratic or authoritarian regimes that had supported drastic neoliberal reforms were met by harsh protests that eventually brought about a rebalancing of free market and social protection. One after another, the governments that had supported the neoliberal shock therapy of free market reform lost support among the citizenship, which still considered it the responsibility of the state to grant some minimum level of incorporation.

The Latin American case shows that, as Polanyi's countermovements developed in the continent since the mid-1990s, their characteristics and outcomes also in democracies were strongly influenced by political opportunities and constraints provided by the party system. As Kenneth Roberts (2014) notices, as 'Social and political resistance to market liberalization intensified in the post-adjustment era, helping to revive leftist parties, strengthen social movements and push populism back towards more statist and redistributive policy orientations', 'the specific form of this Polanyian backlash, however, depended heavily on the politics of market liberalization in each country and in particular on partisan alignments around the process of market reform.' In particular:

Where conservative actors led the process of market reform and a major party of the left was consistently present as an opposition force, the Polanyian backlash in the post-adjustment era was largely contained within institutional channels. Indeed, societal resistance to market orthodoxy strengthened established parties of the left and eventually enabled them to win the presidency in countries like Chile, Brazil, Uruguay and El Salvador. In each case, levels of social protest were relatively moderate in the post-adjustment era, established parties remained electorally dominant and anti-establishment populist figures made little headway in the electoral arena. The political legacies of market liberalization and the political opportunity structure for mass social or electoral protest, were strikingly different where center-left or labor-based populist parties played a major role in the process of structural adjustment. In the short-term, 'bait-and-switch' market reforms imposed by parties that campaigned against them and historically championed more statist and redistributive policies contributed to the broad technocratic consensus around the neoliberal model in the late 1980s and early 1990s – what aptly came to be known as the 'Washington Consensus'. Such bait-and-switch patterns of reform, however, proved to be highly destabilizing in the post-adjustment era, as they de-aligned party systems programmatically and left them without institutionalized outlets for dissent from market orthodoxy. Such dissent, therefore, was often channeled into social protest movements and varied forms of electoral protest, including support for populist outsiders or new 'movement parties' on the left. In countries like Argentina, Bolivia, Ecuador and Venezuela, bait-and-switch market reforms left a sequel of explosive social protest that directly or indirectly toppled presidents, led to partial or complete party system breakdowns and (in the latter three cases) ushered in the election of an anti-system populist figure or a new movement party of the left. (Roberts 2014).

In short, party politics influenced social protests, which became all the more disruptive where the party system did not provide for institutional channels to challenge neoliberal reforms. The *Caracazo* in Venezuela in 1989, the waves of indigenous protests in Ecuador in the 1990s and early 2000s, *piqueteros* in Argentina in the early 2000s, 'water wars' and 'gas wars' in Bolivia in the same period produced indeed large institutional transformations and political changes.

As we will see in what follows, in so-called established democracies as well, the crisis of responsibility brought about a drop in trust in institutions, even if this was not translated into either apathy or radical positions. While in the rampant years of neoliberal capitalism movements still seemed hopeful for the reform of existing institutions, engaging with them in dialogue and control, the anti-austerity protests seem to have lost hope for reform. The political parties of the Left, which had been criticized by the GJM but were still open to collaboration, are no longer considered as potential allies by the anti-austerity protesters.

Alterpolitics in the Global Justice Movement

The criticism of the political consequences of neoliberalism in terms of malfunctioning of democracy was a central concern for the GJM, which indeed asked for participatory and deliberative forms of democracy in the face of what was perceived as a decline in the quality of representative democracy resulting from increasing power of the market and of international organizations. The search for an alternative politics was in fact very visible, with strong criticism of existing institutions leading to demands for their reform.

One central feature is mistrust of parties and representative institutions. The common location of activists on the left of the political spectrum is blended with a high interest in politics, defined as politics 'from below', but mistrust in the actors of institutional politics. Critical attitudes towards political institutions could be singled out in the opinions expressed by the activists interviewed during several editions of the ESF. Data on the second and the fourth ESF confirm the general mistrust in representative democratic institutions (Table 4.1), especially in national governments, followed by the EU and then the UN (which were more trusted by the activists in Florence and in Paris). There was more trust in local institutions (although much less than in the first and second ESFs) (della Porta 2007). Among other actors and institutions, we might notice a much lower level of trust in the church and mass media, as well as in the unions in general and a similarly low trust in the judiciary and (even lower) in political parties. Activists continued to trust instead social movements (and, a bit less, NGOs) as actors of a democracy from below.

Table 4.1. *Trust in institutions of ESF participants in Florence, Paris and Athens (valid cases only)*

Type of institution	Florence 2002		Paris 2003		Athens 2006	
	%	N	%	N	%	N
Local institutions	46.1	2,365	43.1	2,034	26.6	1,122
National government	6.1	2,451	11.6	1,997	11.5	1,126
National parliament	14.9	2,428	–	–	20.5	1,130
European Union	26.9	2,444	17.3	2,002	14.5	1,141
United Nations	29.6	2,444	31.7	1,985	18.1	1,136
Political parties	20.4	2,423	23.0	2,007	21.2	1,120
Unions	16.1	–	57.5	2,025	49.0	1,122
Social movements/NGOs	–	–	90.0	2,067	85.7	1,139

Source: della Porta and Giugni 2009, 89.

Mistrust is higher among the surveyed activists in 2006 than in 2002 and 2003.

This also resonated with the positions taken by the social movement organizations that collaborated in the encounters of the European Social Forums (della Porta 2009a, b).

A look at the minutes of the debates and other documents about the ESF helps us to locate the criticism of representative institutions in a broader frame where, in particular, the EU is stigmatized because of its neoliberalism and lack of democratic accountability. While the EU is seen as 'shaped under neoliberal politics' (cited in della Porta 2009a), there is in fact a perception of a decline in citizens' capacity to affect decisions which move upwards in scale – as an activist notes, 'at the local level we have very little influence on the decision-making process, but our influence becomes null when it comes to questions such as the European constitution or the directives of the WTO or the IMF. We are even criminalized when we attempt it...' (della Porta and Giugni 2009, 90). Moreover, relations with political parties were certainly tense. While the WSF, in its Charter of Principle, described itself as an open space for the civil society, it also explicitly defined it as a 'non-governmental and non-party context'. Like military organizations, parties as such were also excluded from participation. Even if the ESF relaxed this clause, political parties of the centre-left and traditional unions were criticized for having opened the door to neoliberal reforms in the past, as well as for their consideration of the movement as at best able to put forward demands but not to find answers (Andretta and Reiter 2009).

Within this critical political vision, however, many social movement organizations were open to interactions with institutions of multilevel governance, this still indicating a belief in the reformability of representative institutions. Within the Demos project document analysis of about 250 organizations participating in the ESF showed that even though about half of those groups (concentrated particularly in some countries) did not mention relationships with institutions, when they did, they were quite open to interaction with them, also often accepting collaboration on specific problems. As we can see in Table 4.2, in relation to representative institutions in general, statements of open refusal of collaboration were indeed rare (11.5 per cent), while an attitude of either collaboration or democratic control was more frequent (about one-third each).

There were some differences in the attitudes towards the various territorial levels of governance. Collaboration with IGOs and economic actors was less frequent than with national institutions, but still relevant. Additionally, the refusal of collaboration was mentioned more often for institutions at the national level than at the local or supranational ones.

Table 4.2.   Relationships with institutions and economic actors according to main documents (% no. of cases 244)

	Representative institutions	Local institutions	National institutions	IGOs	Economic actors
Collaboration	26.6	22.5	24.6	18.9	14.3
Democratic control	32.4	21.3	32.0	27.9	22.5
Refusal	11.5	4.5	9.0	7.4	14.8

Source: della Porta 2009f, 104.

Differences in attitudes towards institutions at different territorial levels were limited, however. Although the refusal of interactions increased going from the local to the transnational and from the state to the market, the differences were smaller than one might have expected. In particular, the transnational level was recognized as an important institutional level for collaboration by about one-fifth of the surveyed groups (that is, two-fifths of those who mentioned relationships with institutions in their documents). Nevertheless, our organizations tended to be critical of institutions, perceiving their own role as the active engagement in citizens' control of institutional politics, through the implementation of channels of discursive accountability (della Porta and Giugni 2009; Andretta and della Porta 2009).

The results of the interviews conducted during the Demos project with representatives of social movement organizations on declared practices of their groups tend to confirm those on organizational ideology (Table 4.3). First of all, answers to the question 'how does your group relate to public institutions at different territorial levels?' confirm the openness of the surveyed organizations towards collaboration with institutions. Refusal of any collaboration was still very rare: from a very low 4.4 per cent for local institutions, to 11.8 per cent for the national and 13.5 per cent for the international level. The refusal rate was highest for IGOs, but still only a couple of percentage points higher than for national institutions and, in general terms, still very low. The groups that declared a lack of collaboration either due to indifference towards relations with institutions or rejection of institutions was larger, but still limited to between one-fifth at the local and national levels and one-third at the supranational one. The rest of the sampled organizations tended to collaborate, especially with local (as many as 70 per cent) and national (67 per cent) institutions, but also with IGOs (almost half of our sample). Moreover, many groups declared collaborations with various territorial levels at the same time, showing an adaptation to multilevel governance.

Table 4.3.   Relationship with institutions according to interviewees (%; no. of cases 210)

	Local institutions	National institutions	International institutions
Refusal of collaboration	8.4	11.8	13.5
Indifference / no contacts / denial of collaboration by authorities	22.8	21.2	32.5
Critical / selective collaboration	29.7	34.5	24.5
Collaboration	39.1	32.5	29.5
Total	202 (100%)	203 (100%)	200 (100%)

Source: della Porta 2009f, 105.

Here as well, however, interviewees often qualified their collaboration with institutions as critical or selective, with less critical attitudes towards local governments and growing criticism towards the national and supranational levels (della Porta and Giugni 2009).

Aiming at reform, the organizations participating in the ESF were particularly concerned with the accountability of IGOs, considered as the main carriers of the neoliberal globalization project. If, however, the international economic organizations (WTO, World Bank and FMI) were stigmatized as 'antidemocratic', the search of a democratic alternative to neoliberal globalization was stated as a main aim.

The orientation towards strengthening the institutions of global governance, but at the same time democratizing them, is particularly strong when addressing the United Nations or the European Union. Against the existing Europe, the image of 'another Europe' (rather than 'no Europe') was often stressed in the debates (della Porta and Caiani 2009, ch. 5). During the second ESF, the Assembly of the Unemployed and Precarious Workers in Struggle stated that 'For the European Union, Europe is only a large free-exchange area. We want a Europe based on democracy, citizenship, equality, peace, a job and revenue in order to live. Another Europe for another World.' In this vision, the building of 'another Europe imposes putting the democratic transformation of institutions at the centre of elaboration and mobilization. We can, we should have great political ambition for Europe... *Cessons de subir l'Europe: prenons la en mains*' (http://workspace.fse-esf.org/mem/Act2223). Unions and other groups active in public service proclaimed 'the European level as the pertinent level of resistance', among others against national decisions. The 'No to the EU Constitutional draft' was combined with demands for a 'legitimate European constitution' produced through public consultation, 'a European constitution constructed from below'. Many agreed that 'the Europe we have to build is a Europe of rights and participatory democracy is its engine'. In this vision, 'the European Social Forum constitutes the peoples as constitutional power, the only legitimate power' (della Porta and Giugni 2009, 93).

Finally, the social movement organizations and their activists show a strong concern with politics – which is at odds with interpretations of social movement activists as only protesting in the street or even as 'antipolitical' in nature. The documents of the organizations surveyed during the Demos project frequently mention the need to get involved in politics, although with varying meanings and emphasis; indeed, politics is perceived as part of the very self-definition of many of our organizations (della Porta 2009e).

Concluding, while already pointing at the challenges to civil, political and economic rights that neoliberalism brought about at its peak, the GJM still showed some trust in the possibility of reform, through critical but often intense contacts with some particular institutions. Similarly, while criticized as too lenient in their defence of welfare and oligarchic in their organizations, political parties often did provide for logistic and symbolic resources used during the forum process (Andretta and Reiter 2009).

Antipolitics in the anti-austerity movements?

The legitimacy crisis of late neoliberalism and the multiple challenges to governments' responsiveness are reflected in anti-austerity protests, first and foremost, in the fall of trust in representative democracy, that is visible in the contentious politics of the 2010s. Protesters in Puerta del Sol, or those in Zuccotti Park in New York, did indeed contest the very meaning of democracy.

Occupying against corruption

As the political system reinforced market failures rather than correcting them, 'the protesters have called into question whether there is a real democracy' (Stiglitz 2012b, 17). The slogans at anti-austerity protests pointed in fact at the *collusion of business and politicians*, as responsible for the fact that 'banks got bailed out, we got sold out'. Institutional democracy in particular is seen as representative not of people, but of banks and financial power. So, in Tunisia and Egypt the corruption of the rulers and their family, targeted by alternative media, raised indignation. Significantly, in their call for participation in an Antibanks day, the

Italian Draghi Ribelli group (a play on the surname of the Italian president of the European Central Bank, Mario Draghi, meaning 'rebellious dragons') stigmatized the 'economic dictatorship'.[13] PPLeaks and PSOELeaks denounced in Spain the corruption of respectively the centre right and the centre left party (Castells 2013, xxxvii). Adbusters proposed one single claim when they organized the Occupy Wall Street's first day: 'we demand that Barack Obama ordains a Presidential Commission tasked with ending the influence money has over our representatives in Washington' (Kerton 2012, 395). On 29 September, the New York general assembly declared, 'We come to you at a time when corporations, which places power over people, self-interest over justice and oppression over equality, run our government' (van Gelder et al. 2011, 111).

In fact, to be blamed is the *corruption* of representative institutions. With neoliberalism, 'A system evolved in which the top financiers administered to themselves the rewards of self-dealing, squeezed through revolving doors, practised deregulation and administrative collusion, organized themselves into combinations in the name of competition' (Gitlin 2012, 11). In Spain, the slogan 'We are not commodities in the hands of politicians and bankers' is linked to the denunciation of the corruption of representative democracy. The appeal to take the street on 15 May 2011, *'toma la calle'*, was completed with statements like: 'because our politicians rule for the market and not for the citizenry', 'because the minimum salary of a congressman is Euro 3996', 'because the current electoral law benefits big parties, those that are indicted in 700 corruption trials' and 'because when you no longer have a job, your parents no longer have a pension, the price of mortgage goes up and they take away your home, you will still be owing money to the bank' (*toma la calle*, 15.05.11).

Similarly, in the US the greedy 1% was targeted. David Graeber, an anthropologist and activist of the OWS, pointed at the 'collusion between Wall Street financial advisors and local politicians', which forces municipalities into bankruptcy, as 'in every case, a share of the resulting profits is funnelled back to politicians through lobbyists and PACs' (2012, xx). This would 'make it impossible to imagine the American government as having anything to do with the popular will, or even popular consent' (Graeber 2012, xxi). Not surprisingly, corruption is also a recurring theme to emerge in the frame analysis of Italian social movement organizations (della Porta et al. 2014). Mentions of mafia involvement in political decision making also fit into this discourse, especially among anti-mafia groups: citizens groups active on the waste disposal crisis in Campania and others from the earthquake-struck L'Aquila blame bad decisions on corrupt politicians and contract-seeking mafiosi. Generally, the diagnosis is, as presented by the antimafia network Libera, that 'Corruption pollutes the processes of politics, threatens the standing and the credibility of institutions, pollutes and seriously distorts the economy, sucks resources destined for the good of the community, corrodes civic responsibility and democratic culture itself' (in della Porta et al. 2014).

Given the perceived corruption of representative democracy, there is in fact a persistent demand for accountability of public affairs and prosecution of political corruption, as people stigmatize the injustice of, for example, paying the 'bills of a crisis whose authors continue to enjoy record benefits' (cit. in Perugorría and Tejerina 2013, 436). In Greece, in Syntagma Square, MPs were considered as traitors as they had violated a basic democratic contract (Sotirakopoulos and Sotiropoulos 2013). The occupants of Zuccotti Park declared 'no true democracy is attainable when the process is determined by economic power' (van Gelder et al. 2011, 36). In fact, at the OWS general assembly there was the stigmatization of a political disenfranchisement to which the movement reacted:

> ... on September 17, 2011, people from all across the United States of America and the world came to protest the blatant injustices of our times perpetuated by the economic and political elites. On the seventeenth, we as individuals rose up against political disenfranchisement and social and economic injustice, spoke out, resisted and successfully Occupied Wall Street. Today, we proudly remain in Liberty Plaza (also known as Zuccotti Park) constituting ourselves as autonomous political beings aged in nonviolent civil disobedience and building solidarity based on mutual respect, acceptance and love. (van Gelder et al. 2011, 25)

In a similar vein, the *indignados*/Italian Revolution group stigmatized politicians as non-democratic: 'We do not represent any party or association, and nobody represents us! And we say ENOUGH, ENOUGH of there being no way for the active and direct participation of citizens in decisions (...) BE OUTRAGED TOO!!! FEWER POLITICIANS AND MORE DEMOCRACY!!!'[14]

Beyond the condemnation of corruption, the slogan 'they don't represent us' also expresses a deeper criticism of the degeneration of liberal democracy, linked in turn to elected politicians' failure to 'do politics'. The latter are in fact considered as united in spreading a narrative suggesting that no alternatives are available to cuts in budget and deregulation – a narrative that protesters do not accept. In Spain in particular, the movement asked for proportional reforms to the electoral law, denouncing the reduced weight given to citizen participation inherent to the majority system, where the main political parties tend to form cartels and electors see their choices as extremely limited. Also in other countries, among other proposals for restoring the influence of citizens are those that call for direct democracy and to give electors the possibility to express their opinions on the important economic and social choices. In this vein, greater possibilities for referenda are called for, with reduced quorums (for signatures and electors) and increased thematic areas subject to decisions through referenda. The perceived failures of representative democracy bring about proposals for shifting decision making and power back down to local levels and to the citizens. These positions are for instance widespread among social movement organizations mobilizing against austerity policies in Italy. In sum:

> Some groups speak of rejuvenated and empowered local government (Action-diritti in movimento, citizens' committees from L'Aquila, comitato 'no tubo'), self-determination (citizens' committees in Campania) and subsidiarity (Libertà e Giustizia, the World Social Forum); but all groups share the general view that (non-violent) participation is an essential component of true and direct democracy. For Libertà e Giustizia, among others, citizen participation is sparked by their wish to look after 'common goods' and is seen as the best way of interacting with institutions that should fulfil that role. For other groups – including Arci, Assemblea San Giovanni, the Indignados – participatory democracy is built on the model of assemblies held in squares, where citizens deliberate upon decisions. Common goods and citizens' assemblies form the bases of two main sources of inspiration for practicing these democratic ideals in a concrete manner. (della Porta et al. 2014)

The calls for direct democracy became particularly audible during the referendum campaign against the privatization of water and nuclear power plants, later won by a very large margin by the movements that had promoted it in the name of common goods. For the Forum dell'Acqua, struggling for water as a common good, 'To save Italy from crisis (...) large investment in common goods, in culture and in democracy, is needed. And only participation can restore dignity and value to a new politics, capable of carrying the country out of the disaster. All this is possible' (della Porta et al. 2014). The 'really existing democracies' – in Robert Dahl's (2000) definition – are also criticized for having allowed the abduction of democracy, not only by financial powers, but also by international organizations, above all the International Monetary Fund and the European Union. Pacts for the Euro and stability, imposed in exchange for loans, are considered as anti-constitutional forms of blackmail, depriving citizens of their sovereignty. Starting in 2011 with the petition Another Road to Europe, a network of social movement organizations suggested numerous reforms at the EU level in order to get control of financial markets, among other means through the introduction of a Financial Transaction Tax, political supervision on banks, the dismissal of a public role for (private) rating agencies and the creation of public ones, as well as higher taxes on capital and strategies for economic growth (see also Pianta 2012, ch. 4). In fact, these recommendations were accompanied by claims for more transnational democracy.

Criticism of representative democracy as degenerating into an elitist and secretive caste emerged very strongly in the discourse of the various groupings that mobilized against austerity policies. This vision is clear in the *indignados*/Italian Revolution group, who wrote, 'We know very well that whoever has or will in the future be in government will never be on the people's side, nobody has ever listened to our needs and in this system nobody ever will.' Similarly, the No Tav group, mobilized against the building of a high-speed rail link between Turin and Lyon in France, stated 'The caste is deaf, blind, cruel: while the country goes bankrupt, political and economic oligarchies are inflicting contested choices on local populations and institutions, countering with the heavy deployment of public forces' (in della Porta et al. 2014).

The EU, as it is now, is blamed as being dominated by the European Central Bank and other supranational economic and unelected institutions, aiming only at defending the EMU – a 'Europe of the banks' responsible for cuts and austerity. It is criticized for the contested Bologna reform of the university system, accused of transforming education into merchandise, as well as for the lack of a political response to emergencies elsewhere in the world. As the Italian cultural association ARCI stated: 'There would be much to discuss concerning the prescriptions the European powers are using to face the debt crisis; on the error of re-proposing financial instruments that caused the crisis; on the failure of a Europe built solely on the single currency; on the necessity of the full realization of the Union's political dimension' (della Porta et al. 2014).

Not only is the content of civil right enforcement at stake, but also its forms. If the welfare state of the Fordist period was accused of interfering with the lifeworld of the individuals (Habermas 1976), imposing norms from above, the movements' claim for human rights is increasingly framed within a conception of participation of citizens in the planning and implementation of social services. Claims in Puerta del Sol included free and secular education, democratization of educational structures, proportional representation, the 'fight against corruption through norms aiming at establishing a total political transparency', as well as the 'creation of a mechanism of citizens control to claim a real political responsibility' and effective separation of powers (Nez 2011a, b). This is also related with a new discovery of 'the commons' as spaces in which the common goods are to be managed through the participation of all those affected by them. While institutions claim for (depoliticized) technical expertise, protest movements repoliticize the provision of common goods through an emphasis on the practical knowledge citizens hold. The commons are constructed as de-commodification of what is essential to life, with the self-management and self-government of these resources through the participation of the community (Council of Europe 2013, 164; Fattori 2013). The idea of a re-establishment of the common and of a 'commonification' (rather than commodification) of public services is in fact bridged with a participatory approach. The commons are also 'commoned' through the involvement of all stakeholders in their protection, as 'democratic participation is at the heart of the management of the commons' (Fattori 2013, 347). In a processual vision, one can say that the very definition of goods as commons helps in the creation of communities and solidarities (Fattori 2013, 327).

So, protests and campaigns against welfare retrenchment have not just aimed at protecting the material conditions of users of social services and workers in social services, but also contributed to elaborate a different conception of public service as common good, opposing its neoliberal conception as merchandise. If social services in the nation-state had been claimed as rights of citizenship, the rights to a life with dignity (a house, food, health, a job) are increasingly framed as human rights: poverty means an attack against the rights of a person, as it jeopardizes the very recognition of civil, political and social rights. The framework of charity has been challenged by a frame of human rights and the symbolic and material creation of isolated spaces for the *classes dangereux* by a conception of the common. Indignant is a definition of the self that manifests outrage at the disrespect for the rights of a human being, which then resonate with a widespread claim: dignity.

Mistrustful but empowered: European activists face the crisis

The very negative visions of those in power are reflected in very low levels of trust in the institutions of representative democracy. The mentioned surveys of protesters in seven European countries showed that very high levels of mistrust addressed representative institutions in particular. Based on self-positioning on a 5-point scale (Likert) which ranges from 1 (do not trust at all) to 5 (trust very much), among political institutions and actors only trade unions and the judicial systems received a mean of trust that slightly overcomes 3 points on the scale (that is, on average, they are trusted a little more than 'somewhat'). The demonstrators of those countries that were hit harder by the economic crisis, cuts in public expenditures and related increasing inequalities were also those who expressed, in general, lower levels of trust (Table 4.4). In particular, Spanish and (especially) Italian demonstrators expressed much less trust in the institutions and actors of representative democracy (parliament and political parties) than Northern and Continental Europeans did. UK demonstrators fell in between the two groups in terms of their judgements on national parliament and government, but were as mistrustful as the Spaniards as far as political parties were concerned. This trend also holds for unions, although with much higher levels of trust than for parties or parliaments: for instance, even though Italians were the most mistrustful of the unions as institutions, almost five times more trusted them than those who responded that they at least 'quite trust' political parties; the pattern in Spain was similar. The relevance of discontent on economic issues is also testified for by the higher degree of mistrust that we found, in all covered countries, among protesters in demonstrations called for by so-called old social movements, which traditionally represent the class cleavage, than by the new social movements (Figure 4.1) as well as in demonstrations on socioeconomic issues (Figure 4.2).

Also in Italy, protesters express very low trust in traditional politics (Table 4.5). Not only is the national government (even when supported by the centre-left) highly distrusted, but parliaments and political parties have a very low average mean (around 2), with an even lower level for the No Monti Day, but also for the LGTBQ pride march. Moreover, average trust declines when moving from retired people (2.25 average trust in parliament and 2.39 in parties) to part-time workers and unemployed (respectively, 1.88 and 1.89 and 1.90 and 1.92), with low average scores also for students (1.96 and 1.94), and full-time workers (1.97 and 2.07) in between. Trust also declines by age (especially for parties and unions). Additionally, the satisfaction with democracy is low: on a scale from 1 (very dissatisfied) to 5 (very satisfied), protesters express an average satisfaction of 2.8, but with particularly low score of about 2 among the protesters at marches on socioeconomic issues.

Comparing these data with those collected on the same battery of questions at other marches in Italy since 2001, we can note that trust in national institutions and traditional actors (parliaments, parties and trade unions) is now much lower in comparison with the scores registered at the demonstrations surveyed at the beginning of the decade (della Porta et al. 2006) (see Table 4.1, above). The decline of trust in political parties and the parliament is the most striking, with those trusting it 'much' or 'enough' dropping from about a quarter of marchers to just 7 per cent for political parties and from about one fifth to just 6 per cent

Table 4.4. *Percentage of participants declaring at least 'I quite trust', by country*

Countries	Trust in...						No. of Demos
	National Government	National Parliament	Parties	Unions	Judiciary	EU	
Belgium	22.2	24.9	12.5	55.3	35.4	29.6	9
Italy	3.6	5.9	5.9	28.0	52.0	43.6	5
Netherlands	17.1	26.8	20.4	45.3	60.0	25.7	11
Spain	12.0	12.8	7.3	30.2	15.4	13.4	7
Sweden	15.7	37.6	35.2	53.8	54.7	13.4	9
Switzerl.	37.8	29.0	20.6	60.6	53.4	19.5	8
UK	12.3	15.8	7.4	34.5	41.2	25.1	12
Total %	18.4	23.1	16.2	45.3	45.9	23.8	61
Valid Cases	12,571	12,504	12,486	12,522	12,523	12,534	
Cr. V	.24***	.21***	.25***	.23***	.27***	.19***	

Source: della Porta, Andretta and Bosi 2013.

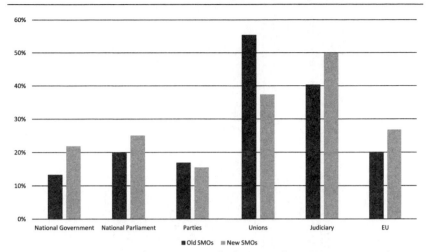

Figure 4.1   Percentage of participants declaring at least 'I quite trust', by type of SMOs staging demonstrations
Legend: Cr. V (Institutions/Actors by SMOs type) respectively, .11**; .06***; N.s.; .18***; .10***; .08***
Source: Data from della Porta, Andretta and Bosi 2013

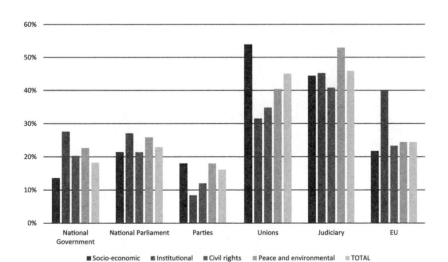

Figure 4.2   Percentage of participants declaring at least 'I quite trust', by demonstrations' issues
Legend: Cr. V (Institutions/Actors by demonstration issue), .12***; .05***; .09***; .18***; .09***; .11***
Source: Data from della Porta, Andretta and Bosi 2013

Table 4.5. Trust in political actors and institutions in demonstrations in Italy 2011–2013 (Likert 1–5, means)

	Trust in...						
	National Government	National Parliament	Parties	Unions	Judiciary	EU	United Nations
Euromayday, Milan	1.28	1.72	1.88	2.67	3.19	3.08	2.63
Mayday, Florence	1.30	2.26	2.53	3.50	3.80	3.46	3.08
General Strike, Florence	1.21	1.97	2.26	3.20	3.59	3.25	2.77
Perugia-Assisi Peace March	1.44	2.03	2.19	2.93	3.45	3.26	3.05
Gay Pride, Bologna	2.11	1.85	1.73	2.52	2.96	3.15	2.88
No Monti day	1.44	1.44	1.76	2.43	2.96	2.02	2.10
Florence 10+10	1.89	1.95	1.89	2.72	3.11	2.45	2.47
Anti Mafia	2.36	2.59	2.21	2.64	3.51	3.36	3.30
No Muos	1.85	2.09	1.87	2.14	2.90	2.46	2.56
TOTAL	1.66	1.99	2.04	2.75	3.28	2.97	2.78

for the parliament. The data on the Italian participants in the first European Social Forum (ESF) in Florence in 2002 and in the Global Day of Action against the war on Iraq on 15 February 2003 (especially compared with data on the Peace March from Perugia to Assisi which took place after September 11 2001), had already registered this declining trend.

Following with the Italian case, globalization is in general seen as creating inequalities and a new global level of governance rather than an opportunity to grow (Table 4.6) – all the more so among lower classes (by self-location and job position) and older people. Comparing cross-demonstrations, we note that the stronger critiques of globalization are to be found among marchers at the anti-austerity protests, as the Florence 10+10 and for the No Monti Day marchers and the participants in the general strike, a bit less so for those who participated in the anti-mafia protest. It seems, that is, that anti-austerity protesters in particular fear the socioeconomic challenge of globalization. Similarly, the EU is perceived as reinforcing globalization rather than mitigating its effects or attempting to save a European social model. The EU is especially stigmatized as reinforcing globalization among participants in the anti-austerity marches, such as the Euromayday, the No Monti Day, Florence 10+10 – less so among anti-mafia and peace activists. Here as well, sceptical views are more widespread among those who self-locate as workers.

Going back to the cross-national analysis, another battery of questions confirms the low level of confidence in parties and representative institutions, as politicians are considered as failing to fulfil their promises. There is in fact broad agreement (four out of five participants in demonstrations) that 'most politicians make a lot of promises but do not actually do anything'. It is worth noting that their means by countries (Figure 4.3) reflect the patterns of variation pointed out for trust in political institutions: Southern Europeans are more likely to feel that their politicians are not to be trusted (from 96 per cent of Italians to 88 per cent of Spaniards) than are Swedes (70 per cent mistrustful) or Dutch (76 per cent), while other countries remain around the average. Here too, looking at the answers by the Italian participants on two items for which we have comparative data on past protests (in particular with the Global Day of Action in 2003), we note a strong increase of mistrust in politicians (from 66.9 to 95.1 per cent). (See Figure 4.3.)

However, while not trusting political institutions, demonstrators – almost paradoxically – believe in their capacity to change the system. The mentioned surveys show in fact a very high confidence in potential for own, collective and transnational efficacy (as belief in the effectiveness of their action), with the percentage of those who agree and strongly

Table 4.6. Degree of agreement with statements on globalization (Likert 1–4, means)

	Globalization opportunity to grow	Globalization creates inequality	Globalization creates new global level governance	EU reinforces globalization	EU mitigates negative effects of globalization	EU attempt to save EU social model
Euromayday, Milan (mean)	1.83	3.21	2.93	2.14	1.87	3.25
Mayday, Florence (mean)	1.63	3.42	2.58	2.34	2.33	3.18
General strike, Florence (mean)	1.61	3.43	2.57	2.25	2.23	3.30
Peace March (mean)	1.74	3.46	2.65	2.24	2.21	3.24
Gay Pride, Bologna (mean)	1.95	3.22	2.70	2.31	2.15	3.09
No Monti day (mean)	1.28	2.86	3.24	1.87	1.63	3.52
Florence 10+10 (mean)	1.40	3.09	3.17	2.02	1.78	3.46
Anti Mafia (mean)	1.97	3.48	2.59	2.31	2.17	3.01
No Muos (mean)	1.57	3.06	2.98	2.02	1.80	3.18
Total Mean	1.68	3.27	2.80	2.17	2.04	3.24
N	1530	1538	1484	1478	1472	1552
Std. Deviation	.767	.856	.824	.776	.826	.840
ETA	.289***	.243**	.299***	.198***	.276***	.187***

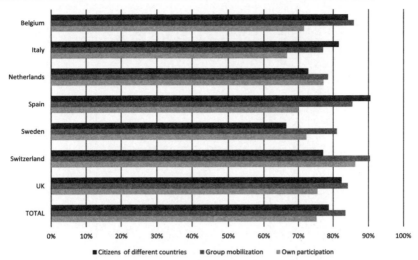

Figure 4.3   Percentage that agree and strongly agree with statements 'Own participation is effective', 'Group mobilization is effective' and 'Citizens mobilizing from different countries are effective', by country
Legend: Cr. V (Efficacy by country) respectively, .13***; .11***; .17***
Source: Data from della Porta, Andretta and Bosi 2013

agree reaching 3/4 of participants on average. While there is high consensus that 'Most politicians make a lot of promises but do not actually do anything' and opinions are instead more split on the statement 'I don't see the use of voting, parties do whatever they want anyway', protesters believe that 'My participation can have an impact on public policy in this country', that 'Organized groups of citizens can have a lot of impact on public policies in this country' and that 'If citizens from different countries join forces, they can have a lot of impact on international politics.' While collective participation is believed to be especially efficacious, one's own involvement and transnational participation is also very highly valued.

Looking at the Italian protesters (Table 4.7), we might observe that, in general, if we compare protest events, we find some congruence on all three items, with the Florence 10+10 and the No Muos demonstrators showing the highest level of trust in self, participants in protests directly related to labour rights and the LGTBQ parade the least. However, there are also some differences, with the anti-mafia protesters trusting individuals more and the No Monti protesters more trustful in transnational action. This can be linked, in fact, to the different social backgrounds of those demonstrators, with younger protesters tending to prefer

Table 4.7. Degree of agreement with statements of trust, in Italian demonstrations, 2011–2013 (Likert 1–5, means)

	Politicians' promises	Voting is useless	I have an impact	Groups have an impact	International cooperation has an impact	Considered decisions
Euromayday, Milan	4.72	2.61	3.65	3.97	4.14	4.04
Mayday, Florence	4.39	2.04	3.85	3.95	4.05	4.00
General Strike, Florence	4.56	2.45	3.70	3.93	4.09	3.92
Perugia-Assisi Peace March	4.44	2.44	3.81	3.97	4.13	4.02
Gay Pride, Bologna	4.04	2.67	3.56	3.90	4.00	3.97
No Monti day	4.15	2.62	3.72	4.16	4.34	4.09
Florence 10+10	3.99	2.47	3.89	4.27	4.43	3.91
Anti Mafia	3.67	1.89	3.95	4.05	4.01	3.96
No Muos	4.12	2.83	3.81	4.24	4.21	4.06
TOTAL	4.23	2.45	3.77	4.04	4.14	3.99
Cr. V.	.337***	.205***	.128***	.154***	.175***	N.S.

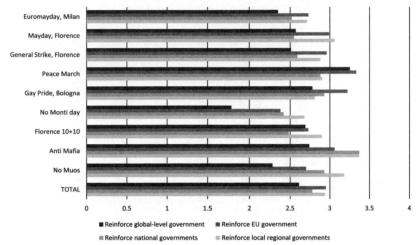

Figure 4.4   Degree of agreement with statements on government (Likert 1–5, means)
Legend: ETA respectively, .224***; .276***; .289***; .369***

individualized action and older ones still more oriented towards transnational action. We can add that protesters present themselves as interested in politics (average of 3.3) and frequently talking about politics (average of 4.0).

While extremely critical of the working of existing institutions, activists expressed in fact a very strong attachment to politics – to the point of demanding a strengthening of the very institutions they mistrust (see also della Porta and Reiter 2012a; della Porta and Andretta 2013). Resonating with the organizational frames presented above are in fact the political positions of the protesters we interviewed. When moving from the assessment of responsibility to potential solutions, Italian protesters tend to agree with the statement that it is important to strengthen governments at various levels: especially local and European, but also national and (a bit less) global. More disagreement with these statements is to be found in the anti-austerity marches of the Euromayday, the anti-Monti day and the Florence 10+10, whose organizers were located more on the left, but also among participants in the general strike; in contrast, there is more support among anti-mafia protesters, as well as among participants in peace and gay pride marches (with the exception, in the last two cases, of the local level) (see Figure 4.4).

Critical feelings towards institutional politics emerge also in answers about electoral choices. Self-located on the left (Figure 4.5), in most

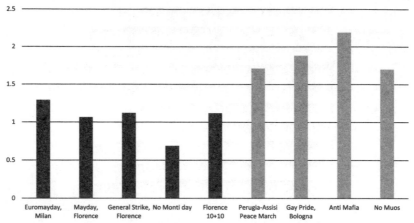

Figure 4.5 Left–right placement of participants in Italian demonstrations, 2011–2013 (average: 0 left – 10 right; ETA: .286***)

cases, they vote for parties on the left rather than on the center-left (Table 4.8). In fact, only among participants in the peace march and the anti-mafia protests (followed by labour protests) are there high percentages for the centre-left Partito Democratico (PD). Support for PD is instead particularly low among Euromayday paraders, who also have the lowest trust in parties and unions but very high confidence in transnational mobilization. In many cases (about 20 per cent), however, protesters cannot find a party with which to identify; this is especially the case not only of the (young) No Muos and LGTBQ participants, but also of one-third of those who participated in the No Monti Day (see Figure 4.5).

In sum, there is no doubt that today's crisis is a crisis of democracy as well as, or even more than, a financial crisis. Neoliberalism is, as mentioned, a political doctrine that brings with it a minimalist vision of the public and democracy (Crouch 2004). It foresees not only the reduction of political interventions oriented to balance the market (and consequent liberalization, privatization and deregulation), but also an elitist conception of citizen participation (electoral only and therefore occasional and potentially distorted) and an increased level of influence for lobbies and strong interests.

Citizens are therefore not presented by the activists as passive subjects in the hands of irresponsible politicians, but rather as being capable of reinventing democracy. If mistrust could lead to a general critique of institutional politics and state intervention, this is however not the case among the anti-austerity protesters we surveyed. Rather, the activists'

Table 4.8. *Party identification by type of demonstration (%, Cramer's V: .18***)*

Party family	Euro MD, Milan	May Day, Florence	General Strike, Florence	No Monti day	Florence 10+10	Perugia-Assisi	Gay Pride, Bologna	Anti Mafia	No Muos	Total
No party	21.7	9.0	14.8	29.1	20.0	15.4	24.9	9.7	28.6	19.1
Left-liberal	10.4	4.0	8.6	15.9	8.6	8.9	16.4	8.6	22.2	11.6
Green	0.0	0.0	0.5	0.0	5.7	1.6	1.0	0.0	1.6	1.0
Social democratic	13.9	46.0	38.3	4.4	14.3	35.0	17.4	49.7	8.7	26.5
Left socialist	0.0	0.0	1.4	0.0	3.8	0.0	0.0	3.2	3.2	1.2
Communist	53.9	39.0	35.9	50.5	46.7	37.0	37.8	25.9	35.7	39.3
Other	0.0	2.0	0.5	0.0	1.0	2.0	2.5	2.7	0.0	1.3
Total	115	100	209	182	105	246	201	185	126	1469
	100.0	100.0	100.0	100.0	100.0	100.0	100.0	100.0	100.0	100.0

discourse on democracy is articulate and complex, taking up some of the principal criticisms of the ever-decreasing quality of liberal democracies, but also putting forward some proposals inspired by democratic qualities other than representation. These proposals resonate with (more traditional) participatory visions, but also with new deliberative conceptions that underline the importance of creating multiple public spaces, egalitarian but plural (see also Chapter 5).

A crisis of responsibility: a conclusion

Concluding, the explosion of social inequalities even in advanced democracies is not only a cause of economic crisis, given reduced consumption and saving, but also a challenge for the image of political equality – a challenge the reference by Occupy Wall Street to the 1% against the 99% symbolizes very well. We can indeed conclude that there is a challenge since, as Tilly noted (2007, 110), 'social inequality impedes democratization and undermines democracy under two conditions: first, the crystallization of continuous differences…into everyday categorical differences by race, gender, class, ethnicity, religion and similar broad groupings, second, the direct translation of those categorical difference into public policies'. This is what is happening now, reducing trust in liberal institutions, but also creating spaces for other models of democracy and construction of critical trust.

In this chapter, I have singled out within neoliberal states a crisis of legitimacy, which took the specific form of a crisis of responsibility – that is, one linked not to too much but rather to too little state intervention, given the decline in public competence and loss of sovereignty accompanied by a rhetoric of depoliticization. This was achieved not through the functioning of a long, hidden hand of the market, but rather through political decisions, often obtained through lobbying and collusion.

Delegitimation of political institutions was related in part to the betrayal of the promises on which neoliberalism had tried to legitimize itself. First and foremost, the deep and long financial crisis was per se a denial of the promises of economic growth and societal well-being that had to come from the free market supporters. So-called technical governance was patently unsuccessful in producing progress, but instead hit hard, according to some economists, nine out of ten European citizens (Pianta 2012). While neoliberalism presented itself as capable of rewarding merit and commitment, in reality even those who played according to those rules of the game were often mercilessly punished. After promising the separation of market and state, it was plagued by scandals of corruption, aggressive lobbying, conflicts of interest. Disillusionment with the betrayal of those promises was quick to emerge among the population when and where the financial crisis exploded.

While fascination with the free market seemed a short, temporary fashion, what emerged with the crisis was rather the evidence of the rootedness of some values linked with social protection. After, step by step, old and new states had been built upon the commitment to protect some main citizens' rights, including social rights, neoliberalism presented a challenge to widespread visions of social justice and political legitimacy. As political culture has shown high levels of resilience, trust in institutions seemed indeed to be influenced by their capacity to act towards some conceptions of justice which – in Western democracies as well as in 'real socialism' in the East or developmental conceptions in the South – meant that the state was supposed to take responsibility for insuring (at least) a modicum of welfare, including rights to housing, employment, health and education. Instead, even in the face of the crisis, public institutions remained attached to a free market vision that had failed to meet its promises.

This is why the crisis emerged, in fact, as a crisis of democracy as well as, or even more than, a financial crisis. Above all, the protesters criticized the ever more evident shortcomings of representative democracies, mirroring a declining trust in the ability of parties to channel emerging demands in the political system. Neoliberalism was and, in fact, is, a political doctrine that brings with it a minimalist vision of the citizens and democracy – as Colin Crouch (2004) demonstrates so well in his *Post-democracy*. It foresees not only the reduction of political interventions to balance the market (and consequent liberalization, privatization and deregulation), but also an elitist concept of citizen participation (electoral only and therefore occasional and potentially distorted) and an increased level of influence for lobbies and strong interests.

This crisis of responsibility, driven by the choice of free market over social protection, had an effect in terms of sudden drops in trust, which punctuated a long-term decline. Mistrust spread, as political authorities were considered unable to meet both the old promises of justice and the new assurances of growth. While the turns towards capitalism with social protection had been seen as compromises between capital and labour – legitimating the state as promoter of security and guarantor of that compromise – neoliberalism denied that need for political legitimacy, stripping public institutions of their competencies and sources of loyalty. If corruption *strictu sensu* spread with the increasing convergence of politics and business, the perception also developed of a rampant corruption *latu sensu*, as betrayal of those very bases of legitimacy in the promises about justice and democracy. In turn, collusion between politics and business produced an array of laws and regulations that made political inequality all the more blatant.

Representative conceptions of democracy have been the most challenged by the developments towards what has been defined as a 'neoliberal' (or 'post-democratic') conception of democracy, which reduces the role of citizens to that of electors if not of consumers (Crouch 2004). The need develops, therefore, to think about other democratic qualities that are better able to put citizens' capacity of surveillance to good use (Rosanvallon 2006). This does not imply a disavowal of the function of the state, but rather a request of politics as capable to reduce economic inequalities and their inefficiencies, together with unfairness. In fact, democratic states have legitimated themselves not only in terms of political equality (and negative freedom) but also (in the output) because they claim to provide some welfare to their citizens.

The protest framing addresses indeed some of the general trends of abdicating responsibility singled out above, with a very high degree of stigmatization of the corruption of so-called representative institutions, which are claimed to be unable to represent the citizens. Representative democracy is also criticized for having allowed the abduction of democracy, not only by financial powers, but also by international organizations, above all the International Monetary Fund and the European Union. Pacts for the Euro and stability, imposed in exchange for loans, are considered as anti-constitutional forms of blackmail, depriving citizens of their sovereignty. Liberal democracy is thus presented as eroded by the market as well as by international institutions. In fact, as we will see in Chapter 5, rather than calling for a return to liberal democracy, the protesters propose and practise different visions of democracy. Around the world, *indignados* citizens have occupied squares, transforming them into public spheres made up of 'normal citizens'. It is an attempt to create high quality discursive democracy, recognizing the equal rights of all (not only delegates and experts) to speak (and to respect) in a public and plural space, open to discussion and deliberation on themes that range from situations suffered to concrete solutions to specific problems, from the elaboration of proposals on common goods to the formation of collective solidarity and emerging identities.

Here as well, the comparison of the GJM in a moment of still rampant neoliberalism with anti-austerity protests during its crisis is telling. While at the beginning of the twenty-first century much research had identified a declining trust in representative institutions (signalled in particular by declining membership in parties, party loyalty and identification, participation in elections, together with increasing rate of participation through unconventional means), since 2011 protests have reflected and accelerated a further dramatic drop in institutional trust. Even if both waves of protest were characterized by multiple strategies, the social movements of rampant neoliberalism were still confident in their capacity to influence public institutions through different channels, including lobbying, and oriented towards the search for democratic global governance, while the social movements in the crisis of neoliberalism have lost faith in accessing public institutions. Similarly, if the relations between movements and parties were tense in the GJM, with some parties offering however important resources for mobilization, the political parties have been kept virulently out of the anti-austerity movement. More and more, the corruption of an entire political class is pointed at as the mechanism through which the profits of the few prevailed over the need – the very human rights – of the many. In opposition to the corrupt elites, the protesters define themselves as part of the large majority of those suffering from social and political inequalities.

These differences notwithstanding, not only is neoliberalism a target for both, but the latter also advocates for the strengthening of public institutions. While post-Marxist conceptions of the state were predicated upon the independence of the political, neoliberalism seems to be challenging those assumptions through increasing dependency of politicians on business, of national governments on big corporations. In terms of the political opportunity approach, while institutions tended to be considered as an arena in which allies and opponents of social movements competed with each other and sympathetic bureaucracies could emerge, with neoliberal developments activists seem to perceive fewer and fewer opportunities for access in an institutional system which emerges as alltogether hostile. The (even critical) trust that pushed movements to engage with public institutions seems to be quickly fading away, as perceptions of political inequalities increase.

In sum, while mistrust does not imply apathy, the political crisis of responsiveness within neoliberal post-democracies for sure brings about shrinking political opportunities, with rebellious reaction against a perceived corruption of democracy through the collusion of business power and political power. As we will see more in depth in the next chapter, mistrust of parties and other associational forms brings about mobilization which are not mediated through traditional actors, with more attention to prefigurative politics than to interactions with institutions.

The relationship with politics was however somewhat different in different countries: while the Arab Spring had immediate political goals in the change of the regime, the Occupy movement refused to address specific claims to the Obama administration; the movement positions in

Southern Europe tended to be in between, with simultaneous articulation of political demands and claims of total autonomy (see also Chapter 5). Future research will be needed in order to investigate more in depth the relations between economic crisis and political ones at the macro, country level, but also at the meso level of various types of movement networks and at the micro, individual level. The question of the specific interactions between center-left versus center-right governments – democratic as well as non-democratic – with movement demands in the developments of the crisis of neoliberalism also remains open for further systematic research.

5

Democracy Is Not a Spectator Sport: Changing Conceptions of Democracy in Social Movements

We want a new model of society, based on the participation of all persons, an effective participatory democracy, where people can take part in decisions on the social, economic and political plans. (From a statement in Puerta del Sol, cited in Nez 2012, 80)

Inclusion. The strength of this movement is that we are many and different...the spaces that make us strong, happy and active are those that everyone can perceive as her own. (*Toma la plaza*, 12/8/2011, cited in Romanos 2011)

In the 2010s, beyond contentious politics as marches in the street, which have also been very relevant in anti-austerity mobilizations, protest politics has taken a variety of forms. For example, collective opposition to eviction has frequently been manifested in civil disobedience, coupled with campaigns of public information against those responsible for the evictions. Public information has also been central in the protest in the educational sectors, in the form of lectures in public places such as squares or trains. Flash mobs have contributed to communicate the dramatic conditions of the poor and the excluded. Social gardening and communal kitchen, together with direct actions against eviction, have addressed the immediate need of a growing population. Especially, today's movements have been called 'square movements' (Pleyers and Glasius 2013), reflecting the symbolic impact of the *acampadas* in public spaces. While not identifying all anti-austerity protests, the camp can be taken as a main expression of a specific organizational model, developed during the crisis of neoliberal capitalism and indeed influenced by its social and cultural implications.

In general, there has always been innovation in the organizational forms of social movements. Traditionally, in the labour movement, centralized and deep-rooted parties and unions contributed to structure the class cleavage (Bartolini 2000). However, there were also moments of pressure for more participatory structures. So Judith Stepan-Norris and Maurice Zeitlin (2003) stressed the unions' need for genuine rank-and-file democracy – as 'democracy makes a real difference in the daily lives of workers: A union with a democratic constitution, organized opposition and an active membership tends to constitute the workers' immediate political community, sustaining both a sense of identification between them and their leaders and class solidarity; as a result, the union also tends to defy the hegemony of capital in the sphere of production' (Stepan-Norris and Zeitlin 2003, 187).

Looking beyond the labour movement, network structures have been put at the basis of social movements' very definition (Diani 1992). An even more loose network has been noted as the main organizational structure of the GJM, which privileged large and loose forums (della Porta 2007). This organizational form could be considered already as an adaptation to the type of fragmented social basis that I have described as linked to the development of neoliberalism. During its evolution, the move from the forum to the camps can be considered as reflecting the further growth of precariousness and insecurity, as well as the related declining trust not only in institutions, but also in associational forms. On the one hand, in fact, neoliberalism weakens the very potential constituencies for unions and formal NGOs by reducing stability, availability of time and material resources to contribute to collective efforts. Civil and political rights become, that is, more difficult to implement in the traditional forms. On the other hand, the related cultural development towards liquid societies increases citizens' preferences for more fluid and less structured forms of mobilization.

The evident challenges to a liberal conception and practice of democracy have been accompanied by the (re)emergence of different conceptions of democracy, elaborated and practised by – among others – movements that today are opposing a neoliberal solution to the financial crisis, accused of further depressing consumption and thereby jeopardizing any prospects for development (whether sustainable or not). Sometimes promoted by social movements, experiments at the institutional level, such as participatory budgeting, reflect this conception of commitments by the citizens, through their common deliberation (Fonts et al. 2014).

As we will see in this chapter, after reviewing some main contributions in social movement studies on the organizational aspects of protest, the emphasis on horizontality that characterizes this anti-austerity wave of protest much more than the previous ones reflects not only the restatement of the role of the 'simple' citizens ('Without us, you're nothing'), but also a search for democratic alternatives that do not need to go through existing hierarchical institutions. The lack of responsiveness by public institutions can explain why recent movements have emphasized the need to build alternatives, rather than looking for party alliances (della Porta 2013c). Looking at the organizational dynamics within social movements, I will address the search for a prefigurative politics that characterized the most visible moments of the anti-austerity protest, the *acampadas* (as long-lasting protest camps in public spaces), comparing them with the most innovative organizational form of the GJM, the forum. I will explain some changes in the conception of democracy with the turns in capitalist development, with social, cultural and political implications.

Old, new and newest movements: the organizational debate

Cleavage theory has stressed the role of organizations (mainly but not only parties) in structuring social conflicts, developing common visions, politicizing and mobilizing. In a parallel way, social movement studies have stressed the role of mobilizing structures. Movements aim at constructing organizations which are, or at least are perceived to be, at the same time efficient and just. Decision making in social movements is not only about how to better promote protests; rather, the organizational forms it takes affect many characteristics of a movement. As we will see, although strategic elements are certainly recognized in organizational choices, they are limited by political, social and cultural constraints. Prefigurative aims are moreover considered, together with strategic ones, as enacted organizational models that change the relations within the movement by activating cognitive, affective and relational mechanisms. Conceptions and practices of democracy acquire central relevance in this evolution.

In social movement studies, the resource mobilization approach has long stressed the need for mobilizing structures that can transform grievances into collective action. Protest is indeed not an individual act; rather, it requires planning, coordination and collective choices. In this perspective, research focused especially on the strategic dimension of organizing: social movement activists, like other collective actors, have long debates (and often controversies) about the best formula to use for recruiting members, keeping commitments, influencing public opinion and reaching out to decision makers. Social movement organizations indeed act strategically – at least, as much as other political organizations do.

Social movement organizational structures are in fact complex, connecting, within networks of different shapes, myriad types of groups: formalized associations and informal groupings, cooperatives and squats, media outlets and unions, or even movement parties. Various classifications have indeed distinguished professional social movement organizations from participatory ones, while empirical research has pointed at their interactions in social movement networks. Research has recognized, moreover, the many organizational dilemmas brought about by the contemporary performances of the various tasks (Jasper 2006). As for the forms of protest, complex and plural repertoires have been identified, with various combinations of moderate versus radical and inward- versus outward-oriented forms (della Porta and Diani 2006).

Strategy is, however, only part of the story. The very notion of a repertoire of action, but also of an organizational repertoire, reflects the observation that the range of choices is limited. In the influential definition by Charles Tilly, 'The existing repertoire constrains collective action; far from the image we sometimes hold of mindless crowds, people tend to act within known limits, to innovate at the margins of the existing forms and to miss many opportunities available to them in principle' (1986, 390). Rooted in the shared culture of the activists, repertoires contain the options considered practicable, while excluding others: 'These varieties of action constitute a repertoire in something like the theatrical or musical sense of the word; but the repertoire in question resembles that of *commedia dell'arte* or jazz more than that of a strictly classical ensemble: people know the general rules of performance more or less well and vary the performance to meet the purpose at hand' (Tilly 1986, 390). Repertoires are not static, but they change slowly, mainly through marginal moves.

We can identify some main types of constraints upon organizational strategies, linked to all dimensions of the cleavages we have addressed. First, like any organizational population, social movement organizations are subject to environmental selection. This means that in each wave of protest, various models are tried and tested; but only a few survive, usually transformed in order to adapt to the quick evolution (ups and downs) of the mobilization. The context within which they interact strongly influences the range of choices available, especially the successful ones. In social movement studies, some reflections have indeed developed on the effects of political institutions, with inclusive systems said to allow for the development of large, unitary and moderate movement organizational structures and exclusive systems instead favouring weak, fragmented and radical ones (e.g. Kriesi 1996). These observations dovetail with those in the literature on cleavages, which proved that the national labour movements and their parties adapted to their environment, growing strong and unitary where they met institutional inclusions, weak and fragmented where they were repressed (e.g. Bartolini 2000; Marks 1989).

The presence of dense but informal *networks* distinguishes social movements from other collective actors, who instead have clear organizational boundaries. In social movements, individuals and organizations, while keeping their autonomous identities, engage in sustained exchanges of resources oriented to the pursuit of a common goal: 'The coordination of specific initiatives, the regulation of individual actors' conduct and the definition of strategies all depend on permanent negotiations between the individuals and the organizations involved in collective action. No single organized actor, no matter how powerful, can claim to represent a movement as a whole' (della Porta and Diani 2006, 21). In new social movements, a networked, loosely coordinated structure emerged as a better fit to address the various and variable needs of mobilization as well as those of survival in the doldrums (Diani 1995; Taylor and van Dyke 2004). The network structure allows movements to maintain a plural repertoire, testing various potential options and combining their effects. The capacity to form and sustain these networks is therefore a very central task in resource mobilization: categorical traits (such as class) are not sufficient for collective action; they need to be supported by dense network ties.

Another contextual constraint that social movement studies have only sporadically addressed resides in the social characteristics of their potential basis of mobilization, as it is affected by *socio-economic structures*. While researchers have established that social movement organizations adapt to the types of networks existing in their environment (Diani 2005), stressing the need to make organizational supply and mobilizing demand meet (Klandermans 2013a), literature on the specific effects of sociographic characteristics of activists on social movement organizations has been sporadic. Observing that social movements have a greater opportunity to spread in groups endowed with material resources and dense ties, new social movement theorists have linked the decline of a hierarchical organizational model to the weakening of the reference basis of industrial workers, who had supported that model. Organizational adaptation then required a shift from hierarchy to networks. Literature on cleavages has indeed pointed at the challenges faced by traditional political parties and unions, given the numerical decline in their core constituency. In particular, the disappearance of the ideological mass party, whose spread had been considered a victory of the labour movement, has been related to the de-freezing of the traditional political divisions along the left–right continuum. The search for an expansion of the electoral basis towards the middle class in fact brought about the (as yet unachieved) search for new party organizational formulas. New social movements have been said in fact to represent new social groups, which have more heterogeneous categorical tracts and are spatially less concentrated (Offe 1985). We might expect the shift from an inclusive to an exclusive capitalist model to reduce traditional resources for collective action. Not only have unions and associations been formally weakened by a reduction of unionization rights and an increase in the number of less-protected workers, but they have been also delegitimated through either their incapacity or their unwillingness to oppose the spread of neoliberalism (Boltanski and Chiapello 2005; see also Chapter 3).

Beyond social structures, however, *normative preferences*, influenced by cultural change, also affect the choice of an organizational formula. As Elisabeth Clemens observed, an organizational model is more likely to be adopted to the extent that it 'is believed to work, involves practices and organizational relations that are already familiar and is consonant with the organization of the rest of those individuals' social world' (1996, 154). Organizations have in fact been defined as arenas for conversation (Eliasoph 1998). As symbolic incentives are particularly important for activists, in order to be rewarding, participation requires social movement organizations that embody the activists' norms and values, as well as adapting to the characteristics of the movements' social bases.

Flexible (and light) organizational forms

Research on recent social movements has in fact linked new organizational forms to cultural as well as social changes in neoliberal societies. Recent cultural transformations have been said to bring about the need to adapt mobilizing strategies to multiple identities, with organizational structures that allow for multiple choices and give voice to individuals (Roggeband and Duyvendak 2013, 99). Some attention is paid to the emergence of 'light communities' – with light identities, loose ties, short-term engagement and low identification – as people are less and less willing to create strong collective bonds (Roggeband and Duyvendak 2013, 95). In this direction, various research pointed at the 'shifting balance between organizations and individuals' (Walgrave 2013, 207), with decreasing availability to organize one's whole personal life around an activist identity. Although old types of organizations still stage protest events, mobilization processes are increasingly based on more informal coordination forms. The assumption is that, 'In late modern societies, people become increasingly connected as individuals rather than as members of a community or group; they operate their own personal community networks. Traditional greedy institutions, such as trade unions and churches, which made significant demands on members' time, loyalty and energy, are replaced by light groups and associations that are loose, easy to join and easy to leave' (van Stekelenburg and Boekkooi 2013, 218). That is, in a society that is more fragmented, differentiated, plural, identities tend to be less and less pervasive (as broadly applied) and salient (Snow 2013b). Organizational formats must adapt to these cultural changes, inventing organizational repertoires that resonate with a higher degree of subjectivity and individualism.

An additional expected characteristic of organizational developments in the crisis of neoliberalism is an increasing detachment from institutional politics, with a preference for prefigurative (rather than instrumental) forms of mobilization. Research on organizational sociology stresses the positive role played by the coherence and authenticity of organizational identities and of organizational learning as knowledge sharing (Soule 2013). In a similar direction, research on social movements has pointed at the importance of prefigurative organizational forms – prefigurative politics meaning 'a political orientation based on the premise that the ends a social movement achieves are fundamentally shaped by the means it employs and that movements should therefore do their best to choose means that embody or "prefigure" the kind of society they want to bring about' (Leach 2013, 1004). In this sense, activists must seek to develop 'counterhegemonic institutions and modes of interactions that embody the desired transformations' (Leach 2013), in particular through consensus and participatory democracy. As Francesca Polletta has suggested, movement organizational format, even when inefficient, can be preferred by many activists for its expressive and redemptive characteristics: as 'by enacting within the movement itself values of radical equality, freedom and community, activists have sought to bring into being a society marked by those values' (Polletta 2013, 908).

The prefigurative capacity of protest is linked to its eventful characters insofar as protesting changes relations (della Porta 2008; see also della Porta 2014a).[15] Especially during cycles of protest, some contingent events tend to affect the given relations by fuelling mechanisms of social change: organizational networks develop; frames are bridged; personal links foster reciprocal trust. In this sense, protest events constitute processes during which collective experiences develop through the interactions of different individual and collective actors, which take part in it with different roles and aims. They have transformative effects 'by constituting and empowering new groups of actors or by re-empowering existing groups in new ways' (Sewell 1996, 271), thus putting in motion social processes that 'are inherently contingent, discontinuous and open ended' (Sewell 1996, 272). Many protests have, in fact, cognitive, affective and relational impacts on the very movements that carry them out (della Porta 2014a). Some forms of action or specific campaigns have a particularly high degree of 'eventfulness', producing 'profound effects on the group spirit of their participants' (Rochon 1998, 115) and promoting a sense of collective identity (Pizzorno 1993). Looking at internal democracy also means addressing the capacity of protest events to produce relations, by facilitating communication as well as effective ties (della Porta 2009a and 2009b).

In what follows, I will address the mentioned debates by looking at the characteristics of emerging organizational formats and conceptions of democracy in progressive movements targeting neoliberal capitalism.

Changing conceptions of democracy

The normative reflection on organizational forms within social movements has addressed the broad topic of conceptions of democracy. In the neoliberal era criticisms of representative democracy have pushed not towards anti-politics, but rather towards calls for more participation and deliberation. The intense debate in normative theory addressed two main dimensions of democratic conceptions that are relevant for our reflections on social movements. The first dimension refers to the recognition of participation as an integral part of democracy; the second looks at the construction of political identities as endogenous (rather than exogenous) to the democratic process.

First of all, while the ideal of democracy as government of, by and for the people locates the source of all power in the citizenry at large, *representative* institutions restrict the number of decision makers and select them on the basis of some specific qualities. A distinction is usually made between the (utopistic) conception of a *democracy of the ancients*, in which all citizens participate directly in the decisions about the public goods and a (realistic) *democracy of the moderns*, where an elected few govern. The size and complexity of decision making in the modern state is often seen as imposing constraints on the participation in public deci-sions of the many and, especially, for normal citizens – often considered as too inexperienced, if not too emotional, to take part in the choices that will affect them. Electoral accountability should then give legitimacy to the process, by allocating to the citizen-electors the power periodically to reward or punish those in government. If liberal theories have under-lined delegation and electoral accountability, participatory theorists have affirmed the importance of creating multiple occasions for participation (Arnstein 1969; Pateman 1970). Elections are at best too rare to grant citizens sufficient power to control the elected. Additionally, elections offer only limited choices, leaving several themes out of the electoral debate and citizens' assessment. What is more, elections are shown to be manipulated given the greater capacity of some candidates to attract licit or illicit financing, as well as to command privileged access to mass media. Instead, a multiplication of channels of participation is praised as contributing to create schools of democracy that are capable of con-structing good citizens through interaction and empowerment (della Porta 2013a).

Together with delegation, the value and legitimacy of majoritarian decision making has also been contested. A 'minimalist' view of democ-racy as the power of the majority has been considered not only as risky in terms of thwarting the rights of the minorities, but also as reducing the quality of decision making. As there is no logical assumption that grants more wisdom to the preferences that are (simply) more numerous, other decision-making principles should at least temper the majoritarian one. In normative debates, deliberative theories have in fact promoted spaces of communication, the exchange of reasons, the construction of shared definitions of the public good, as fundamental for the legitimation of public decisions (among others, Dryzek 2000; Cohen 1989; Elster 1998; Habermas 1981; 1996). Here, it is not the number of pre-existing preferences, but the quality of the decisions that would grant legitimacy, as well as efficacy of decision making. By relating to each other – recog-nizing the others and being recognized by them – citizens would have the chance to understand the reasons of the others, assessing them against emerging standards of fairness. Communication not only permits the development of better solutions, by allowing for carriers of different knowledge and expertise to interact, but it would also change the percep-tion of one's own preferences, making participants less concerned with individual, material interests and more with collective goods.

Participation and deliberation are in fact democratic qualities in tension with those of representation and majority decisions and along-side these in a precarious equilibrium in the different conceptions and specific institutional practices of democracy. Building upon normative democratic theory, I have defined a participatory-deliberative model as made up of the following elements (della Porta 2009a, b; 2013a):

(a) *Preference (trans)formation*, as 'deliberative democracy requires the transformation of preferences in interaction' (Dryzek 2000, 79).
(b) *Orientation to the public good*, as it 'draws identities and citizens' interests in ways that contribute to public building of public good' (Cohen 1989, 18–19).
(c) *Rational argumentations*, as people are convinced by the force of the better argument (Habermas 1981, 1996).
(d) *Consensus*, as decisions must be approvable by all participants.
(e) *Equality*, as deliberation takes place among free and equal citizens (as 'free deliberation among equals', Cohen 1989, 20).
(f) *Inclusiveness*, as all citizens with a stake in the decisions to be taken must be included in the process and able to express their voice.
(g) *Transparency*, as a deliberative democracy is 'an association whose affairs are governed by the public deliberation of its members' (Cohen 1989, 17).

These seven elements might be distinguished in terms of conditions, means and effects: we have participatory deliberative democracy when, under conditions of equality, inclusiveness and transparency, a communicative process based on reason (the strength of the good argument) is able to transform individual preferences and reach decisions oriented to the public good (della Porta 2009a).

As we will see, all of these elements, often imported from anti-austerity protests in the semi-periphery and periphery of the capitalist world system are present in the GJM of the early 2000s as well as in the anti-austerity protests of the 2010s, although with some different emphases and in different combinations. In particular, I will point at the shifts synthesized in Table 5.1. As I will argue, while the social forums mixed both associational and assembly based forms, with an emphasis on consensus, the *acampadas* refused associations, privileging the participation of the person – the citizen, the member of the community. From the relational point of view, whereas the social forum process was oriented to associational networking, the *acampadas* follow a more aggregative logic aiming at offering spaces to the individual participants (Juris 2012). From the cognitive point of view, while the forum aimed at building political alternatives, the *acampadas* were more prefigurative. These differences are in part the product of learning processes, after a perceived decline in the innovative capacity of the social forum process. However, they also reflect adaptation to a context characterized by a legitimacy crisis of late neoliberalism and by its social and political consequences,

Table 5.1.   Dimensions of democracy: from the forum to the camps

	Forum	Camps
Transparency	Open meeting places	In the open-air space
Equality	In associational democracy	In communitarian/ direct democracy
Consensus	Within spokes-council and SMOs	In the assemblies, open to all
Argumentation	Rational/political	Prefigurative/emotional
Orientation	Cognitive work towards the public good	The construction of the common
Preference transformation	In the GJM	In the 99%

but also to national opportunities and constraints. In fact, referring to existing research on Tahrir Square, Puerta del Sol and Place de Cataluna, Syntagma Square, Zuccotti Park (but also to the failed *acampadas* in Italy), I will single out in what follows many similarities but also some differences.

Constructing new organizational repertoires: organizing against neoliberalism in the periphery

The protests that developed against austerity since the 1990s in the world-system periphery were path-breaking, not only from the perspective of the emergence of new collective identities, but also from the organizational point of view. In fact, while unions and other historical institutions of the developmental state were targeted by neoliberal reforms as jeopardizing the free market, new organizational forms gradually developed, promoting and practising alternative models of democracy. The ideas of democracy developed from the Zapatistas in Mexico, the Sem Terra in Brazil, the *picqueteros* in Argentina, the indigenous communities in Bolivia, Peru or Equador, travelled all around the world, challenging the representative and majoritarian models dominating in the West.

First and foremost, all these experiences promoted participatory and deliberative formulae, with an emphasis on the equal role of all citizens, of consensus building through argumentation, in recognition of differences but also of the common aim of constructing the commons.

The importance of differences and ways to accommodate them was addressed by the Zapatistas in Mexico, that influenced then the GJM. The positive stress on the encounters of diverse people open to mutual understanding is deep-rooted. Often quoted is subcomandante Marcos' greeting to the activists participating in the first intercontinental encounter in the Lacandon Rainforest: 'Some of the best rebels from the five continents came to the mountains of the Mexican South-East. All brought things, brought words and ears, brought their ideas, their hearts, their worlds. To meet with other ideas, with other hearts, with other worlds...A world made of many worlds is to be met these days... A world made of many worlds opens its space and conquers its right to be possible...A world of all worlds that rebel and resist the power.' In fact, consensus is rooted in communitarian forms of democracy: 'No major strategic or policy decision is made until it has been considered and approved by consensus in every community's assembly.' Here, 'There is little imposed order or structure to the discussion; it proceeds organically until eventually two or three ideas or positions emerge and the coordinator summarizes them. The process continues in the same lively, chaotic manner until eventually someone asks, "Acuedo, ya?" (Do we have agreement?)' (Starr, Martinez-Torres and Rosset 2011, 105). Good communication implies an often promoted capacity to listen as well as a training to act as mediator in assemblies of different types. The stress on the inclusion of citizens as equal is visible in the compulsory form of participation as well as in the rotation of tasks. Participation also in governmental roles is indeed considered as a school of democracy for the citizens as it also teaches to hold governmental actors accountable.

Also the Argentinean *picqueteros*, which emerged in 1996 calling for full employment and reincorporations of the poor, formed as an alliance of groups going from Christian-based communities to communist and from unions to human rights associations. At the pickets, community ties were built around the occupation and expressed in the assemblies, where decisions about agreements with the state were made (Svampa and Pereyra 2003; Rossi 2013). Claims for 'cleaner government, greater transparency and improved accountability' were also reflected in internal forms of democracy that relied upon transparent, open and inclusive processes. The multi-sectoral mobilization was in fact organized through 'assembly style of decision making, which later became generalized as popular assemblies. Popular assemblies were new brokerage instruments because they were open-air, freewheeling gatherings', with a progressive shift of power from organizational leaders to rank-and-file activists (Silva 2009, 74). Also, on the tradition of the popular protests in Argentina, 'olla popular were organized, creating spaces where people congregated, exchanged experiences, recognized their common plight and took courage' (Silva 2009, 84).

In the long occupation of the Sem Terra in Brazil as encampments were created and then run by land-less peasants, a similar emphasis was put on inclusion of all members in the decision-making processes that often addressed main choices in the everyday management of the occupied land. In fact, 'immediately, everyone is participating in governance and building trust and community' (Starr, Martinez-Torres and Rosset 2011, 109). Rotation in main position has to ensure broad involvement. Consensus through high-quality communication is considered as a main value, as 'In the MST people are in meetings much of the time' (Starr, Martinez-Torres and Rosset 2011, 109). Self-governed communities aimed at the construction of different conception of politics and humanity.

The importance of gradually constructing new organizational forms, alternative to the corporatist ones that neoliberalism had weakened, emerges as central from research on Latin America. In general, episodes of contention began with separate streams of protests, which then linked, as 'the common origin of highly varied grievances and demands facilitated the articulation of horizontal linkages among protest organizations' (Silva 2009, 41). Brokerage mechanisms included summit meetings, organizational networks, open assemblies and communal forms of social organization. In these developments, the indigenous conceptions of democracy as involving the whole community in discursive interactions spread to other movements.

This type of evolution has been described in the Bolivia case, where anti-neoliberal contestation grew up during three waves of protest before Evo Morales' election as president in 2005 (Silva 2009). The only country to experience a social revolution, Bolivia had militant and independent unions. After the 1952 revolution, in the 1950s and 1960s, the National Revolutionary Movement (MNR) had built the national populist state and corporatist system, with strict links with the union (COB). In the 1960s and 1970s, under a populist military rule, the military promised a land reform, which was only partially accomplished. After transition in 1982, since 1985 protests developed against IMF sponsored neoliberal reform – in particular the New Economic Policy, based on an economic stabilization programme that eliminated state control on prices, wage controls and public sector salaries. As shock treatments caused political and economic exclusion, weakening the unions (about 500 unionists were arrested in 1985), the COB framed resistance in a Polanyi-like defence of formal sector employment, pay and working conditions and nationalist state intervention. As many former miners had become coca growers, they organized roadblocks against coca eradication, stressing the cultural and identity framing of coca use. Local mobilizations of *cocaleros* put the basis for transformation in the popular sector. The years 1993–7 brought about a large increase in anti-neoliberal contention, with alliances of campesinos, urban workers and low-land indigenous population plus teachers, *cocaleros* and students.

It was during these protests that coordination increased, exploiting dense ties in community networks. After the 'March for Life, Coca and National Sovereignty', a new wave of contestation developed in 1995, with the growth of coordination during water and gas wars in the early 2000s. Initially, these were characterized by mutual support and loose coordination. The so-called 'water war' then developed against the privatization of water in Cochabamba, as private entrepreneurs asked for changes in customary water rights. The new law in fact advantaged large private corporations against local cooperatives and neighbourhood associations, resulting in price increases and expropriation of water access rights, with ensuing disruption of everyday life. A loose alliance of various groupings converged then in the Coordinadora of civic committees, which organized roadblocks in April 2000, linking rural peasant irrigators, water collectives, urban workers, middle classes, shantytown dwellers and the traditional Left (Silva 2009, 127). Coca-growers blocked roads to Cochabamba, while neighbourhood assemblies claimed 'water is ours', 'Pachamama, Woracocha and Tata dios gave it to us to live, not to do business with' (Silva 2009, 128). Unions of *cocaleros* and campesinos joined in against neoliberalism. In this process, there was a development through traditional *ayllus*, of self-government, with revival of *ayllu* democracy. Claims included suspension of the general water law, *cocalero* union participation in policy making, reestablishment of a state bank, creation of an agrarian university, titling of indigenous areas and direct administration of protected areas. The alliances strengthened thanks to a horizontal structure, based around assembleary conceptions of direct democracy;

> The Coordinadora was very open and tolerant; it welcomed any organization interested in joining the struggle; it helped interested groups, such as shantytown dwellers whom traditional unions had ignored, to organize. It promoted an assembly style of decision making to build confidence and support for its decision. The Coordinadora introduced the idea of direct democracy to the political agenda as a means to overcome persistent government neglect and denial of the legitimacy of the popular sector. Last, but not least, the Coordinadora framed the issue as an assault on the necessities of life for all in the interest of international capital and its domestic allies who were in cahoots with corrupt government officials. (Silva 2009, 131)

A third wave of protest then spread with the 'gas war' in 2003. Again, *cocaleros* staged roadblocks, pensioners joined in asking for adjustments in pensions, workers revolted against income taxes (rather than corpo-rate taxes). Here as well, local networks were mobilized. Protest started in El Alto, with a close-knit system of community associations created to meet basic needs on the territory. Local syndicates also organized informal workers, with a quick snowballing of contention. As the framing of the conflict pointed at 'us', the Bolivian people and 'them', the politi-cians and businessmen betraying the country, indigenous frames stressed a reciprocal obligation to mobilize the community. A gas *coordinadora* was then built on the example of the water *coordinadora*. Demands included referenda on energy policy, industrialization of natural gas, a constituent assembly to reform political institutions, withdrawal from the free trade agreement with the United States and ending the eradica-tion of coca. After 20 September 2003, protests were brutally repressed: five peasants were killed and twenty more died in October, as rage increased around the image of the defiant indigenous. New left-wing protest then developed in 2005, helping Morales and the MAS (Movimiento al Socialismo) to win elections with 53.7 per cent (67 per cent in the referendum of 2008), with state control of oil, gas and mineral reserves.

A similar history of slow accumulation of organizational resources and adaptation of mobilization strategy to changing social, cultural and political conditions also characterized Ecuador, where national pop-ulism, with the military in power in the 1960s and 1970s, had expanded state planning and services, subsidized food, energy and transport and introduced agrarian reforms. After the return to electoral democracy in 1979, under IMF and US pressure neoliberal reforms developed in the mid-1980s to address the debt crisis. Since the beginning, protests against neoliberalism attempts involved weak urban labour but very strong indigenous groups, against the increasing power of the executive. During the first wave, organized labour strengthened its protests, timing them with congressional opposition. Even though the first wave of protest was weak, it forged unity and militancy. In 1990, the first indigenous uprising saw the participation of union members. The alliance of lowland and highland Indians developed against an exclusionary, hegemonic, antide-mocratic and repressive state, bridging claims based on ethnicity, equal access to services and class (claims for peasants' rights to land, fair prices).

As in Bolivia, the local community was key to mobilization and 'assembly style decision making facilitated consensus building' (Silva 2009, 159). A community authority structure strengthened reciprocal obligation and village participation. The leadership was open to collabo-ration with non indigenous social movements of the popular sector, as they felt indigenous people were immersed in the various societal groups.

Between 1992 and 1996, as radicalized neoliberalism eliminated state subsidies on fuel, food and transport and also introduced new cuts in public services, a second and more intense wave of protest addressed the 'modernization law' in 1993, which increased the power of the executive. A Mobilization for life then developed on a reformist platform for indigenous claims and recognition of representatives, achieving some results in terms of credit, alliances of indigenous peoples including self-help, artisans, labour, public sector unions, teachers and so on; but also new social movements (including human rights, environment, gender) and Christian base communities.

A third wave of protests targeted neoliberal reforms in 1996–2000, peaking against the collapse of the private banking sector in 1998 as well as predatory and corrupt business. Protests also addressed new policies increasing the value-added tax and privatizing oil, electricity, telecommunication, plus flexible work. A sixty-day state of emergency increased rage, desperation and frustration. The reformist demands of indigenous and other social movements included the return to the state of money given to the bank and repealing announced economic measures, legal proceedings against corrupt business and politicians and the lowering of fuel prices. After increasing protest in 1999, with indigenous uprisings, union mobilizations and roadblocks, frustration over unfulfilled promises fuelled requests for radical constitutional reform and even flirted with the military. In 2006, Rafael Carrera was elected and implemented a programme of anti-neoliberal reforms.

In Mexico, in the same period, protests developed among electricians, steelworkers, railroad workers, airport employees, textile workers and miners, as well as students, teachers, lawyers and writers (Williams 2001). Unions weakened, however, as unionists were the first to be dismissed, annual contracts were abolished and unemployment grew. Social movement organizations grew, with regular general assemblies of workers, departmental assemblies and delegates, votes on strikes. While the discourse that the private sector can create more jobs and security than the public seems resonant with the economic growth in early 1990s, the struggle was fuelled as those promises failed to materialize. Traditions of workers' mobilization survived through developments of new conflicts and use of direct action, relying on developmental ideology. Each new juncture helped in forging alliances, as in the main strikes in 1977, 1979, 1985 and 1989, with the involvement of the community as shopkeepers and their wives helped along with students, farmers and fishermen and neighbourhood settings, street-sellers, cab drivers. Participatory forms of democracy facilitated coordination among different social and political groups.

Democracy and organization in the Global Justice Movement

In the GJM, criticism of representative democracy, even if with openness to interaction with institutions and parties, was embedded in a specific vision of democracy within the movement, with a strong emphasis on values of participation and deliberation (see also Chapter 4).

The networking of concrete initiatives

Shared in the GJM was the idea of the social forum as a place for *networking*, with a positive emphasis on diversity (della Porta 2009c). In its normative self-conception, the ESF is an inclusive public sphere. The main organizational challenge is indeed to combine coordination (through structures such as the European Preparatory Assembly, charged with the preparation of the forum), but also the informal role played by a network of cosmopolitan activists) with respect for the autonomy of the various organizations and activists that participate in the forum process. Switching from norms to practices, the forum appeared as capable of mobilizing thousands of groups, networking them in various combinations.

Focus groups with activists of the Social Forums in Florence confirmed that a main strength of the movement was seen as its capacity to *network* associations and individuals, bringing together 'many situations...that in previous years, especially the last ten, did not come together enough...the fact of being in contact and in a network is one of the most important factors...this is the positive thing...the value of the Social Forums' (4G, p. 89). The network was defined as more than a sum of groups, for it is in the network that the activist 'gets to know people, forms relationships, becomes a community...' (4A, p. 92). The search for 'another possible world' was contrasted with the specialized, fragmented action of foregoing decades. While the activists shared previous experiences in associations, the movement also develops from a critique of life in associations in the 1990s – being defined, indeed, as 'the coming together of people who were no longer finding answers to the everyday problems they had to face, day after day, in the various associations they were members of, or else people who weren't in any association because they didn't trust any' (3A, p. 62). The added value of the movement was thus seen in its capacity to bring together single-issue knowledge and mobilizations, bridging them within a more general framework. During the focus groups with activists of the Florence Social

Forum, the movement was significantly defined as 'a big building site' (1E, p. 26), its strength 'coming just from all those people working in their own *little* way in their own *little* associations' (1D, p. 24).

Agreement among different kinds of people was searched for around *concrete action*. The very cross-fertilization among the 'various souls of the movement' was seen as made possible by common initiatives, daily conduct and interaction among individuals rather than organizations. During common campaigns, tolerant identities developed from the direct experience of acting together with different people and groups. The movement originated in mobilizations of diverse, initially barely related groups that had turned against a number of international organizations. Contacts among the various affiliations had been built up over time, during previous mobilizations, such as the campaigns against NAFTA and then the Multilateral Agreement on Investments (MAI) or the first protests at EU Summits. A strongly felt common aim helped in overcoming ideological differences: 'one person maybe has a photo of Stalin and another a photo of Jesus over his bed, all in all it doesn't matter too much, if both believe that Nestlé has to be boycotted... because with ideologies, extreme objectives, dogmatism, you can't ever get anywhere' (2G, p. 42). Interaction around concrete objectives helped, in the activists' view, in the building of an ever more solid common base. A 'strength of the movement', 'its richness', 'a strategically winning choice' was singled out in its going 'forward for a long time coming together around particular points, leaving aside more systematic discussions, theoretical ones and so on'. From an initially instrumental impetus to act as a coalition, there ensued the start of a process of building a collective identification – albeit partial, given that 'the relationship with any organization ought properly to be to take a critical position but try to form part of a general scheme *even not taking totally on board everything that's offered to you, but at any rate belonging to something*' (IG, p. 19).

Solidarity developed, indeed, in concrete protest events, which allowed for contamination in action (della Porta and Mosca 2007) – or, as the activists said, in the search for a new way of doing politics founded on *immediately gratifying action* rather than on sacrifice for the sake of a distant future. The search for a new type of activist, oriented to immediate transformation in everyday life, brought together the new generations with the old ones, building in both cases upon experiences with voluntary associations. In the words of a member of the '68 generation, voluntary works, as 'doing politics because it was doing society, doing action in society, in the neighborhoods etc.' is contrasted with 'the endurance of the old-style militancy, sort of... today I'm busting my ass, sacrificing myself, so that tomorrow I can shift political equilibria, get into government and through government change society and make it better. In the present, sacrifice is the mode of politics, happiness is for after the victory when things can be changed' (5E, pp. 122–3). Again in the words of an activist, the movement's value was in 'regaining universal categories of politics, in short, a much higher level of politics' than in the specialization of the 1980s and 1990s – as one activist remarked, 'I feel my generation's, growing up in the second half of the Eighties and in the Nineties...had to do with a sort of specialization of politics, with no general vision of politics and especially no direction to aim at: this movement has instead regained universal categories, as shown by the basic slogan, "another possible world". For me this is a very important fact, that has given me enthusiasm and passion in politics' (3E, p. 63). The strength of the movement came, indeed, 'from the fact that various experiences intersect, so that if I was concerned until yesterday more with human rights, I have been able to interweave my experience with someone more concerned with economics, with work, or so many other things' (3E, p. 63).

The search for a deliberative element emerged particularly in the acknowledgement of the importance of *dialogue*. As an activist put it, 'the Forum has something evangelical, that is, something new, something we were waiting for, something there was a need of...how is it new? It's new particularly...in the way of arguing, the way of confronting each other, in its caution, its different mode of approach, avoiding opposi- tions: it's bringing together components that are very far from each other and very different, that see each other a different way today...' (6G, p. 144). The movement is therefore described as a discursive arena: 'a network bringing into communication a whole series of environments, of people with a common sense of things they want to change, even if among them the differences are profound'.

Research on the GJM stressed in fact the importance of a networking logic, which has been said to reflect and at the same time contribute to, the spreading of a 'cultural logic', as embedded sets of values oriented towards the building of decentralized coordination of autonomous units and the free circulation of information facilitated by the Internet (Juris 2004; Juris 2005b). Perceived by the activists as a 'new way of doing politics', networking implied reliance on non-hierarchical struc- tures, open access to information, direct participation and consensual methods of decision making (Juris 2004). Differently from 'old politics' based upon unitary strategy and a logic of representation, this 'new politics' invoked the creation of open spaces, with limited convergences of diverse actors that are connected, but with respect for their specifici- ties. Calls for democracy tend to be particularly lively in network struc- tures – in the words of activists (cited in Juris 2004), 'Participatory democracy is not only a transversal theme in our work, it constitutes our model of… operation' and the 'building of these networks is the world we want to create'. Networks are in fact perceived as structures that allow groups to 'balance freedom with coordination, autonomy with collective work, self-organization with effectiveness'.

Networking involves different and diverse actors. In the ESF, as in the WSF, this has been nurtured under the conception of internal democracy as based on the *consensual* 'open space method', which should make plurality a strength. What seemed to make cognitive exchanges especially relevant for the GJM in general and for the social forums in particular, was the positive value given to the openness towards 'the others', considered in some activists' comments as a most relevant attitude in order to 'build nets from the local, to the national and the supranational' (see e.g. http://www.lokabass.com/scriba/eventi.php?id_eve=62). The development of inclusive arenas for the creation of knowledge emerged as a main aspiration in the social forum process. This value is widespread among activists across ideological and national borders. Beyond the social forum process, common to the GJM is the respect for diversity, including its own internal diversity, based on the recognition of the history of the various organizations that converge in it.

Together with respect for diversity, *horizontality*, as lack of vertical power, was a founding value of the ESF as well as the WSF. Although the lack of acknowledgement of the presence of power inside the forum was considered as risky by some activists, as a value horizontality had in fact a mobilizing and legitimizing effect. Although the ESF per se did not take decisions, the European Preparatory Assembly and the Assembly of the European Social Movements decided by consensus and refused delegation (including a permanent steering committee).

Nurtured in the social forums, but not limited to them, is also the strong *transnational* dimension of networking. The social forum processes developed from the convergence of different movements with previous experiences of common transnational mobilizations. The first Intercontinental Encounter for Humanity and Against Neoliberalism in Chiapas in 1997, together with the campaigns against the Multilateral Investment Agreement in 1998, were important steps in the process of globalization of protest. In the year 2000, 'protest intensifies and spreads geographically to every continent; the social arc of organizations participating in them appears to have expanded and enriched itself in terms of demands and proposals' (Seoane and Taddei 2002, 110). Together with the Zapatistas in Mexico, the peasants protesting the privatization of water in Cochabamba, the World Women's March, the peasants meeting in Bangalore and the EU counter-summit in Nice all converged in the year 2000 into a common path of contestation of IGOs. Even though internationalism is not new for social movements of the Left, the share size of an ESF (or, even more, a WSF) is much bigger than similar international meetings of the labour movement or even of new social movements. What is more, notwithstanding the institutionalization of the social forum process, those travelling and participating in them were far from being only national leaders. Research results pointed in fact at the permanence of national levels of organization, evident in the role of the national organization committees of the country that hosts the ESF, but also in the national delegations that take part in the EPA (della Porta 2009a). However, they also stressed the role of informal networks of cosmopolitan actors that feel themselves and are felt as developing a primary loyalty to the transnational nature of the process (see Chapter 3).

Multiple strategies

While most of the analysed groups took part in transnational action, their strategies did vary, as the multiplicity of concerns and values was reflected in a multiplicity of forms of action. A plural repertoire confirmed the pluralistic nature of the movement. In the documents of the organizations sampled during the Demos project, while protest was mentioned by a large majority of the groups (69.3 per cent), a similarly large share mentioned influencing the media, spreading alternative information and raising awareness as a main logic of action of their groups (68.0 per cent) and almost half of the organizations mentioned the political education of citizens (42.6 per cent). Although smaller, the significant number of groups mentioning political representation (11.5 per cent), defence of specific interests (18.4 per cent), advocacy (27.5 per cent), provision of services (21.7 per cent) and self-help (13.9 per cent) signals that most organizations engage in various types of activities. Even larger percentages also referred to lobbying (35.7 per cent). Most of the groups did not limit themselves to a single strategy but mixed multiple strategies.

Similar results come from the interviews with representatives of social movement organizations. As Table 5.2 shows, almost 90 per cent of the groups valued cognitive activities such as disseminating information, organizing conferences, seminars and workshops, publishing research reports and so on. Around three-quarters of the groups reported performing protest activities and the same proportion engaging in the construction of concrete alternatives. About one-half of the groups employed a strategy of lobbying with direct pressure on public decision makers. Contrary to the assumption that lobbying and protest are opposite

Table 5.2. Main strategies of the groups by country (%)

Main strategies of the group	Country							
	France	Germany	Italy	Netherlands	Spain	Sweden	UK	Total
Protest	78.6	73.1	81.1	59.3	97.1	75.0	75.9	78.1
Building concrete alternatives	85.7	61.5	64.9	88.9	62.9	89.3	79.3	75.2
Lobbying	42.9	57.7	51.4	70.4	37.1	57.1	69.0	54.3
Political education / raising awareness	78.6	100.0	89.2	92.6	82.9	96.4	89.7	89.5
Number of overlapping strategies								
0–1	10.7	7.7	8.1	5.7	3.6	10.3	7.4	7.6
2	21.4	34.6	21.6	31.4	10.7	6.9	22.2	21.4
3	39.3	15.4	43.2	40.0	50.0	41.4	22.2	36.7
4	28.6	42.3	27.0	22.9	35.7	41.4	48.1	34.3
Total	13.3	12.4	17.6	16.7	13.3	13.8	12.9	100.0
(N)	(28)	(26)	(37)	(35)	(28)	(29)	(27)	(210)

Cramer's V is: 0.257** (protest); 0.269** (alternatives); 0.232* (lobbying); n.s. (political education).
NB – overall % of column can sum above 100% because of the possibility of multiple responses.
Source: della Porta 2009e, 31.

Table 5.3.   Strategies the Global Movement has to use in order to enhance democracy

	Practise democracy in group life	Take to the streets	Spread information to public	Promote alternative models	Contact political leaders
Most important	27.6	15.8	26.7	35.7	7.4
Second most important	18.1	15.3	31.5	27.1	10.6
Third most important	21.5	22.1	24.9	18.4	9.3
Fourth most important	22.7	30.2	13.9	13.5	13.9
Fifth most important	10.2	16.6	3.0	5.2	58.9
Total	100.0	100.0	100.0	100.0	100.0
N	1,072	1,064	1,073	1,080	1,060

Source: della Porta and Giugni 2009, 98.

strategies used by different actors, there was evidence of the use of both by a significant percentage of our groups.

At the individual level, when participants at the 4th ESF were asked to rank strategies oriented to enhance democracy according to their perceived importance (Table 5.3), the most traditional form of political participation, contacting political leaders, had the lowest level of support. While parties were criticized for their elitist conception of politics as an activity for professionals, even more than opposition to specific policy choices, the movement was praised by the activists to nurture 'a completely different model of self-representation, etc., that doesn't fit, doesn't gel with a party's way of selection from above' (in della Porta 2005, 196). The demand for politics coincided with a demand for participation against parties that were perceived as bureaucracies founded upon delegation, promoting the (wrong) idea of politics as undertaken by professionals, interested at most in electorally exploiting the movement, while still denying its political nature. In fact, respondents considered spreading information to the public to be more relevant than contacting politicians.

If the New Left in the 1970s was fascinated by a possible revolutionary seizure of power, activists in the GJM tended instead to present their action as oriented towards slow and gradual change. In this sense, one activist intervening in a focus group compared the movement to a river: 'the broader the river, the slower it flows...sometimes it even seems as if it flows underground, just because it's so broad...the movement is like water permeating and flowing everywhere, so that when it knocks the wall down it already owns the field...' (in della Porta 2005, 196). Even more, the activists stressed the importance of building alternative spheres of political engagement and discussion. They very often ranked as most relevant the practising of democracy in group life and, still more, the promotion of alternative political and social models. In the activists' perception, politics involves the search, through debates, for an emerging conception of the common good.

Although significantly better supported, the participatory option of reliance upon protest as a main means of putting pressure upon decision makers is considered as a priority (first or second option) by less than one-third of our interviewees. The movement's objective was in fact designed as oriented to 'make the world aware': in the words of one focus group participant, it 'does not have the objective of taking power, but of changing society in its relationships, in feelings, in relations with people, of building a different world; and a different world is built from below' (della Porta 2005).

These values were embedded in the dense political and social networks to which the alter-globalists belonged. The activists surveyed during the ESF had individual experiences of multiple memberships in different kinds of organizations and on different issues. The functioning of the forum allowed for the production and reproduction of specific networks and campaigns, combining the various interests and identities of participants in multiple ways. The networks in the forum emerged as dense, with a particularly high embeddedness of those activists sharing a long tradition of attention to transnational issues, nurtured in previous mobilizations on issues such as solidarity with the South and peace. A plurality of backgrounds is confirmed by data on previous involvement of participants in the ESF (Table 5.4), which indicated that about one-third of the 4th ESF participants were members of parties, unions and pacifist, international solidarity or pro-migrant right organizations; the same proportion participated in the more specifically alter-globalist local social forum and organizations against neoliberal globalization. Additionally, about one-fifth had been members of feminist, ecologist, or student organizations and around 10 per cent participated in charities, pro-unemployed and gay–lesbian–transgender groups. ESF participants were members of many organizations and on different issues: only 6 per cent of participants at the fourth edition of the ESF in Athens did not declare membership in any of the types of organizations listed; only 19 per cent were members of only two, while half of the sample declared more than four memberships and one-quarter declared seven or more.

A similar capacity for networking has been stressed for the WSF. According to the UC-Riverside survey at the WSF 2005, about 70 per

Table 5.4. *Organizational affiliations of participants in European Social Forums (Survey Data; Percentage of All Respondents)*

Type of Organization	Florence 2002	Paris 2003	Athens 2006
Students	57.4	7	20.1
Youth	n.a.	7	n.a.
Social movements	52.7	n.a.	n.a.
Voluntary associations	51.2	12 (also charity)	11.1 (also charity)
Sports	50.9	n.a.	n.a.
Environment	43.1	18	20.6
NGOs	41.5	n.a.	n.a.
Parties	34.6	18	32.2
Immigrants	33.6	12	31.4 (also anti-racist)
Social centers	32.2	5	8.2
Unions	31.9	3	25.9
Local committee	21.8	8	n.a.
Women	21.7	8	19.0
Religious	19.2	6	3.5
Homeless	n.a.	7	n.a.
International solidarity	n.a.	n.a.	31.6
Peace	n.a.	17	31.2
Human rights	n.a.	16	30.3
Humanitarian	n.a.	22	n.a.
Local social forum	n.a.	n.a.	26.9
Anti neo-liberal	n.a.	40	22.7
Consumerism/fair trade	n.a.	5	18.0
Development aid	n.a.	n.a.	16.8
LGBT	n.a.	4	7.7
Socialist	n.a.	n.a.	15.8
Communist	n.a.	n.a.	15.0
Alternative media	n.a.	n.a.	13.4
Trotskyist	n.a.	n.a.	10.2
Unemployed	n.a.	6	8.0
Peasant / farmer	n.a.	3	3.7
Anarchist	n.a.	n.a.	2.9
N	2,475–2,503	2,198	1,186–1,187

Source: For Florence, della Porta et al. 2006; Paris, Fillieuleaud Blanchard 2006; Athens, della Porta 2009b.

cent of WSF participants claimed that they were 'actively involved' in at least one social movement, while about 40 per cent were actively involved in three or more types of social movements. However, the identification with traditional ideologies is limited both in the ESF and in the WSF: in the 4th ESF, 16 per cent declared membership in socialist groups, 17 per cent in Communist, 3 per cent in anarchist (versus respectively 14 per cent, 5 per cent and 3 per cent in the WFS in 2005) (Smith et al. 2007, 63–4).

Critical self-reflection

The organizational model of the forum adopted instruments from the past, but also attempted to adapt them: it proved useful in some moments, but also showed limits that were often stigmatized by the same activists. The 'movement of movements' built itself upon a dense and rich network of movement organizations, often the product of previous protest cycles: this meant that it built upon experiences of organizational institutionalization, but also upon reflexive criticism of it. These networks of networks provided important resources, but also the challenges of maintaining open public spaces without discouraging individual participation. The presence of internal social, ideological and generational differences has stimulated the search for forms of participation that respect individual 'subjectivity', avoiding exclusive commitments and vertical control; consensus rules were privileged *vis-à-vis* majority rules; direct participation was emphasized over representative mechanisms; leaders were considered as 'speakers' or 'facilitators'. While the assembly remained one of the principal arenas of internal democracy, there was nonetheless a search for new rules (the presence of facilitators, limitation of delegation, orientation towards consensus) that could mitigate the traditional problems of direct democracy. Delegation was strongly criticized: according to the Charter of the WSF, no one is authorized to speak on its behalf (Haug et al. 2009).

In terms of building internal public spheres, the challenge was the maintenance of a deliberative form of communication as opposed to a strategic one. Innovation was visible in a value system that stressed diversity, rather than homogeneity; subjectivity, rather than obedience to the organizational demands; transparency, even at the cost of efficacy; open confrontations oriented to consensus building over decisions; contamination rather than ideological puritanism. These values have been incorporated in the social forum processes that functioned for many years, building arenas for public debates. Even though intermittently, with particular success in the stages of mobilization, the movement succeeded in the delicate task of building plural and tolerant identities. In fact, participant observation at meetings of social movement organizations linked to the GJM showed that consensus building through respect for the others were strongly supported values (della Porta and Rucht 2013).

There was, however, a gap between aspiration and reality, which activists critically noted. The ESF has been indeed an arena for debate and networking, but also a space where various conceptions of democracy have emerged and been developed. In addition to calls for a fluid, open and inclusive organizational structure, the internal debate about the implementation of conceptions of democracy was already emerging at the first ESF in Florence in 2002. The representatives of local social forums called for a 'rootedness in the territory', the creation of open assemblies and a fluid structure, stressing the importance of the non-organized (see Haug et al. 2009). By the second ESF, a main criticism addressed the role of the more 'institutional' organizations, accused of imposing a hierarchical and non-transparent structure on what was supposed to be an open and consensual process (Sommier 2005). The local social forums were particularly critical of a 'top down' approach and those critiques were instrumental in the creation of autonomous spaces (Andretta and della Porta 2009, 65).

First and foremost, some activists considered the real capacity to overcome vertical power in the social forum process as too limited. As we observed, in the ESF assemblies the differential weight of various individuals was in fact (informally) recognized, according to their reputation within a sort of 'complex representation'. There was thus 'a process of closure due to relevance of personal networks of trust and shared experience. The EPA leadership is not inaccessible, as they welcome any help and "expertise" to contribute to the process. But they welcome especially *new* expertise and because of the immense experience accumulated within the leadership group, *new* expertise is difficult to find. People who can *contribute to the process* are highly valued; but what is considered as a valuable contribution is defined by those who are already there' (Haug et al. 2009, 41).

Similarly for the WSF, the activist and sociologist Teivo Teivainen stressed that although 'it is strategically and morally desirable that movements that want to radically democratize the world apply democratic principles to themselves', 'pretending that there is no relations of power that should be made visible within the WSF process is the most harmful of these depoliticizing elements' (2004, 2–3). Although reflected in the grass-roots workshop activities, the ideal of horizontality was indeed little represented in the governing body of the WSF (Pleyers 2005, 512). The tensions between those who perceived the forum as mainly a space for exchanging ideas and networking and those who instead privileged the constitution of a unitary actor capable of political mobilization, has characterized not only the WSF, but also its European counterpart. The degree of inclusiveness of the European Preparatory Assembly, which organized the various ESF editions, was often discussed and various groups have preferred to organize autonomous spaces outside of the official forums.

The history of the social forums testifies, therefore, to the difficulties brought about by the implementation of many democratic aspirations. The ESF, like the WSF, emerged in fact as a 'contested space' (Osterweil 2004, 187) where different forms of power play a role in the preparatory process as well as in the days of the forum. In both, 'ideological differences were largely coded as disagreement over organizational process and form' (Juris 2005a, 264). Differences are especially visible in conceptions of democracy that contrast horizontal versus vertical visions. If from the normative point of view the forum stressed 'horizontality', the organizations taking part in the forum as well as the activists favour different organizational models. In various moments (especially around the 3rd edition of the ESF), tensions between a 'vertical' versus a 'horizontal' organizational vision indeed emerged. The same divisions have been noted in the WSF, where:

> The 'horizontals' favor more decentralized, loosely knit movement networks and organizations with flat, open, non-hierarchical and more directly democratic decision-making processes. They often are self conscious about prefiguring the type of society they want to create. However, they often lack mechanisms to ensure that those actually participating are accountable to, or represent the concerns of, constituents. The 'verticals', on the other hand, accept the need for hierarchy, institutionalism, professionalism and representative structures. They include larger professional NGOs, trade unions and affiliated parties. While some of these organizations, such as unions and parties, include mechanisms, such as elections or formal decision-making processes, to try to keep leaders accountable to their members or constituents, larger professional NGOs often lack these mechanisms. (Smith et al. 2007, 27–8)

These positions have been described as going beyond the preferred internal decision making, aligning along two different registers: 'Whereas one side (the horizontals) sees culture itself as a political terrain – a site where real change is effected – the other (the verticals) believes that culture, form and structure are subservient to real politics' (Osterweil 2004, 501). As Juris observed, 'the broadest convergence spaces, including the social forums, involve a complex amalgam of diverse organizational forms' (Juris 2005a, 257).

Self-reflecting on the tensions between norms and practices, the ESF organizational structure has often been reformed on such issues as the plenaries with invited speakers or the division of tasks among the national organizing committees of the various ESF editions and the EPAs. Similarly, the WSF process has also been repeatedly transformed, responding to some of the criticisms and appeals for more participatory and transparent decision making (Teivainen 2002; Smith 2004, 417, 419; Pleyers 2007, 61). The constant restructuring of the organizational format testifies to the perceived gap between norms and practices (on the ESF, see della Porta 2007; on the WSF, Smith et al. 2007). Dissatisfaction with the democratic process had an effect in terms of declining mobilization, as research on ESF participants indicated that 'activists' satisfaction in the GJM meetings is higher when they perceive that those who defend different and conflicting opinions treat each other as equals and especially when the full participation of all those who are interested is promoted' (Andretta and della Porta 2009, 83).

Since 2008, new waves of protest – for example, in schools and universities – were led by a new generation of activists that pushed forward new ideas that built upon, but also went beyond, the social forum process (Zamponi 2013). At times, however, these protests lacked the capacity to expand beyond the established social movement milieu, fuelling a debate about better mobilization strategies and practices. The failure of previous attempts to expand protests beyond the small circles of activists is stressed in Spain (Sampedro Blanco and Sánchez Duarte 2011), as well as in the United States – where, Graeber noted, following 'the idea that the organizational form that an activist group takes should embody the kind of society we wish to create, the problem was breaking these ideas out of the activist ghetto and getting them in front of a wider public' (2012, 23).

This sort of learning process through movements continued with the anti-austerity protests. Participation and deliberation are central also in the *acampada*, even though with a larger emphasis on what the *indignados* termed as direct democracy. In the *acampadas*, indeed, the horizontal vision prevailed, while the more associational model survived in other anti-austerity protests.

Democracy and organization in the anti-austerity protests

Those who protested in Tahrir, Kasbah, Sol, Syntagma or Zuccotti have not just criticized existing representative democracy as deeply corrupted, but also experimented with different models of democracy. In part, conceptions and practices of democracy were inspired by the participatory and deliberative models of previous citizens' mobilizations. In part, however, they also innovated on them, in a process of collective learning from detected weaknesses of those models in the past and adaptation to new endogenous and exogenous challenges. Accused by the centre-left parties of being apolitical and populist (not to mention without ideas) and by the Right of being radical leftists, these movements have in reality placed what Claus Offe (1985) long ago defined as the 'meta-question' of democracy at the centre of their action.

The camps as continuity and rupture

The *acampada* – at the same time forms of protest and organizational form – represented a major democratic experiment, adopted and adapted from one context to the next. If the social forums had been the democratic invention of the GJM of the previous decade, the *acampadas* represented in part an updating of those, but in part also a development oriented to overcome their perceived failures and an adaptation to changing times. Conceptions of participation from below, cherished by the progressive social movements, are in fact combined with a special attention to the creation of egalitarian and inclusive public spheres.

The anti-austerity activists' discourse on democracy is articulate and complex, taking up some of the principal criticisms of the ever-decreasing quality of liberal democracies, but also some proposals inspired by democratic qualities other than representation. These proposals resonate with (more traditional) participatory visions, but also with new deliberative conceptions that underline the importance of creating multiple public spaces, egalitarian but plural.

To a certain extent, the *acampada* can in fact be seen in continuity with the social forum model, although with increased emphasis on some democratic qualities of participation and deliberation. As we will see, the very space where a camp is set is open to all, to enforce the public and transparent nature of the process. Meeting in public spaces is also a way to stress the inclusiveness of the process and the refusal of delegates represents a further emphasis upon equality. The method of consensus is oriented towards establishing the basis of good communication that could achieve a synthesis of diverse opinions, finding solutions oriented to the public good. Some differences emerge, however, between this conception – of real, direct, or radical democracy – and the democracy of the GJM.

As I will argue, while the social forums mixed both associational and open participatory (assembly based) forms, with an emphasis on consensus, the *acampadas* refused associations privileging the participation of the person – the citizen, the member of the community. From the relational point of view, whereas the social forum process was oriented to networking, the *acampadas* follow a more aggregative logic (Juris 2012). From the cognitive point of view, while the forum aimed at building political alternatives, the *acampadas* were more prefigurative. These differences are in part the product of learning processes, after a perceived decline in the innovative capacity of the social forum process. However, they also reflect adaptation to a context characterized by a legitimacy crisis of late neoliberalism and by its social and political consequences, but also to national opportunities and constraints. In fact, referring to existing research on Tahrir Square, Puerta del Sol and Place de Cataluna, Syntagma Square, Zuccotti Park (but also to the failed *acampadas* in Italy), I will single out in what follows many similarities but also some differences.

The social forums have been an innovative experiment promoted by the GJM. Distinct from a counter-summit, which is mainly oriented towards public protest, the social forum is a space of debate among activists. The format of the social forum epitomized the cognitive processes that developed within protest events as arenas for encounters. The charter of the WSF defines it as an 'open meeting place', as participation is indeed open to all civil society groups, with the exception of those advocating racist ideas and those using terrorist means, as well as political parties. Its functioning involves the organization of hundreds of workshops and dozens of conferences (with invited experts) during a very short span of time and testifies to the importance given (at least in principle) to the production and exchange of knowledge. In fact, the WSF has been defined as 'a market place for (sometimes competing) causes and an "ideas fair" for exchanging information, ideas and experiences horizontally' (Schoenleitner 2003, 140). Writing on the ESF in Paris, the sociologists Agrikoliansky and Cardon (2005, 47) noted that it 'does not indeed resemble anything already clearly identified. It is not really a conference, even if we find a programme, debates and paper-givers. It is not a congress, even if there are tribunes, militants and mots d'ordre. It is not just a demonstration, even if there are marches, occupations and demonstrations in the street. It is neither a political festival, even if we find stands, leaflets and recreational activities. The social forums concentrate in a unit of time and space such a large diversity of forms of commitment that exhaustive participation in all of them is impossible.'

These different activities converged on the aim of providing a meeting space for the loosely coupled, huge number of groups in order to lay the groundwork for a broader mutual understanding. Far from aiming at eliminating differences, the open debates were designed to increase awareness of each other's concerns and beliefs. The purpose of networking-through-debating was in fact openly stated as early as the first ESF in Florence, where the Declaration of the European social movements read: 'We have come together to strengthen and enlarge our alliances because the construction of another Europe and another world is now urgent...' (della Porta 2009a).

In the GJM, diversity and transparency in the forum were highly valued, but difficult to practise. If the organizational process of social forums wanted to be open, in reality at the global level some main associations, as mentioned, tended to dominate decision making. In Europe, the preparatory assemblies were open to all participants, but still held in closed places. With the occupation of the public squares, the *indignados* movements stressed even more the open and transparent nature of their democratic model, as the very essence of parks and squares is their being public, open spaces. Not only were Tahrir, Kasba, Puerta del Sol and Syntagma open air spaces, but they were also most important points of encounters for the citizens. Keeping the main site of protest in the open, the movements also put a special emphasis on the inclusivity of the process, aiming at involving the entire agora.

So, in Egypt, in a society characterized by gated communities for the rich and slums for the masses of poor, the encounters at Tahrir but also the painting of murals represented a reappropriation of the public space, especially after thirty years of emergency law had prevented gatherings (Winegard 2012). A member of a citizens' committee thus described the spirit of the camp the protesters built there: 'I cannot describe my joy...we were waiting for something to happen but never expected that it would be a revolution of this sort. It surprised us as much as it surprised the world. And it was not just what happened in Tahrir Square: in every village and in every hamlet of every village was another square like Tahrir' (cit. in Abu-Lughod 2012, 25). The heterogeneity of the participants was mentioned with pride – 'people of different backgrounds, of different classes, just sitting together talking' (Gerbaudo 2012, 69).

Direct democracy was often called for. In Spain, the assemblies in the encampments were described by activists as 'primarily a massive, transparent exercise in direct democracy'. The *acampadas* were to reconstruct a public sphere in which problems could be discussed and solutions looked for. So, an American activist defined Zuccotti Park as 'a sort of beautiful, exciting thing, which does not happen in public space in New York. Public space here is not really utilized in the way that it is utilized in the rest of the world.' She recounts one of the first evenings spent in Zuccotti Park: 'there were people who maybe they were there supporting like a union, or there were people who were there with signs saying they were professors...we just stayed there and talked, it was a beautiful fall night...and we stayed there on an edge of the park...and sort of just listened to other people's conversations and there were a lot of debates...It was like a spirit, something that had life in it and it was really reaffirming' (Gerbaudo 2012, 122–3).

The general assemblies as main institutions of the *acampada* testified to an inclusive effort. In the social forum process, the assemblies were important but somehow separated from the forum itself through the formula of the 'social movement assemblies', usually held after the forums. In the forum itself, the main structuration was around workshops, where activists exchanged information and networked, rather than properly deciding. Consensual methods were adopted by several (but not all) organizations of the forum process in their internal decision making, but they were actually practised in different ways by different groups (della Porta 2009b).

In the *indignados* movement, the assemblies took instead a central role for the elaboration of strategic and tactical decisions for the movement: from the creation of a general programme, either specific claims or at least statements of intent, but even more for the everyday management of the camps. Through inclusivity and respect for the opinions of the others, a collective thought is expected to emerge. In Spain, on the model of the one in Puerta del Sol, all general assemblies in Madrid neighbourhoods worked as spaces that had to be 'transparent, horizontal, where all persons can participate in an equal way' (Nez 2012, 84).[16] Inclusion, absolute and of all, was a main principle – as 'the aim is to promote in all movement assemblies a transparent and horizontal way of functioning that would allow to each person to participate on an equal foot' (Nez 2011a). General assemblies often broke down into committees, which then reconvened within them. In Spain, the spokes of the various commissions referred to the general assemblies. Commissions on topics such as communication, mutual respect, infrastructure, laws and action coordinated working groups that worked through consensus. Liaison persons had to keep contacts between the various subgroups (Botella-Ordinas 2011). Thousands of propositions were thus put forward and in part approved by consensus: on politics, economy, ecology, education.

In the United States as in Spain, 'each camp quickly developed a few core institutions: if it was any size, at least there would be a free kitchen, medical tent, library, media/communication, center where activists would cluster together with laptops and information center for visitors and new arrivals' (Graeber 2012, 240). The importance of an inclusive communication process is well illustrated by the people's-mic, developed in OWS, at first as a tactical solution to power cuts but ultimately becoming an instrument of improved, horizontal communication. So, the practice and its meaning is reported by activists:

> ...at the center of this movement are general assemblies, where decisions are made by consensus. Facilitators are charged with managing the process so that all have a chance to be heard and everyone has a chance to express approval, disapproval, or to block consensus by means of hand signals. The use of the people's microphone is a central feature of the general assemblies. To use the people's mic, a person first grabs the attention of the crowd by shouting, 'Mic check!' Then, he or she begins to speak, saying a few words at a time, so that others can shout the words on to those behind them in the crowd. Originally developed as a way to circumvent bans on amplification at many occupation sites, the people's mic has developed into much more than that. It encourages deeper listening, because audience members must actively repeat the language of the speaker. It encourages consensus because hearing oneself repeat a point of view one doesn't agree with has a way of opening one's mind. And it provides a great example of how community organizing works best when it's people-powered and resilient. This technique allows crowds of thousands to communicate and also allows groups involved in direct street action to make democratic decisions on the fly. The occupation zones are not just places to talk about a new society. They are becoming twenty-four-hour-a-day experiments in egalitarian living. (van Gelder et al. 2011, 8)

Another main democratic formula, coming from the GJM but further elaborated in the anti-austerity protests, is the consensual method. In Spain, consensual deliberative methods are promoted especially by the young activists of the autonomous squatted centers and anarchist groupings. While in previous movements direct democracy through consensus had been experimented with in spokes-councils, during the *acampadas* it was applied to the general assemblies, involving often hundreds of thousands of people. The aim was, according to a Spanish activist, to 'try to convince the other and if the other disagree, develop the discussion in a constructive way' (Nez 2011a). Consensual methods were similarly elaborated in the Occupy movement in the United States, where a horizontal decision-making process developed – sponsored by the younger generations (which had, by two-thirds, voted for Obama) – based on the continuous formation of small groups, which then reconvened in the larger assembly. According to David Graeber, 'The process towards creative thinking is really the essence of the thing' (Graeber 2012, 23).

Deliberation was in fact seen as an instrument against bureaucratization, but also against the routinization of the assembly and a way to build a community. While the GJM used street parties, with puppets and a carnival-like atmosphere, it was noted that 'OWS, in contrast, is not a party, it's a community' (Graeber 2012, 240). It is said to have 'created a crisis of legitimacy within the entire system by providing a glimpse of what real democracy might be like' (Graeber 2012, xvii). In Sol, participants presented themselves as persons who came in a free and voluntary way to claim dignity and social and political consciousness: 'We do not represent any party or associations. What unites us is a desire of change' (Nez 2011a).

Inclusivity does not mean that assemblies were not regulated: just the opposite. Building upon the experimentations in the 'horizontal' side of the GJM, the *indignados* further developed rules that had to implement equality and inclusivity. In Spain, rules in the assemblies included limits on times for talking, hand gestures, rotating speakers, the preparation of *compte rendus* (read at the next assembly meeting). A commission on conflicts, managed by students, used techniques of psychology and group dynamics. Organizers also developed special techniques for assemblies; for example, participants were arranged in semicircles, with corridors that allowed them to move around, with mediators and so on. In Occupy Wall Street, following the principle of direct democracy, 'everyone affected by a project should have a say in how it is conducted' (Graeber 2012, 230). Following horizontal practices, anyone could call for a working group; people then divided into small circles, coming back together after some time, with a speaker reporting on the debate in each group. There was moreover also the acknowledgement that 'consensus process only works if it is combined with a principle of decentralization' (Graeber 2012, 227) and 'decisions should be made on the smallest scale, the lowest level, possible' (Graeber 2012, 229). In the United States, instead of voting up or down on a controversial proposal, groups that made decisions by consensus worked to refine them until everyone found a solution acceptable (Taylor et al. 2011, 47).

Participation and protest were seen as transformative, as a means of living out 'real' democracy. The Italian Revolution or Indignati group so sums up the idea, stating that 'doing the thing that you wish to say is the best way of saying it. In this case, thousands of citizens are calling for democracy by practicing it in the first person in the square and sharing this practice with thousands of others who feel the same need' (see della Porta et al. 2014).[17]

The functioning of democracy: prefiguring a different society

The more or less permanent occupations of squares were thus seen as creating a new agora in publicly owned spaces ('Because the squares belong to us and they are locations of a new communitarian and participatory democracy')[18] and experiments with new forms of democracy as a way to address problems of representative democracy all the way up to the global level (della Porta 2014b). In Spain, the assemblies in the encampments were described by activists as 'primarily a massive, transparent exercise in direct democracy'. So, they declared, 'We feel part of the movement because we contribute to creating it, spreading it, growing it' (@galapita and @hibai 2011, cited in Postill 2012).

Cognitive, affective and relational mechanisms developed during the protests – especially during most intense moments such as the *acampadas*.

The cognitive mechanisms

Similarly to the social forum, the *acampadas* have been sites of contention, but also of exchange of information, reciprocal learning, individual socialization and knowledge building. Cognitive mechanisms of frame bridging were very important in the social forum process. During the forums themselves, but also during their preparation – sometimes up to a year long – a most important aim was the sharing of knowledge by activists from different countries, groups, ages and so on. In this process, alternative visions were built about globalization, Europeanization, the development of capitalism. Knowledge was exchanged mainly among activists and in many cases exchanges were facilitated by associations of various types. In the *acampadas*, the cognitive function was central, but its production extended – so to speak – from the activists to the citizens. The aim was often stated as building a community.

With the creation of a protest camp, Tahrir Square became the heart of the mobilization in Egypt, 'participants ranging from Cairo's poor to middle and upper-class people, across the political spectrum, as well as across religious divides' (Warkotsch 2012). Slogans were shouted such as 'bread, freedom and dignity', as well as 'the people want the removal of the regime' and bystanders were called to join in. Cognitive processes were indeed very important, as 'Tahrir was not all fun and festivity. The space was also infused with serious politics: fierce battles were waged against government thugs trying to break in, fiery speeches were delivered denouncing the regime and animated discussions about Egypt's political future resounded in the night air' (Shokr 2012, 43). Debates developed in the many Tahrir squares that were built all over Egypt, where there was an atmosphere of permanent parties ('like a night of Ramadan') but also political speeches. There was talk of the old Egypt and frequent ironic references to the revolution (revolutionary eating, revolutionary hunger, revolutionary joints).

Cognitive mechanisms were even more explicitly reflected upon as Tahrir spread to Europe and the United States. While the forums had been described as sort of universities, where abstract knowledge was embedded in specific contexts, the *acampadas* privileged the personal knowledge of the individual participants and their direct experiences.

In Spain, as it organized assemblies in the streets and the squares, the 15M introduced a political logic in this space (Pestaña Moreno 2013), thus allowing new people to learn new skills. Assemblies aimed at mobilizing the common people, not (just) activists but communities of persons, with personalized hand-made placards and individualized messages. As an activist noted, 'What unites us are problems and ways of thinking that are common to many people in a very transversal way...we want to begin with concrete problem, not ideologies' (Perugorría and Tejerina 2013, 435). The squares become spaces for intense cognitive exchanges among people who were previously strangers to each other. Postill (2012) vividly recalls, 'the strong sense of connection to the strangers I spoke to during that fleeting moment...Under normal circumstances – say, on an underground train – we would have found no reason to talk to one another, but the present situation was anything but normal. The 15-M movement had brought us together and the sense of "contextual fellowship"...cutting across divides of age, class and race was very powerful.'

Consensus was in fact defined as based on a specific cognitive process, which wants to be first of all inclusive and respectful of people's individual experiences. As Graeber (2012, 2011) noted about OWS, 'anyone who feels they have something relevant to say about a proposal ought to have their perspectives carefully considered. Everyone who has strong concerns or objections should have those concerns or objections taken into account and, if possible, addressed in the final form of the proposal. Anyone who feels a proposal violates a fundamental principle shared by the group should have the opportunity to veto ("block") the proposal.' So, after someone made a proposal, the facilitator, after asking for clarifying questions, started to look for consensus. This process foresaw friendly amendments, 'temperature checks' (to ensure that the atmosphere remains relaxed) and hand signals (Graeber 2012, 214–15).

Consensus was thus assigned a deep meaning as capable of developing a truly collective thought, as very different from the sum of individual ideas. In Spain, the *Rapide guide for the dynamization of the popular assemblies* thus explained: 'Two people with different ideas put their energy together to construct something. It is not a question of my idea or yours. It is the two ideas together that will build something new that before neither of us knew. It is for this reason that an attentive listening, during which we are not just busy preparing our answer, is necessary. The collective thought is born when we understand that all opinions, ours and the different ones, are necessary in order to form consensus' (*toma la plaza*, 31/5/2011, cit. in Romanos 2011). So, 'To take the square is not just an occupation as the others but an act that locates at the center of the public space the experimentation with a participatory and deliberative decision making' (Romanos 2011).

The emotional mechanisms

Cognition must not be separated from emotion (Goodwin et al. 2001). Camps are places of talking and listening, where however the building of collective identities is sustained through the development of strong emotions. While the social forum process was also fed by the intense moments of transnational encounters, as the GJM activist Naomi Klein herself observed, the stationary nature of the camps help in building longer-lasting relations. So, the GJM had chosen summits as targets and 'summits are transient by their nature; they only last a week. That made us transient too. We'd appear, grab world headlines and disappear' (van Gelder et al. 2011, 46). In contrast, she noted, *acampadas* put no end to their presence and 'this is wise. Only when you stay put can you grow roots' (van Gelder et al. 2011). Emotions were particularly strong in Egypt, given the danger of the action and the dimension of the change; but they seem to have been more reflected upon in OWS, where the political culture of the activists most involved in the camp was more oriented to address individual feelings.

Emotional charge was mentioned about the camps in Tahrir, whose establishment on 28 January 2011 was said to represent an acceleration of history, with a cognitive shift from a language of demonstration to a language of revolution (El Chazli 2012). So an activist reminded us that, while there, 'We had no idea that the world was following us, we had no idea of what the media was saying, what the TV was saying, what Al-Jazeera was reporting, what the people in the streets were doing...we were living in another dimension' (in Gerbaudo 2012, 69). Another recalled, 'It was one of the most profound moments of my life. The sight of the square filled with tens of thousands heralded the long-awaited dawn. As we entered the square, the crowds installed there cheered the coming of a new battalion, greeting us with joy. I wept' (cited in El-Ghobashy 2011). Tahrir has been described as 'the square that sings, dances, cries and hopes' (Guibal and Tangi 2011, 39), as 'Tahir vibre, Tahir exulte' (Guibal and Tangi 2011, 40), a quasi-utopian community with a noble ethics of solidarity (Holmes 2012, 405–6). The protests were presented as part of a moment of epiphany: as a 'truly historical moment', a 'revolutionary moment' – in the words of an activist, 'everybody understood that it was, in fact, a moment' (Nigam 2012, 54).

In Spain, as elsewhere, activists talked of the joy of being together, developing a narrative of becoming (Perugorría and Tejerina 2013, 437). Open public spaces in fact facilitated the creation of intense ties, through encounters among diverse people who suddenly felt they shared a common belonging. Positive emotions develop: participants in the camps 'later reported a range of psychosomatic reactions such as goose bumps (*carne de gallina*) or tears of joy. I felt as if a switch had been turned on, a gestalt switch and I had now awakened to a new political reality. I was no longer merely a participant observer of the movement, I was the movement' (Postill 2012). In the same vein, in this Spanish activist's recollection, the encounters of so many and so different people produced an intense atmosphere of expectation: 'When I arrived to Calle de Alcalá and I saw all the people there I was very happy. And to see that there were so many people of different age and to see that it was growing and to see that we were a lot...and now that I am telling you this I get goosebumps...really I was so happy. When we arrived to Puerta del Sol, people started sticking big posters on the buildings. People who were there were so unbelievably happy.'

Emotionally charged, participation was then not a cost, but a reward in itself. In Spain, 'The square in central Madrid was turned in an "acampada", a protest camp, which also, thanks to the intense social media messaging radiating from it, came to act as an almost irresistible *magnetic gathering* or *trending place* for the thousands of Spaniards who would flock there in the following days' (Gerbaudo 2012, 91–2). Similarly in the United States, the activities in the OWS are defined by participants as energizing, inspiring, producing 'tears of inspiration. I did not know that popular power could bring with it such an overwhelming sensation. It is a chill...a tremble that is both incredibly powerful...and also a little scary, feeling how much power we can actually have together, side by side' (Taylor et al. 2011, 31).

The relational mechanisms

Both cognitive and affective mechanisms are embedded into networks of relations. As mentioned, the social forums constituted an organizational format aiming at building and consolidating large (and loose) organizational networks. While to a certain extent prefigurative in their nurturing of values of plurality and tolerance, the forums had a very strong orientation towards externally oriented action.

Camps are spaces to express protest, but even more to prefigure new relations. Here, however, the latter aim seems to predominate. Differently from the very temporary global convergence spaces of the social forums, the *acampadas* are 'rather occupation and subversion of prominent urban public spaces' (Halvorsen 2012, 431). As an activist wrote, 'democracy starts with people caring about one another and acting responsibly on that sense of care, taking responsibility both for oneself and for one's family, community, country, people in general and the planet' (Langman 2013). While a strategic view tended to dominate in Tahrir, the prefigurative dimension was more emphasized in the OWS, with the Spanish and Greek *indignados* somewhere in between.

The prefiguration of different relations was important for those who camped in Tahrir. This concern developed during the occupation, as 'when protesters arrived at Tahrir on 29 January, they did not come with the intention of creating a radical utopia...In many ways, Tahrir had come to represent the overall decline of public space – people could barely congregate or mingle, let alone protest – under Mubarak's thirty-year rule. The commune that Tahrir was to become was wholly improvised through the lived experience of sharing the area and protecting it from the regime encroachment. As the revolution unfolded, Tahrir was elevated from a rally site to a model for an alternative society' (Shokr 2012, 42).

Also in Spain, Greece and the United States, in their discontent with mainstream politics, the *indignados* saw the *acampadas* as experimentation with another form of democracy, nurtured by different interpersonal relations. Spanish activists declared that 'With 15M we have recovered that part of person who wants to share, a part we had long forgotten.' The *acampadas* are therefore not just ludic rendez vous, but rather the building of 'cities in the city', with their own sets of fluid relations. As activists noted, 'we recovered and utilize the public space; we occupied the squares and the streets of our cities to meet and work in a collective open and visible way. We inform and invite every citizen to participate. We debate problems, look for solution and organize actions and mobilizations. Our digital tools and networks are open: all the information is available on the Internet, in the streets, in the squares' (15M manifesto, 'How to cook a nonviolent revolution', cit. in Perugorría and Tejerina 2013, 436).

Similarly, American activists stress the prefigurative value of the camps: 'What they want...is to do exactly what they are doing. They want to occupy Wall Street. They have built a campsite full of life, where power is exercised according to their voices...they are practicing the politics of space, the politics of building a truly public space....It has become many things. Public square. Carnival. Place to get news. Daycare center. Health care center. Concert venue. Library. Performance space. School' (cit. in Castañeda 2012). When Occupy Wall Street started in the United States, quickly spreading in thousands of American cities, the occupations represented not only occasions to protest but also experimentations with participatory and deliberative forms of democracy in the everyday life. In the OWS, decisions about how to spend the relevant sums donated and how to manage the camp took much time. In Zuccotti, opposition to the wasting of people resources and the call for respect, sobriety and cooperation was also expressed in posters such as 'Keep it clean. This plaza and the flowers are important for the community' (Liboiron 2012, 386). Describing Occupy Boston and citing an activist who talked about the 'small slice of utopia we are creating', Juris (2012, 268) singled out some tactical, incubating and infrastructural roles of the occupied free spaces: among the first were attracting media attention and inspiring participation; among the second, 'providing a space for grassroots participatory democracy; ritual and community building, strategizing and action planning, public education and prefiguring alternative worlds that embody movement visions'; among the third, networking and coordination.

Differently from the movements of the previous decades, which had used a varied and plural repertoire, the *acampadas* became much entrenched with the very identity of the movement, not just, as in occupations for other social movements, an action form among others. Beyond the prefiguration of a different society, which the activists already imagined, these spaces, as Razsa and Kurnik (2012) noted, were also important in the invention of alternative, but not yet imagined, futures, through what has been called a 'politics of becoming'. In the Occupy movement they studied in Slovenia, the encounters of diverse minorities transformed their visions. Occupied spaces have been seen, in fact, as 'vibrant sites of human interaction that modelled alternative communities and generated intense feeling of solidarity' (Juris 2012, 268). Aims included 'engaging in direct and transparent participatory democracy, exercising personal and collective responsibility...

empowering one another against all forms of oppression' (van Gelder et al. 2011, 25).

With more emphasis than in the social forums, what is considered as important is the process, even more than the outcome. In the United States, 'the encampments were consistently unwilling to make the effort to coalesce around what would conventionally be called demands and programmes. Instead, what they seemed to relish most was themselves: their community and esprit, their direct democracy, the joy of becoming transformed into a movement, a presence, a phenomenon that was known to strangers and discovering with delight just how much energy they had liberated. For indeed, in a matter of days, their sparks had ignited a fire' (Gitlin 2012, 29).

Empowerment thus goes through the development of space where the creativity of a normal people can be developed. A primer on the NC General Assembly website explains, 'Consensus is a creative thinking process: When we vote, we decide between two alternatives. With consensus, we take an issue, hear the range of enthusiasm, ideas and concerns about it and synthesize a proposal that best serves everybody's vision' (Taylor et al. 2011, 47.). In fact, 'Consensus at its best offers a cooperative model of reaching group unity, an essential step in creating a culture that values cooperation over competition' (Taylor et al. 2011, 47). Through these practices, the movement aimed at changing things by presenting a new narrative, offering everyone a chance to create something, proposing an 'ethic and practice of deep democracy and community'. In the hopes of the activists, 'Patient decision making translate into wisdom and common commitment when everyone is heard. Occupy sites are communities where anyone can discuss grievances, hopes and dreams in an atmosphere of mutual support' (Taylor et al. 2011, 13).

Beyond *acampadas*: still networked activists?

In addition to the *acampadas*, protests took different forms involving different actors. In fact, mobilization of various types, as mentioned, existed before and, especially, after the camps. Workers and users of public services organized together to oppose public budget cuts to basic rights such as health or education. Groups organized self-help and advocacy at the local level, providing material support to the victims of the economic crisis. New political parties emerged to bring the movement claims inside institutions. Referenda were organized to oppose privatization of the commons.

As in the GJM, the repertoire of action was in fact broad. The protesters we interviewed stressed their experiences with different forms of

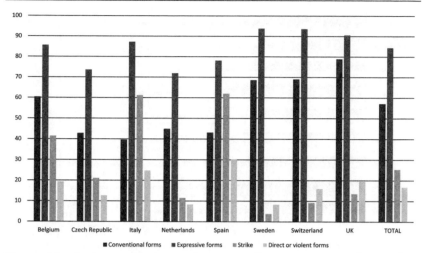

Figure 5.1   Action repertoires and country (Percentage responding 'I have done it')
Conventional forms = contacted politician/donated money; expressive forms = boycott/bought products/bought badge/sticker
Legend: ETA (values by repertoire) respectively, .29***; .23***; .49***; .19***

political participation, from conventional to unconventional. As the data from surveys indicate (Figure 5.1), however, there are also some cross-national differences in terms of experiences with action repertoires. In fact, while conventional and expressive forms are more widespread among protesters in the United Kingdom, Switzerland and Sweden, experiences with strikes are much more common in Belgium and especially in Italy and Spain (more than 60 per cent in both cases) – but much less so in Sweden, Switzerland, the Netherlands and the United Kingdom, where it remains below 15 per cent (even just 4 per cent in Sweden). In parallel, in the Southern European countries, direct action is more frequent, with up to 30 per cent in Spain and 25 per cent in Italy, against an average of 17 per cent (and just 8 per cent in Sweden or the Netherlands). More disruptive forms of protest are, that is, more widespread where the crisis of neoliberal capitalism hit harder.

Protesters also emerge as well networked (Figure 5.2), with – reflecting general trends in the population – less frequent organizational membership in Spain and Italy as well as in the Czech Republic. Differences are particularly impressive as far as party membership is concerned: around 20 per cent in the countries more hit by the financial crisis and instead

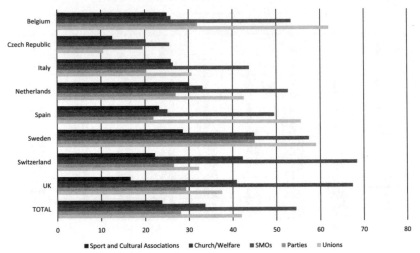

Figure 5.2   Membership in types of organizations, by country (%)
Cr. V, respectively, .29***; .16***; .23***; .17***; .13***

up to 45 per cent in Sweden. Union membership also varies cross-country, but with no clear relation with the socio-economic conditions, as unionized participants are more frequent in Belgium, Sweden and Spain and less in the Czech Republic and Italy, but also in Switzerland (where SMOs are instead over-represented).

The surveys at marches in Italy point to the variety of not only social but also political groups involved in the protests, as well as at their location in complex networks, allowing us to observe differences among different protests. The protesters we have surveyed are first of all endowed with previous experiences in protest participation and are well embedded in networks of associations. While the protests without a doubt involved also firstcomers, most protesters have frequent experiences of participation in protest, in the last twelve months as well as in general (Figure 5.3). They are not atomized citizens, but rather endowed with multiple memberships in various types of associations (Figure 5.4). Types of membership vary however by demonstrations. So, union membership is more common at labour protests (with the exception of the Euromayday, where participation in unions is half that of the Labour Day marches and participation in social movement organizations is twice as much). Church/welfare memberships are more common at peace and anti-mafia demonstrations – participation in social movement

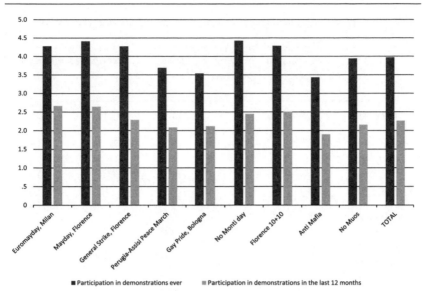

Figure 5.3   Participation in past demonstrations (ever and in the last 12 months)
(Likert 1 (never) – 5 (more than 21), means)

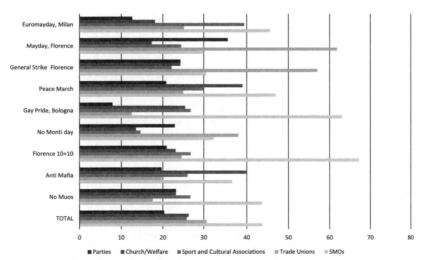

Figure 5.4   Organizational membership (active and passive) by type of demon-stration in Italy 2011–2013 (%)

Table 5.5. Forms of participant action by type of demonstration in Italy, 2011–2013 (%)

	Expressive forms	Signing a petition	Strike	Conventional forms	Direct or violent forms
Euromayday, Milan	93.7	87.4	55.9	27.6	33.9
Mayday, Florence	73.6	74.5	70.9	45.5	12.7
General Strike, Florence	87.0	75.8	91.8	40.3	16.0
Perugia-Assisi Peace March	89.9	83.3	54.7	30.2	16.7
Gay Pride, Bologna	88.7	78.8	50.0	35.8	25.0
No Monti day	87.8	87.3	73.0	44.4	33.9
Florence 10+10	93.1	94.6	66.9	61.5	41.5
Anti Mafia	89.6	74.6	39.3	37.8	15.9
No Muos	84.2	84.2	53.2	47.5	41.7
TOTAL	88.0	81.7	61.7	39.9	24.9
Cr. V	.14***	.16***	.32***	.18***	.24***

Conventional forms = contacted politician/donated money; expressive forms = boycott/bought products/bought badge/sticker

organizations is very widespread and even membership in parties was reported by one protester out of five (with the exception of the LGTBQ parade). Moreover, protesters have broad experiences with various forms of unconventional participation: strikes, but also direct action (direct action especially in the Euromayday, where strikes and conventional forms are lower) – particularly among those who participate in the anti-austerity protests (Table 5.5).

Participants' conceptions of politics are also expressed in their motivations for collective mobilization. Overall, the defence of interests tends to come last, while raising awareness is the dominant motivation, followed by the expression of solidarity and of one's own views. Pressing politicians and moral obligations come only after (with a slight preference for interest expression in protests on labour issues and for expression of moral obligation in peace protests and antimafia demonstrations) (Table 5.6).

Concluding, even in the context of neoliberalism and its crisis, participation in protest marches is facilitated by existing networks of different types as well as previous experiences with contentious politics.

Table 5.6. Motives for participation by type of demonstration (Likert 1–5, means)

	Defend interest	Express view	Press politicians	Raise awareness	Express solidarity	Moral obligation
Euromayday, Milan	3.5763	4.3525	3.8934	4.5410	4.5081	2.8417
Mayday, Florence	3.2338	4.4096	4.3085	4.5843	4.6344	3.3614
General Strike, Florence	3.6564	4.4569	4.4524	4.6256	4.5101	3.3958
Perugia-Assisi Peace March	2.2311	4.4681	4.3109	4.7339	4.5943	3.9234
Gay Pride, Bologna	3.6779	4.4218	4.3774	4.7934	4.4057	3.3158
No Monti day	3.6905	4.4419	4.0175	4.6944	4.3210	3.9639
Florence 10+10	3.1504	3.8407	3.7672	4.3689	4.2672	3.4831
Anti Mafia	3.0389	4.2527	4.3854	4.7538	4.6186	3.9362
No Muos	3.8739	4.3871	4.4361	4.6154	4.4640	3.9672
TOTAL	3.3137	4.3597	4.2507	4.6612	4.4871	3.6148
Cr. V	.377***	.210***	.225***	.180***	.150***	.268***

Communicating beyond the squares

New *technologies* have been considered as linked to emerging organizational forms, not only as an enhancing instrument of protest, but also as capable of shaping the organizational format through their influence on the culture of participation. In general, social media (and new digital technologies in general) are expected to change participation in protest, as they make protesting less risky and help in forming and joining groups; but they are also less capable of producing strong bonds of solidarity (Polletta et al. 2013, 19). While even virtual collective identity seems able to mobilize, digital technologies tend to facilitate especially some limited forms of commitment such as consumption-based forms of sociability rather than more political forms of commitment (Polletta et al. 2013, 30). In fact, personalization of politics has been linked to different organizational models, in particular through the use of digital media that allow for very light mobilizing structures. As Lance Bennett and Alexandra Segerberg (2013) observed, personalized politics is not necessarily ineffective or disorganized, but can be organized in different ways. In particular, connective action can be activated when 'interpersonal networks are enabled by technological platforms of various designs that coordinate and scale the networks' (Bennett and Segerberg 2013, 35). In fact, 'in place of content that is distributed and relationships that are brokered by hierarchical organizations, *connective action* networks involve co-production and co-distribution, revealing a different economic and psychological logic: peer production and sharing based on personalized expression' (Bennett and Segerberg 2013, 35, italics mine). In this vein, connective action can be organizationally enabled, when loose networks of organizations sponsor it, or crowd-enabled, with 'dense, fine grained networks of individuals in which digital media platforms are the most visible and integrative organizational mechanisms' (Bennett and Segerberg 2013, 13). In this sense, communication does not only serve to exchange information but rather 'communication routines can, under some conditions, create patterned relationships among people that lend organization and structure to many aspects of social life' (Bennett and Segerberg 2013, 8). While in the past organizations had played a main role in mobilizing into collective action, new forms of connective action, based on digital media, allow 'individuals to find personally comfortable ways to engage with issues on- and off-line' (Bennett and Segerberg 2013, 145). Spread through the social media, personalized messages (or easily personalized ideas) emerge as persuasive. So, especially the more spontaneous crowd-enabled networks are particularly efficacious in resource allocation, allowing for both short-term and long-term adaptation to changing environments (Bennett and Segerberg 2013, 8).

While the research on the GJM focused on its use of new technologies such as websites or mailing lists (della Porta and Mosca 2009; della Porta 2011), most recent studies of the wave of protest that started with the Arab Spring paid particular attention to the social media and their effects on conceptions and practices of democracy. The Arab Spring has in fact been defined as characterized by 'the instrumental use of social media, especially Facebook, Twitter, YouTube and text messaging by protesters, to bring about political change and democratic transformation' (Khamis and Vaughn 2011, 1). New media facilitated the development of free spaces, networking, planning. They allowed 'citizen journalists' to document the protest activity as well as denouncing police repression. As an activist declared, 'To have a space, an online space, to write and talk [to] people, to give them messages which will increase their anger, this is my favorite way of online activism. This is the way online activism contributed to the revolution. When you asked people to go and demonstrate against the police, they were ready because you had already provided them with materials which made them angry' (in Aouraght and Alexander 2011).

The role of new media was particularly relevant before and during the Egyptian uprising, when they enabled 'cyberactivism, which was a major trigger for street activism; encouraging civic engagement, through aiding the mobilization and organization of protests and other forms of political expression; and promoting a new form of citizen journalism, which provides a platform for ordinary citizens to express themselves and document their own versions of reality' (Khamis and Vaughn 2011). Different new media were used in different ways. Facebook allowed for spreading information from (virtual) friend to (virtual) friend, as it enables participants to send messages to thousands of people, 'with the added benefit that those receiving the messages were already interested and trusted the source' (Idle and Nunns, 2011, 20). The blogging service Twitter (with 175 million registered users in 2010) allowed participants to post their comments and 'tweet' about specific subjects, including hashtags (such as #Jan25 for Egypt or #sidibouzid for Tunisia) that permitted users to launch as well as to follow protest events. In the very first week of the protest, as many as 1.5 million Egypt-related tweets have been counted (Aouraght and Alexander 2011), in many cases allowing for contacts between activists and foreign journalists (Lotan et al. 2011). Digitally encoded video, audio, or text were uploaded on the Internet and were aggregated by topic and by type. For instance, You Tube allowed users to upload user-created content, among them self-made videos. Thanks to the combination of old and new communication techniques, communication overcame borders, as the Egyptian activists received support from a flow of information coming from abroad as well as influencing the public opinion at a transnational level, as Western media used activists' social media in their coverage of the events (della Porta 2013a).

Influenced by the Arab Spring, the protest of the Spanish *indignados* was also highly mediated. Not by chance, at its origin was the *No Les Votes* (Don't Vote For Them) campaign, which asked citizens not to vote for any of the three major parties responsible for a hotly contested bill accused of curtailing copyright infringement on Internet users and attacking digital freedom in favour of media lobbies (as documents published by Wikileaks confirmed). Network organizations emerged during this campaign, among them Youth Without a Future (*Juventud Sin Futuro*) and Real Democracy Now! (*Democracia Real Ya!* DRY), which later promoted the mobilization in 2011 (Flesher Fominaya 2014, 169). Following its roots in campaigns on media rights, the Spanish movement of the *indignados* showed high skills in the use of new technologies. As Postill (2012) well described: 'The key role played in the inception and coordination of the movement by hackers, bloggers, micro-bloggers, technopreneurs and online activists is hard to overestimate.' In fact, 'What is striking about 15-M nanostories is how successfully leading activists used Twitter in the build-up towards the 15 May protests across Spain. By means of Twitter hashtags such as #15M or #15mani (#15mdemo), DRY [Democracia Real Ya] supporters were able not only to rally protesters at short notice but also to set the changing political and emotional tone of the campaign.' In the words of two activists: '[T]he direction (el sentit) is created mostly on Twitter. Hashtags serve not only to organise the debate but also to set the collective mood: #wearenotgoing, #wearenotafraid, #fearlessbcn, #awakenedbarrios, #puigresignation, #15mmarcheson #closetheparliament' (in Postill 2012). In fact, 'The nanostories being shared about specific protests or power abuses may be short-lived, but over time they add up to a powerful sense of common purpose among hundreds of thousands of people. Together, they form a grand narrative of popular struggle against a corrupt political and economic order.'

It was also through Twitter, Facebook and other social media that protest spread to the United States. In the Occupy movement, 'the combination of Twitter and smartphone, in particular, allows individuals to continually post and receive updates as well as to circulate images and texts, constituting real-time, user-generated news feeds' (Juris 2012, 267). In fact, the very characteristics of the technology used by the activists have been said to play an important role in the creation of a participatory ethics that stresses individual involvement over organizational one (Juris 2012).

Even recognizing that media alone do not make social movements, Juris has pointed at the important effects on the dynamics of protest of the different organizational frames which are facilitated by the Web 1.0 versus the Web 2.0 types of technologies, where the latter indicates technological developments that allow users to interact with each other via the World Wide Web, through user-generated content. As he noted, 'whereas the use of listservs and websites in the movements for global justice during the late 1990s and 2000s helped to generate and diffuse distributed networking logics, in the #Occupying movements social media have contributed to powerful logics of aggregation' (2012, 260–1). While the logic of networking aims at connecting diverse collective actors, the logic of aggregation involves the assembling of diverse individuals in physical spaces. Rather than networks of networks, social media facilitate a mass aggregation of individuals (Juris 2012, 267). While personalized shifts have been defined as shallow and inefficient, 'personal action frames that emerge from connective networks often satisfy mass media demand for a simple angle and make it possible to intensify networking within various organizationally enabled and crowd-enabled organizations' (Bennett and Segerberg 2013, 7). Cheaper and easier to use than the previous instruments of online communication, social media allow for more subjective interventions that extend beyond traditional activist communities, but also represent a more submerged and fragmented form of communication.

Learning democracy in action: some conclusions

Organizational structures are, for movements, much more than instruments. Even if choices are often strategic, they are limited by a sort of repertoire of available instruments that is, as an action repertoire, built upon previous knowledge and only marginally innovated (Clemens 1996). Not only knowledge, but also norms define the realm of organizational possibilities. If there is continuity, there is a learning process, too. Movements are, as Alberto Melucci (1989) stressed, self-reflective actors. Even from one generation to the next, the pros and cons, successes and failures of specific democratic devices are reflected and intervened upon. In the short term as well, in the intense moments of mobilizations in protest cycles or waves, movement activists develop their conception of democracy, introducing innovations that then travel across countries and from one movement generation to the next.

In particular, traditionally characterized by an emphasis on participation, left-wing movements have conceived participation in different ways. Criticisms of elitism and appeal to council democracy have been audible in several moments in the development of the labour movements (della Porta 2013a). Left-libertarian movements had been already characterized by a critique of the bureaucratization of the organizational structures of their predecessors, proposing horizontal forms of participation through general assemblies but also small affinity groups (e.g. Rosenthal and Schwartz 1989; Polletta 2002). Reticular organizational formats had dominated the GJM, that had indeed exposed principles of participation and deliberation in the forums.

As we have seen, in the *acampadas*, the principle of deliberative and participatory democracy – inherited from the previous movements – were adapted to the characteristics of a movement of 'common people' rather than activists, that privileged persons over associations (della Porta 2013b, c, d). Equality and inclusivity in public spaces was indeed more radical in the movement's appeals to 'the 99 per cent'. To a certain extent, the emphasis on plurality as a positive value and the related need to encompass large numbers increased with the diversity of the citizens affected by the austerity measures. The search for radical inclusivity, equality and transparency was reflected in the choice of public spaces – such as parks and squares – as the pulsating heart of the movement, where no walls or fences had to reduce the transparency and publicity of the process. The orientation to public goods, to be obtained through the participation of all citizens in a high quality discourse, was embedded in the generalization of the use of consensual methods, even to large assemblies. The alternative management of the commons was indeed prefigured in the camps.

The complex rules and norms of these horizontal conceptions of participation and deliberation were adopted from various groups, more or less embedded in national traditions. Spanish activists thus cited anarchism and US ones pointed to the Quakers as progenitors of horizontalism, but also important were the ways in which the original ideas had been transformed through and by other movements, from the feminist to the anti-nuclear and the autonomous squatted youth centres. In fact, the strength of these streams of national movement cultures influenced and limited the capacity of the *acampadas*, as specific democratic spaces, to travel from one country to the next (Oikonomakis and Roos 2013). Moreover, it affected the adaptation of a long lasting form of protest, the camp, as it travels from Iceland to Egypt and then to Europe and the United States, becoming along the way more and more conceptualized by activists as a prefiguration of a different society.

Learning from previous movements does not, however, mean just adopting their forms by imitation, but rather reflecting upon their mistakes. As mentioned, even the experiences of the GJM, the immediate progenitor, were not taken for granted, but criticized because of an allegedly increasingly associational, or even hierarchical, vision of participation and deliberation, that especially the new generations did not find resonant with their taste and experiences. While representative democracy became increasingly affected by a deep legitimacy crisis, conceptions of direct democracy (re)emerged as more apt to organize highly critical citizens. In addition, the dynamism of the square was counterpoised to the perceived encapsulation of cyberactivism in the digital sphere, with a statement of protagonism of the citizens: *'sin nosotros, no sois nada'* (Sampedro Blanco and Sánchez Duarte 2011).

Finally, the *indignados* also adapted along the way to their perceptions of their own strengths and weaknesses, successes and failures. For example, in order to avoid that a very small dissident minority or even single individuals could block decisions supported by the quasi totality of participants (solutions, such as consensus minus one or two, modified consensus, or supermajority were introduced), provided one could express disagreement that could be argued and accounted for in the minutes of the meetings. In Spain, the commission of assembly dynamization also presented various specific proposals to improve decision making. Additional solutions, such as decentralization, were discussed as, in a declining phase of mobilization, the haemorrhage of participants interacted with the specialization of those who remained – the rotation of spokes stopped working when not enough activists were available to take over specific tasks and the most active developed specific competences with the emergence of a de facto hierarchy (Nez 2012). As the drum circles of the OWS created some organizational problems and tensions with the residents, these were addressed by 'talking and listening' (Taylor et al. 2011). When the perception of the marginalization of various ethnic and social groups emerged in the OWS, moderators increasingly tried to assure a racial and social balance.

In sum, as both social movement theory and cleavage theory would have predicted, organizational structures vary, while collective actors strategize, developing upon previous mistakes. However, both the political opportunities and the social bases of reference constrain strategic choices. Besides, organizational repertoires, as repertoires of protest, are not only chosen instrumentally. Rather, there are strong normative concerns that favour some options, while excluding others.

The hierarchical structure of the labour movement had reflected the high degree of catnet-ness of the working class, as well as the belief in the ethical value of a strong, unitary, professional organization.

Vice-versa, the new social movement, with its plural basis, had privileged a network structure, which resonated with the refusal of planning and the positive emphasis on subjectivity and creativity. These organizational preferences were anchored in conceptions of democracy that more and more emphasized participation as a value. Especially since the 2000s, participatory conceptions of democracy were accompanied by elaborations of deliberative democracy, stressing the importance of building inclusive, egalitarian and transparent public spheres, in which citizens could together develop common visions. If these ideas were already embedded in the social forum as a main invention of the GJM, the *acampadas*, as a main invention of its successors, promoted even more the public location of deliberation (in squares and parks), its openness (to all citizens) and its equalitarian conception (privileging direct over associational formats). With different emphases – less in the Arab Spring, more in the United States, in-between in Southern Europe – the prefigurative value intrinsic in organizational formats that allowed the enactment of an alternative society was put at the core of the movement experience.

Further research is for sure needed on the specific characteristics that movement politics takes in the core, the semiperiphery and the periphery of the neoliberal capitalist system as well as in the varieties of capitalist forms. As we mentioned, the *acampadas*, as forms of action, spread unequally on the globe and even at similar degree of economic stress movements appeared much more able to mobilize in some countries than in others. While social science work on cross-national diffusion had predicted spreading through geographical proximities and attribution of similarity, the camps were for instance a successful means of mobilization in Spain and Greece, but not in Italy or Portugal. In order to understand the relationship between capitalist development and forms of protest, to be investigated is also the path of further spreading of some forms and frames of anti-austerity protest under different social, political and cultural conditions, in countries such as Turkey or Ukraine.

6

Bringing Capitalism Back into Protest Analysis? Some Concluding Remarks

The aim of this book has been exploratory. I have discussed theoretically how social movement studies can be bridged with some trends in political economy and social and political theory in order to illuminate some aspects of protest politics under neoliberalism. In particular, I have looked at the previous engagement of social movement studies with the concept of cleavage as a conceptual instrument that can help understanding contemporary movements by bridging social structures, cultural trends and political organizations. Given that one of my main purposes was making different theoretical approach and fields of knowledge interact, I left space to the presentation of various approaches. As I imagine that, given my own background, this work would talk especially to social movement scholars, I focused even more on those contributions which are not traditionally taken into account in social movement studies. As I cannot pretend I became an expert in either political economy or social and political theory, I admittedly picked only some contributions in these areas, without pretending to offer a complete survey.

While I had (some one could say ambitious) theoretical aims, I did not aim at writing a treatise or develop 'big theory'. Rather, I was interested in activating some theoretical concepts and approaches in order to see what they can tell us which is useful in order to understand contemporary social movements – and, more broadly, societal and political transformations. Empirical evidence was therefore important, but not presented as aiming at theory testing. Rather, I use primary sources as well as secondary ones in order to illustrate the plausibility of some investigative paths. Empirically, I have in fact addressed recent anti-austerity mobilizations under the general question: can we talk of a return of class cleavage? I have used two empirical bases: surveys at protests (both anti-austerity and on other issues) between 2011 and 2013 – as well as more occasional references to surveys at demonstrations in various European countries and secondary analysis of existing research on protests in the same years in other countries (especially Egypt and Tunisia; Spain and Greece; and the United States). I have also surveyed the literature on anti-austerity protests in Latin America, as a sort of predecessor and inspirational source for actual ones and I have used primary empirical evidence from the Demos project on the GJM in Europe in order to point at continuities and discontinuities. The empirical data, even if focusing on Europe, allowed to go more in depth in the analysis of, at the individual level, the effects of social background of activists on their cultural vision and politics, as well as, by comparing demonstrations with each other, the diversity of mobilized arenas and, cross-nationally, the effects of the extent and forms of the crisis on demonstrators in different countries.

In this concluding chapter, I will summarize the results of the empirical research on the three dimensions of the cleavage I have singled out since the beginning, referring to some mechanisms which linked the different levels (see Figure 6.1). I will then reflect more in general about the democratic potential of social movements that target austerity measures. Finally, I will suggest some ideas about urgent empirical and theoretical tasks to perform to indeed bring capitalism back into protest analysis.

A new class cleavage?

Cleavages imply *structuration*. Social movements have been traditionally considered as expressions of either deeply rooted categorical traits or more temporarily felt grievances. This was reflected in their involving especially people sharing some structural characteristics. However, attention to the social basis of the protest tended, with some exception, to fade away, as social movement scholars focused more and more on the 'how' of the protest. Among those who remained concerned with the social basis of protest, new social movement theorists stated either the emergence of new social classes, after the decline and/or incorporation of the working class, or the increasing irrelevance of the class

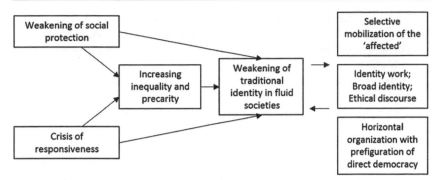

Figure 6.1   Explaining anti-austerity protests

dimension for understanding social movements' mobilizations. Class was more and more rarely referred to as an analytically useful concept for the analysis of contentious politics. Attention to such dimension of collective action remained however alive in specific theorization (as in world-systems theory) or area studies (as in Latin America) and was then revived in recent times in post-Marxian vision of how new capitalist formations bring about new forms of exploitation. If the structuralism of these approaches had the advantage of bringing attention back to big structural changes, social movement theories could however balance the expectation of a sort of spontaneous rebellion of the oppressed, with their traditional concern with specific conditions for mobilization – in particular, the needs to bridge category and networks in order to understand when mobilization appears.

This combination seems indeed of fundamental value if we want to understand nowadays protests. While some research had indicated that the social bases of (left-wing) protest shifted from the industrial working class for the labour movement to the new middle classes for new social movements, protests targeting neoliberal capitalism brought attention back to the mobilization of the losers of globalization. Sometimes called 'multitude' or 'precariat', those who protested represented coalitions of various classes and social groups that perceived themselves as losers of neoliberal development and its crisis. Precariousness was certainly a social and cultural condition for many participants. Overwhelmingly present in protests has been a generation (that in Portugal defines itself as 'without a future') that is characterized by high levels of unemployment and under-employment – that is employment in positions which are ill-paid and un-protected. The most marginalized groups participated in the Arab Spring and those affected by the financial crises mobilized in different forms in Southern Europe (while apparently less so in the Occupy movement, which had a more homogeneous constituency).

These young people are not those who have traditionally been described as losers: they are rather the well educated and the mobile, who were once described as the 'winners' of globalization – but are far from perceiving themselves as such. Together with them, in the same or in different protest events, we found other social groups that have lost most from the neoliberal attacks to social and civil rights: from public employees to retired individuals – those once considered as the most protected social groups and now becoming instead, to larger or smaller extent, precarious themselves in terms of their life conditions, including in terms of losing fundamental rights such as those to health care, housing, education. Similarly, blue-collar workers of the small but also large factories, shut down or at risk of being shut down, have participated in the wave of protest. With high levels of participation by young people and well-educated citizens, the anti-austerity protests brought into the street a sort of (inverted) '2/3' society of those most hit by austerity policies. As we have seen from survey data on protesters, if one-quarter of protesters identified as workers, one-half defined themselves as lower middle class. Overall, only about half (a bit more in the anti-austerity protests) had a permanent position in the labour market. Therefore, the protests brought together coalitions of citizens with different socio-biographic backgrounds, but united by their feeling of having been unjustly treated.

Addressing capitalist dynamics within different temporalities, anti-austerity protests must be located in the crisis of a second 'great transformation', imposing the free market over social protection in the form of neoliberalism. As in the first great transformation, liberalization, deregulation and privatization have driven public policies, this time especially in the interest of huge, transnational corporations and financial capitalism. Debt crises developed particularly in disorganized forms of capitalism, but inequalities also grew in areas of coordinated capitalism, especially in the weaker European economies – which suffered, first, from unfavourable currency exchange rates and then from the impossibility, within the EMU, to devalue due to economic difficulties. The social effects of these crises have been, with different timing at the core and at the periphery of the world economy, a broad precarization of various social groups through youth unemployment or underemployment, declining salaries and labour protection in the once central labour markets of industry and the public sector, cuts in retirement and other subsidies, in what amounts to a generalized loss of rights (Stiglitz 2012a; Streeck 2014). In comparison with the GJM of the beginning of the century – which although denouncing the growing inequalities saw an underrepresentation of the poorer social groups – the anti-austerity protests mobilized a variegated coalition of citizens that felt (unjustly) hit by austerity measures. Not all those with grievances had however equal capacity to mobilize.

In my theoretical model, structuration is linked to *identification* processes. In order to transform discontent in grievance and then claims, the personal situation needs to be linked to a collective one – that indeed, Pizzorno (1993) noted, allows assessing one's own interest in the long term – and to a political identity, which permits to single out targets and choose strategies. If neoliberalism produces a liquid culture, destroying old bases for personal, collective and political identity through forced mobility and related insecurity, identification processes are however still needed. They are not impossible to develop, but not automatic either. Rather, as social movement studies would predict, they assume once again a central role, which is however much shaped by the changing culture of neoliberalism. Concepts coming from social movement studies, such as resonance, authenticity or credibility, are certainly useful to understand the specific challenges of identity work for social movements in times of austerity. They need however to be contextualized within reflection on the specific characteristics of neoliberal cultural systems.

As for the cultural element of the cleavage, in fact, while the labour movement had developed a strong identity – supported by a complex ideology – and new social movements had a focus on specific concerns, the identification processes of anti-austerity protesters seemed to challenge the individualization of liquid society as well as its fear and exclusivism, calling instead for state intervention and inclusive citizenship. Defining themselves broadly – as citizens, persons, or the 99% – activists of the anti-austerity movement elaborated a moral discourse that called for the reinstatement of welfare protections, but they also (indignantly) challenged the injustice of the system. Referring often to the nation, as basis of reference of a community of solidarity (and suffering), they however combined inclusive nationalism with recognition of the need to look for global solutions to global problems.

If scholars reflecting on a liquid society had stressed the presence of multiple individual identities, changing subjective identification and soft (or weak) collective identities, while others had hoped in an insubordination of the multitudes which no longer needed identification, we have observed much identity work oriented to a definition of the self, with the re-emergence of a social criticism of capitalism. As precariousness, as lost security about life development itself, spread from young unemployed and under-employed to large social groups of once protected, identification with the overwhelming majority in the society might provide some certainty. A strong morality framing (especially widespread in the US case) grew to contrast the perceived amorality of neoliberalism and its ideology, with the commodification of public services. The cynical, neoliberal view of personal responsibility for survival and the proclamation of selfish motives as beneficial to the economy have been stigmatized in the name of previous rights, with calls for their re-establishment. An appeal for solidarity and a return to the commons has been juxtaposed to an unjust and inefficient neoliberal ideology. Differently from the GJM, which had presented itself as an alliance of minorities in search of a broad constituency, the anti-austerity movements have constructed a broad definition of the self, as a large majority (contrasted with the network of minorities allied within the GJM) of the citizens. An (inclusive) definition of the nation emerged, in contrast to the wholehearted cosmopolitanism of the GJM, as a reaction to declining national sovereignty. Backward looking, the anti-austerity protests called for the restoration of lost rights, vehemently denouncing the corruption of democracy. However, they also looked forward, combining concerns for social rights with those for cultural inclusivity.

Politicization of social conditions is a relevant mechanism in the formation of a cleavage. While political opportunities have been considered as relevant as either stable (institutional) conditions or contingent ones, a missing link is the analysis of middle-term shifts between stability and crisis. Moreover, while political process approaches have looked at (strictly) political institutions, political economy pushes towards a broadening of attention towards the interaction of politics and the market. If welfare state and party government were taken for granted in traditional reflections of political opportunities, attention to the politics of neoliberalism in post-democracies is all the more important in order to understand how social movements can adapt to and challenge a situation characterized by high level of institutional distrust, reduction of traditional organizations of political consensus and the decline of political competencies.

The economic crisis has been linked in fact to a legitimacy crisis at the political level, which took the specific form of a crisis of political responsibility. Losers feel such not only on the market, but also from the political point of view, as more and more groups in the society consider themselves non-represented within institutions that are more and more seen as captured by big business. While privatization, liberalization and deregulation reduced the capacity of the state to answer citizens' demands, particularly those countries with weaker economies lost large portions of their national sovereignty, as they were forced to accept loans from international financial organizations, with attached conditionalities in terms of implementation of heavy austerity measures. Collusion between economic and political power then emerge stronger and more visible. The effects have been a dramatic acceleration of trends towards declining party membership, loyalty and identification as well as of conventional forms of participation and (especially) institutional trust. In comparison with the GJM, the declining confidence in representative institutions is reflected in the weakening of the search for channels of access to public decision making through lobbying or critical collaboration. Even if there is still a desperate search for politics, its traditional forms are deeply mistrusted and autonomous ones explored (with ever more emphasis in Southern Europe and especially in the US Occupy). Not democracy per se is challenged however but rather its degeneration – as 'they call it democracy, but it is not'.

In sum, social movements active against neoliberalism are embedded in a crisis of legitimacy that takes the particular form of a lack of responsibility towards citizens' demands. They stigmatize the power of big corporations and (unaccountable) international organizations, with the related loss of national governments' sovereignty. What is more, they hold responsible those governments and the political class at large for what they consider an abduction of democracy. However, rather than developing anti-democratic attitudes, they claim that representative democracy has been corrupted by the collusion of economic and political power, calling for participatory democracy and a general return to public concern with common goods. Given the extremely low trust in existing representative institutions, these movements have addressed requests to the state, but also experimented with alternative models of participatory and deliberative democracy. *Acampadas* became places to prefigure new forms of democracy.

In this sense, these movements are not antipolitical but rather propose a different – deliberative and participatory – vision of democracy that they try to prefigure in their own organizational forms. Although appealing to the citizens beyond traditional parties and associations, they are far from widespread definitions of populism as an exclusivist and homogenizing discourse, instead suggesting the importance of developing arenas for encounters among persons with different social backgrounds and political ideas. Deliberation through high-quality discourse rather than charismatic power is called for as a way to find solutions to common problems. In the presence of an institutional system felt as more and more distant, a direct commitment is promoted. This development reflects the perceived challenge in the crisis of neoliberalism: first, the singling out of a large and very critical potential basis of the movement in the heterogeneous social groups who have been hit by the crisis; and, second, the search for radically different forms of politics, which reflects deep disappointment not only with representative institutions and political parties, but also with unions and associations of various types, stigmatized as unwilling or unable to address the financial crisis.

As for the *mobilization* of the cleavage, research has stressed the social movements' capacity – either through learning or through environmental selection – to adapt organizational structures to some characteristics of the social bases and related collective identities. Social structure and culture seems to interact as classes develop specific tastes which resonate not only with their material resources, but also with their normative expectations. In fact, social movement studies have pointed at the instrumental logic in organizational development, but also at its prefigurative function; at the external use of organizational resources, invested as they are in order to reach their aims, but also at its internal use, in consolidating identity by embodying specific values. This combination of instrumentality and normativity is indeed important for understanding the process of mobilization in anti-austerity protests.

Neither the hierarchical structure of the labour movement nor the networked model of the new social movements seems to fit the emerging anti-austerity protests. Even if different strategies are present in different groups, orientation on the left of the political spectrum remains common, along with a strong mistrust in institutions of representative democracy and, instead, confidence in the citizens' capacity to change their world (della Porta and Andretta 2013; della Porta and Reiter 2012b; della Porta et al. 2013). As neoliberalism attacked the corporatist actors that had driven the social pacts of Fordist capitalism, the unions first but also many civil society associations once integrated in the provision of social protection, the idea of a direct democracy of the citizens started to be cherished by the emerging movements.

As predicted by both social movement and cleavage theories, organizational structures have developed following normative preferences, strategic reflections over past successes and failures, but also adapting to the political and social balances of opportunities and constraints. Both the social characteristics of the reference base and its normative preferences are relevant in explaining the search for new organizational forms. Developing upon the GJM's experiences with participatory and deliberative forms of democracy, the anti-austerity protests moved from a 'democracy of the forums' to a 'democracy of the squares', with growing attention to openness, publicity and equality. Deliberative and participatory conceptions and practices of democracy were combined with an emphasis on the direct participation of the citizens rather than through networks of associations. A networking logic has been accompanied by an aggregated one, with growing emphasis on the construction of free spaces when moving from the MENA region, to Southern Europe and then to the United States.

Is class politics then back? More research is of course needed in order to answer this (admittedly ambitious) question. If we understand class cleavage as a strict link between social basis (socio-graphic element), collective identity (cultural element) and parties (organizational elements), we can say that this is long gone. What we noticed, however, is the existence of protest that connects the old labour with the new precarious workers, in broad coalitions of those who feel penalized by neoliberal globalization. Appeals to materialist values are bridged with postmaterialist ideas, in the calls for state intervention and inclusive citizenship. As for the organizational structure of these protests, we noted the presence of different models that converged towards increasing mistrust for representative democracy and increasing demand for direct (participatory and deliberative) forms.

Movements and democracy

Can democracy be saved through these new forms of (alternative) movement politics? While it is too early to provide a definite answer to this question, some observations are in order.

Protests have socialized into politics a new generation – the one potentially hardest hit by the consequences of neoliberalism – as well as many, formerly apolitical, people affected by the crisis. The participation in the collective mobilization might in itself have given dignity to those many citizens that austerity measures have left, not only without basic human rights – such as housing, food, health – but even, as activists claim, politically disenfranchised. Faced with the stigmata of being unemployed, homeless and/or having to pay back unpayable debts, the movement discourse offers these people the opportunity to shift the blame from the individual to the system.

Not only have protests been powerful sites of political socialization; they have socialized participants to democratic politics. Against the xenophobic and elitist discourse of the populist Right (Kriesi et al. 2012), the anti-austerity movement I have analysed has developed a discourse of solidarity and inclusion. With their experimentation with deliberative and participatory forms of democracy, they have shown that democracy has not just one, disqualified, meaning, but can be the basis for people's participation and deliberation.

Their discourse has also spread. Certainly, movements against austerity have been widely supported by public opinion. To take the Spanish example, as many as two-thirds of the citizens declared much or enough sympathy for the *indignados* and 80 per cent of the population asked their government to open a dialogue with them (Llera 2012). Similarly high has been consensus on the movement's aims in the US population (Gitlin 2012) and in Greece. Moreover, the movement reflected dominant requests for increasing taxes for the rich and decreasing the costs of politics (supported by about 90 per cent of the citizens in Spain), as well as a growing opposition to privatization of public services (Llera 2012). Similar trends have been noted in Greece (Ruedig and Karyotis 2013). In the United States as well, about 60 per cent of the citizens declared themselves in favour of progressive economic reforms in order to reduce disparities in wealth (Gitlin 2012). Resonating with general sentiments, the anti-austerity movements have thus been able to sensitize the public opinion. In general, these movements have been seen as effective in bringing the debate on social justice back in. As Stiglitz noted, 'in some ways, the protesters have already accomplished a great deal: think tanks, government agencies and the media have confirmed their allegations, of the high and unjustifiable level of inequality, the failure of the market system' (2012b, 21).

The protesters' mistrust in traditional politics certainly resonates with a large part of the population in the countries more hit by the austerity measures. Suffice it to remember that, with a general decline in trust in the second half of the 2000s – with about two-thirds of citizens dissatisfied by the performance of their governments – the displeasure with the functioning of democracy in Spain reached two citizens out of three in 2011, almost inverting the results of 2007 (when 42 per cent were dissatisfied) (Llera 2012), while trust in parties declined to about one-third of the population, from about half in 2001 (Iglesias 2012). More generally, in Europe opinion polls – including the ones promoted by the European Commission itself through its Eurobarometer – clearly indicate the effects of the financial crisis on support for European institutions by European citizens. In short, they indicate a dramatic drop in citizens' trust in the EU, going from 57 per cent in the Spring of 2007 to 31 per cent in the Autumn of 2013 (Eurobarometer 2013). Growing mistrust is linked to a dramatic increase in the percentage of citizens for whom the EU conjures a negative image, a figure that has nearly doubled (from 15 to 28%), while the percentage of those who have a positive image dropped (from 52 to 31%) between 2007 and 2013 (ibid.).

There are certainly important resources for those who want to save democracy, linking political rights to civic and social rights. Some problems are nevertheless open and difficult to address through movement politics alone. First of all, protests have proven massive in numbers, but fluctuating in mobilizing capacity. Prefiguring new forms of democracy is not that easy: consensual decision making takes time, assemblies can be frustrating, participation goes in waves, material needs often win over solidarity and public commitment. The anti-austerity front is also often divided. Forms of protest such as *acampadas* have spread transnationally, but in a selective way (Roos and Oikonomakis 2014; della Porta and Mattoni 2014): from Spain to Greece and the United States, but not in the United Kingdom, France, Germany, or even Italy or Portugal. If the intensity of the economic crisis can explain non-diffusion in, for example, Germany or France, in the Italian and Portuguese cases one should point instead at the low resonance of very horizontal organizational formats in the movement culture (e.g. Zamponi 2013). Additionally, even in Spain, Greece, or the United States, anti-austerity protests have often taken other, more traditional forms, led by unions and other associations, which have rarely converged with the *acampadas* groups. Organizational divergences have made coalition building difficult, notwithstanding compatible substantial demands. Finally, the *acampadas* are by definition short-lived, even if they prompt the development of important spin-off movements – as, in Spain, the local assemblies that continued protests in popular neighbourhoods, the 'coloured tides' (mareas) that mobilized workers of public services, as well as 'strong cultures of solidarities and creative alternative economies' (Flesher Fominaya 2014, 188).

What is more, even if movements have stressed prefiguration, citizens need a (paradigmatic) change of public policy decisions. What they claim is a return of the public, which also means states and other public institutions taking back competences they had released during neoliberalism. Even if the appeal is to reconstruct (decentralized) commons, robust interventions of legal and institutional character are required.

This is difficult to implement until the movements are able to influence institutional decision making. Social movement studies have indicated the relevance of the party-in-power for the realization of movements' aims. Nowadays, anti-austerity movements in Europe and the United States have been more capable of electorally punishing centre-left parties, considered as blind and deaf towards their electorate's demands, than of promoting alternative coalitions, as has been the case in Latin America. Even if they are able to promote protests inside the parties, the capacity of groups such as OccupyPD to really affect party hierarchy is currently dubious. Recent EU elections showed however that, in the countries which were more hit by the crisis and, especially, where various forms of protests developed to target austerity measures, new renovated parties (such as Podemos in Spain or Syriza in Greece) have been successful in capitalizing in electoral terms from protest politics.

Where to go from here?

In sum, bringing capitalism (systematically) back in research in contentious politics would certainly help our understanding of recent social movements. In this volume, I have tried to bridge some insights from social movement studies with reflections in political economy and political and social theory that I think could provide some new theoretical lenses to guide forthcoming empirical investigations.

Building upon some classical works on broad capitalist developments, I have in particular suggested a look into the following issues.

First, if social movement studies once examined the interactions between protest and capitalism in both its formation and its Fordist development, research must now investigate the effects of the neoliberal turn in capitalism as well as its (contingent, at least) crisis on some characteristics of emerging movements. Particularly, given the shift from protection to free market, it would be central to investigate more systematically the effects of economic restructuring on class structures and, then, the structuration of cleavages that are at the same time the basis for and the product of social movement work.

Second, classic and contemporary literature on capitalism discourses – especially, on its ideology – pushes attention towards the emergence of an immoral economy. As during the first wave of liberalism, the cynical disdain for the poor and the excluded goes hand in hand with the fanatical belief in the virtue of the free market (to the benefit of either the consumer, in the past, or the shareholder now). Cynical discourses (and action) are then resisted by the movement through a call for dignity against the indignity of power, as well as the betrayal of the promises of freedom and welfare. The way in which framing and counterframing are articulated is in this respect a very interesting field for further investigation.

Third, without implying a definitive systemic crisis à la Wallerstein (see Wallerstein 2010), it is important to locate the contemporary movement in a legitimacy crisis which, differently from the one Habermas expected, is determined not by a domination of the public over the private world but rather by a domination of the private over the public (Bauman 2000).[19] How today's legitimacy crises of neoliberalism affect citizens' mobilizations is indeed a central topic for investigation. Reference to the people (or, even more, to the citizens or the persons) certainly goes together with the denunciation of the corruption of those in power, with a radical rejection of the entire political class rather than a focus on the neoliberal institutions that had been targeted by the previous movements (della Porta and Mattoni 2014). While parties and parliaments lose (or give up) their function of reducing inequalities and granting rights, social movements seem to move beyond existing representative democracy, inventing alternative politics and polities.

Fourth, as for research in political economy (Regini 2014), also in social movement studies contemporary developments call for a reflection on the ways in which structures and agencies combine in the collective mobilization processes (della Porta 2013a). While there is no doubt that anti-austerity protests have a genealogy composed of previous movements, among which the GJM is a most proximate relative, the logic of collective action building seems to have changed. Differently from the GJM, which developed as a network of networks of activism (called indeed a 'movement of movements'), the *indignados* and the Occupy movements also mobilized 'first comers', including those who had been hit hardest by austerity measures. While from the point of view of political identities (and socialization) the movements of 2011 are even more diverse than those of the previous decade, they nonetheless present themselves through a unified conception of 'the people', the citizens, or persons. Reference to the common feelings of outrage prevails over a positive definition of common aims (as global justice in the GJM).

Without aiming at being exhaustive, these ways of bringing reflection on capitalism back in the social movement studies seem to me worth investigating further. Some research directions seem indeed most urgent.

First, while I pointed at the fact that the same global crisis took very different forms in different countries, much more systematic comparison are needed between the core and the periphery of capitalism as well as within them. If I suggested to look at anti-austerity movements in Latin America and research about them as a source of inspiration to understand recent anti-austerity movements at the core of the capitalist system and at the Arab Spring as, at least in part, moved by similar claims, the different dynamics in the different peripheries should be comparatively addressed. The example of Latin America also pointed at the interactions between market and politics, capitalist evolution and state evolution, describing specific types of mobilization where traditional left-wing parties were still perceived as pursuing an anti-neoliberal struggle and where instead they were not. Also at the world-systems core, on which the reflection on variety of capitalism focused, research is needed to compare social movements within coordinated versus market-oriented forms of capitalism in their evolution within the great recession of neoliberalism. The combination of private and public debt, the geopolitical location, the constraints and opportunities coming from membership in political and economic international organizations – all can be expected to have an impact on the intensity of protests.

Beyond capitalism diversity, not only the intensity but also the forms of protest varied in space. Camps were central for contentious politics in Egypt, Tunisia, Greece, Spain and the US or Israel – but they did not travel much beyond these cases. Most hit by recession, Ireland, Italy and Portugal have also seen protests, which however took other forms. While also the forums had differential success in different countries, the camps showed even higher degrees of idiosyncracies. Camps spread however cross-time: Gezi Park in Istanbul and Maidan in Kiev represented main arenas of protest in respectively Turkey and Ukraine. As protests for social justice went beyond the declining economies to the (apparently) growing one, systematic cross-national analysis of the interactions between economic development and contentious politics is strongly necessary. As Jeff Juris (2012) noted, a logic of aggregation of individuals supersedes a logic of organizational networking. While our research mainly focused on protest, it would be important to investigate how also other social movement activities address the crisis of late neoliberalism, among others by trying to develop alternative forms of production of public goods and management of the commons.

Second, in this area of study as in most others, there is the need to combine cross-national and transnational approaches. While the crisis itself, with its different timing and developments in different countries, brought attention back to national economics and national politics, it however also highlighted the strength of global actors, as big corporation and international organizations. More than ever, it emerged with much evidence that the high degree of interdependency does not indeed mean convergence: rather, even at macro-regional level, it became clear how little has been done in terms of positive integration. In the EU, the once weakest economies went back to their weak status, after short-lasting illusions of growth and prosperities. Not only the European Monetary Union proved unable to fulfil its promises of well-being, but for many countries the Euros meant forced acceptance of unfavourable monetary policies. As the EU model is driven by the (negative) integration of the markets, the EU became indeed a main promoter of austerity policies, at the cost of quickly dropping support. Unable to face spreading criticism through changes and adaptation, the recipe to address recession has been more of the same: anti-inflationary policies which produce more recession. Similar impact had other macro-regional organizations or international financial institutions, such as the IMF, that are still dominated by the anti-Keynesian paradigm. Analysis should therefore develop a capacity to address national and transnational trends at the same time.

Finally, I defended a relational approach as able to bridge structure and agency and pointed indeed at various mechanisms, with cognitive and affective implications. In looking at social, cultural and organizational dimensions of the cleavages, I traced the genealogy of anti-austerity protests in previous movements, but also stressed their discontinuity and found some explanations for them within the changing characteristics of neoliberal capitalism. I did not go however in depth in the analysis of the anti-austerity movement's interactions within more complex fields. First of all, neoliberalism developed not only through collusive relations between politics and the market, political and business elites, but also through a growing securitization of the relations between states and citizens. As the welfare state leave space to the warfare state, governments are responding to the anger of the citizens by reducing more and more spaces of free political expressions and, especially, the rights to protest. Not only the capacity to control citizens increased, but neoliberalism, especially in its crisis, fuelled illiberal conceptions of civil and political rights. The rhetoric of the war on terror mixed with the one of the sovereignty of the markets (and need to attract investments) brought about growing restriction upon citizens' political expression – often stigmatized as 'populism'. As research on Latin America and the MENA region clearly indicated, this military (or security) aspect of the political economy of neoliberalism needs to be taken into account in order to understand the dynamics of protest.

Moreover, besides the interactions of movement and the state, those – direct or mediated – with the right-wing response to neoliberalism also needs to be taken into account. Those activists calling for direct democracy in Syntagma Square were very different in their visions and claims from those who militate now in Golden Down – as different as the Tea Party is from Occupy. Nevertheless, these movements have something in common – at the very least, the dissatisfaction with neoliberalist developments. In both cases, some ideas spread cross-nationally, with a sort of double diffusion within camps, but also in a continuous exchange of moves and countermoves. A relational perspective must address these types of interactions as well.

Notes

1 http://www.oxforddictionaries.com/definition/english/capitalism.
2 The short face-to-face interviews were given to 20 per cent of the sampled interviewees: interviewers were instructed to administer such short questionnaires to every five people selected. This allowed us to control for possible bias introduced in the return of the questionnaires. The variables included in the short face-to-face questionnaires that can be compared with those in the longer postal questionnaires are: gender, education, age, membership of organizations staging the demonstration, participation in past demonstrations and the extent to which interviewers were determined to participate in the selected demonstrations. Our bias analysis demonstrated that on only two variables (gender and past participation in previous demonstrations) and only in some of the demonstrations were there weak statistically significant differences between the two samples.
3 http://www.protestsurvey.eu/index.php?page=index; http://cosmos.eui.eu/Projects/Contexcontest.aspx.
4 This was confirmed, for example, by Ronald Dore's (2000) research on Japanese mutual trust, by Piore and Sabel (1984) on flexible specialization, by Sorge and Streeck (1988) on diversified quality production, with strong trade unions, institutionalized worker participation on the shop floor and above, with relatively high wages and relatively low wage spread.
5 As Scharpf (2011) noted, democratic institutions have indeed a double political responsibility to avoid crises: responsibility towards the will of the people but also towards the common good.
6 The UK's 'Big Society' programme, launched by Conservative Prime Minister Cameron with the aim: 'to shift responsibility for meeting social needs from the state to individual families and community and to shift service provision

from the public sector to charities, local communities-based groups and business' (Coote and Shaheen 2013, 243), is part of a more general trend in Western democracy, which has the effect of pitting local communities and voluntary groups against each other for access to ever more limited resources.

7   Results from other surveys conducted among WSF participants have confirmed this profile (Ibase 2006; Brunelle 2006).

8   Or, 'The conditions most favorable of the prosperity of agriculture exists when there are no entails, no unalienable endowments, no common lands, no right of redemption, no tithes' (ibid., 180).

9   Moral discourses spread also in movements targeting international actors (Bushy 2010).

10   http://www.italianrevolution.org/italia-indignataalzati-e-cammina

11   Research on lobbying in the EU confirmed in general that 'in terms of representation there is a clear bias in favour of business interests. They constitute by far the biggest group among the participants in Commission consultation' (Kluever 2013, 216).

12   Osa and Corduneanu-Huci (2003) noted in nondemocracies an increasing mobilization, with increases in inflation volatility, together with decreases in trade openness (often as reaction to stress) or growing gaps between GDP and sinking standards of living. In these cases, movements may internally generate resources, overcoming closed opportunities.

13   http://occupiamobankitalia.wordpress.com/appello-12-ottobre

14   http://www.italianrevolution.org/tag/siamo-qui-per-prendercelo. All quotations are taken from Italian documents translated by Louisa Parks.

15   Sewell defines events as a 'relatively rare subclass of happenings that *significantly transform structure*' and an eventful conception of temporality as 'one that takes into account the transformation of structures by events' (1996, emphasis added).

16   They met once a week in a public space, with different types of public in different types of neighbourhoods (Nez 2011b).

17   http://www.italianrevolution.org/276

18   http://www.italianrevolution.org/dal-presidio-permanete-al-presidio-diffuso

19   As he noted, 'it is no more true that the "public" is set on colonizing the "private". The opposite is the case: it is the private that colonizes the public spaces' (ibid., 39), as 'any true liberation calls today for more, not less, of the "public sphere" and "public power"' (ibid., 51).

References

Abu-Lughod, Lila (2012) Living the 'revolution' in an Egyptian village: moral action in a national space. *American Ethnologist* 39(1), 21–5.

Agrikoliansky, Eric and Cardon, Dominique (2005) Un programme de débats: forum, forms et formats. In Agrikoliansky, Eric and Sommier, Isabelle (eds.) *Radiographie du Movement Altermondialiste*. La Dispute, Paris, pp. 45–74.

Alexander, Jeffrey C. (2011) *Performative Revolution in Egypt: An Essay in Cultural Power*. Bloomsbury Academic, London.

Alimi, Eitan Y. (2012) 'Occupy Israel': a tale of startling success and hopeful failure. *Social Movement Studies* 11(3–4), 402–7.

Almeida, Paul D. (2008) *Waves of Protest. Popular Struggle in El Salvador, 1925–2005*. University of Minnesota Press, Minneapolis.

Almeida, Paul D. and Johnston, Hank (2006) Neoliberal globalization and popular movements in Latin America. In Almeida, Paul and Johnston, Hank (eds.) *Latin American Social Movements*. Rowman and Littlefield, Lanham, pp. 3–18.

Amable, Bruno (2011) Morals and politics in the ideology of neoliberalism. *Socio-Economic Review* 9, 3–30.

Andretta, Massimiliano and della Porta, Donatella (2009) Models of democracy: how activists see democracy. In della Porta, Donatella (ed.) *Another Europe*. Routledge, London, pp. 65–85.

Andretta, Massimiliano and Reiter, Herbert (2009) Parties, unions and movements: the European left and the ESF. In della Porta, Donatella (ed.) *Another Europe*. Routledge, London, pp. 173–203.

Andretta, Massimiliano and Sommier, Isabelle (2009) The social bases of the GJM and democratic norms. In della Porta, Donatella (ed.) *Another Europe*. Routledge, London, pp. 111–27.

Andretta, Massimiliano, della Porta, Donatella, Mosca, Lorenzo and Reiter, Herbert (2002) *Global, noglobal, newglobal: Le Proteste di Genova contro il G8*. Laterza, Roma and Bari.

Antonio, Robert J. and Bonanno, Alessandro (1996) A post-Fordism in the United States: the poverty of market-centered democracy. *Current Perspectives on Social Theory* 16, 3–32.

Aouraght, Miriyam and Alexander, Anne (2011) The Egyptian experience: sense and nonsense of the internet revolution. *International Journal of Communication* 5, 1344–58.

Archibugi, Daniele (2003) Cosmopolitical democracy. In Archibugi, Daniele (ed.) *Debating Cosmopolitics*. Verso, London, pp. 1–15.

Arnstein, Sherry R. (1969) A ladder of citizen participation. *Journal of the American Institute of Planners* 35(4), 216–24.

Arrighi, Giovanni, Hopkins, Terence K. and Wallerstein, Immanuel (1989) *Antisystemic Movements*. Verso, London.

Auyero, Javier (2007) *Routine Politics and Violence in Argentina: The Gray Zone of State Power*. Cambridge University Press, Cambridge.

Ayeb, Habib (2011) Social and political geography of the Tunisian revolution: the alfa grass revolution. *Review of African Political Economy* 38(129), 467–79.

Barker, Adam J. (2012) Already occupied: indigenous people, settler colonialism and the Occupy movements in North America. *Social Movement Studies* 11(3–4), 327–34.

Barker, Colin (2013) Marxism and social movements. In Snow, David, della Porta, Donatella, Klandermans, Bert and McAdam, Doug (eds.) *Blackwell Encyclopedia on Social and Political Movements*. Blackwell, Oxford, pp. 713–21.

Barker, Colin, Cox, Laurence, Krinsky, John and Nilsen, Alf Gunvald (eds.) (2013) *Marxism and Social Movements*. Brill, Leiden.

Barker, Colin and Lavalette, Michael (2014) Welfare changes and social movements. In Donatella della Porta and Mario Diani (eds), *Oxford Handbook on Social Movements*. Oxford University Press, Oxford.

Barnes, Samuel, Kaase, Max and Allerbeck, Klaus (1979) *Political Action: Mass Participation in Five Democracies*. Sage, London.

Bartolini, Stefano (2000) *The Political Mobilization of the European Left 1860–1980: The Class Cleavage*. Cambridge University Press, Cambridge.

Bartolini, Stefano and Mair, Peter (1990) *Identity, Competition, and Electoral Availability: the Stabilization of European Electorates – 1885–1985*. Cambridge University Press, Cambridge.

Bauman, Zygmunt (1997) *Postmodernity and its Discontent*. Polity, Cambridge.
– (2000) *Liquid Modernity*. Polity, Cambridge.
– (2007) *Liquid Times: Living in Times of Uncertainty*. Polity, Cambridge.

Baumgarten, Britta (2013) Geração à rasca and beyond: mobilizations in Portugal after 12 March 2011. *Current Sociology*, first published on 17 April.

Beck, Colin J. (2013) Ideology. In Snow, David, della Porta, Donatella, Klandermans, Bert and McAdam, Doug (eds.) *Blackwell Encyclopedia on Social and Political Movements*. Blackwell, Oxford, pp. 586–90.

Beinin, Joel (2011) A workers' social movement on the margin of the global neoliberal order: Egypt 2004–2009. In Benin, Joel and Vairel, Frédéric (eds.) *Social Movements, Mobilization and Contestation in the Middle East and North Africa*. Stanford University Press, Stanford, CA, pp. 181–201.

Benford, Robert (2013) Identity fields. In Snow, David, della Porta, Donatella, Klandermans, Bert and McAdam, Doug (eds.) *Blackwell Encyclopedia on Social and Political Movements*. Blackwell, Oxford, pp. 579–80.

Bennett, Lance and Segerberg, Alexandra (2013) *The Logic of Connective Action: Digital Media and the Personalization of Contentious Politics*. Cambridge University Press, Cambridge.

Benski, Tova and Langman, Lauren (2013) The effects of affects: the place of emotions in the mobilizations of 2011. *Current Sociology*, first published on 17 April.

Benski, Tova, Langman, Lauren, Perugorría, Ignacia and Tejerina, Benjamín (2013) From the streets and squares to social movement studies: what have we learned? *Current Sociology*, first published on 17 April.

Berg-Schlosser, Dirk (2013) Poverty and democracy – chances and conflicts. *Redefining and Combating Poverty: Trends in Social Cohesion* 25, 217–30.

Bernstein, Mary and Taylor, Verta (2013) Identity politics. In Snow, David, della Porta, Donatella, Klandermans, Bert and McAdam, Doug (eds.) *Blackwell Encyclopedia on Social and Political Movements*. Blackwell, Oxford, pp. 580–4.

Beyerlein, Kraig and Bergstrand, Kelly (2013) Biographical availability. In Snow, David, della Porta, Donatella, Klandermans, Bert and McAdam, Doug (eds.) *Blackwell Encyclopedia on Social and Political Movements*. Blackwell, Oxford, pp. 136–8.

Biekart, Kees and Fowler, Alan (2013) Transforming activisms 2010+: exploring ways and waves. *Development and Change* 44(3), 527–46.

Bishara, Dina (2013) The power of workers in Egypt's 2011 uprising. In Korany, Bahgat and El-Mahdy, Rabab (eds.) *The Arab Spring in Egypt: Revolution and Beyond*. The American University in Cairo Press, Cairo.

Bohle, Dorothee and Greskovits, Bela (2012) *Capitalist Diversity on Europe's periphery*. Cornell University Press, Ithaca.

Boltanski, Luc and Chiapello, Eve (2005) *The New Spirit of Capitalism*. Verso, London.

Booth, John (1991) Socioeconomic and political roots of national revolts in Central America. *Latin American Research Review* 26(1), 33–73.

Borland, Elisabeth (2013) Quotidian disruption. In Snow, David, della Porta, Donatella, Klandermans, Bert and McAdam, Doug (eds.) *Blackwell Encyclopedia on Social and Political Movements*. Blackwell, Oxford, pp. 1038–41.

Boswell, Terry and Dixon, William J. (1990) Dependency and rebellion. *American sociological review* 55, 540–59.

Botella-Ordinas, Eva (2011) La démocratie directe de la Puerta del Sol. *La Vie des idées*. www.laviedesidees.fr/La-democratie-directe-de-la-Puerta.html

Bourdieu, Pierre (1977) *Outline of a Theory of Practice*. Cambridge University Press, Cambridge.

Brunelle, Dorvall (2006) *Le Forum social mondial: origine et participants*, Observatoires des Amériques. Online, available at: www.ameriques.uquam.ca

Buchanan, James and Tullock, Gordon (1962) *The Calculus of Consent: Logical Foundation of Constitutional Democracy*. University of Michigan Press, Ann Arbor.

Buechler, Steven M. (2000) *Social Movements in Advanced Capitalism: the Political Economy and Cultural Construction of Social Activism*. Oxford University Press, Oxford.

– (2013) New social movements. In Snow, David, della Porta, Donatella, Klandermans, Bert and McAdam, Doug (eds.) *Blackwell Encyclopedia on Social and Political Movements*. Blackwell, Oxford, pp. 846–55.

Bushy, Joshua W. (2010) *Moral Movements and Foreign Policy*. Cambridge University Press, Cambridge.

Calhoun, Craig J. (1982) *The Question of Class Struggle: Social Foundation of Popular Radicalism during the Industrial Revolution*. Blackwell, Oxford.

Calvo, Kerman (2013) Fighting for a voice: the Spanish 15-M/Indignados movement. In Cox, Laurence and Flesher, Cristina (eds.) *Understanding European Movements*. Routledge, London.

Castañeda, Ernesto (2012) The Indignados of Spain: a precedent to Occupy Wall Street. *Social Movement Studies* 11(3–4), 309–19.

Castells, Manuel (2013) *Communication Power*. Oxford University Press, Oxford.

Chalcraft, John (2011) Labour protest and hegemony in Egypt and the Arab Peninsula. In Motta, Sara C. and Nilsen, Alf G. (eds.) *Social Movements in the Global South*. Palgrave, London, pp. 35–58.

Chomsky, Noam (2012) *Occupy*. Penguin, London.

Clemens, Elisabeth S. (1996) Organizational form as frame: collective identity and political strategy in the American Labor Movement. In McAdam, Doug, McCarthy, John and Zald, Mayer N. (eds.) *Comparative Perspectives on Social Movements: Political Opportunities, Mobilizing Structures, and Cultural Framing*. Cambridge University Press, Cambridge/New York, pp. 205–25.

Cohen, Joshua (1989) Deliberation and democratic legitimacy. In Hamlin, Alan and Pettit, Philip (eds.) *The Good Polity: Normative Analysis of the State*. Basil Blackwell, Oxford, pp. 17–34.

Collier, Ruth Berins and Collier, David (2002) *Shaping the Political Arena: Critical Junctures, the Labour Movement and Regime Dynamics in Latin America*. University of Notre Dame Press, Notre Dame, IN.

Coote, Anna and Shaheen, Faiza (2013) Social justice, deficit reduction and diminishing social rights: lessons from the UK's 'Big Society'. *Redefining and Combating Poverty: Trends in Social Cohesion* 25, 243–64.

Corrigal-Brown, Catherine (2013) Participation in social movements. In Snow, David, della Porta, Donatella, Klandermans, Bert and McAdam, Doug (eds.) *Blackwell Encyclopedia on Social and Political Movements*. Blackwell, Oxford, pp. 900–5

Council of Europe (2013) *Living in Dignity in the 21st Century. Poverty and Inequality in Societies of Human Rights: The Paradox of Democracy*. Council of Union, Strasbourg.

Crossley, Nick (2002) *Making Sense of Social Movements.* Open University Press, Buckingham.

Crouch, Colin (2004) *Post-democracy.* Polity, Oxford.

– (2010) Democracy and the economy. In Pizzorno, Alessandro (ed.) *La democrazia di fronte allo stato democratico.* Feltrinelli, Milan, pp. 181–92.

– (2012) *The Strange Non-Death of Neoliberalism.* Polity, Oxford.

Dabashi, Hamid (2012) *The Arab Spring: The End of Postcolonialism.* Zed Books, London.

Dahl, Robert A. (2000) *On Democracy.* Yale University Press, New Haven.

Dalton, Russell J. (2004) *Democratic Challenges, Democratic Choices: the Erosion of Political Support in Advanced Industrial Democracies.* Oxford University Press, Oxford.

Damen, Marie-Louise (2013) Political alignments and cleavages. In Snow, David, della Porta, Donatella, Klandermans, Bert and McAdam, Doug (eds.) *Blackwell Encyclopedia on Social and Political Movements.* Blackwell, Oxford, pp. 943–46.

della Porta, Donatella (1995) *Social Movements, Political Violence and the State.* Cambridge University Press, Cambridge/New York.

– (2003) Social movements and democracy at the turn of the millennium. In Ibarra, Pedro (ed.) *Social Movements and Democracy.* Palgrave Macmillan, New York, pp. 105–36.

– (2005) Multiple belongings, tolerant identities, and the construction of 'another politics': between the European Social Forum and the Local Social Fora. In della Porta, Donatella and Tarrow, Sidney (eds.) *Transnational Protest and Global Activism.* Rowman and Littlefield, Lanham, MD, pp. 175–202.

– (ed.) (2007) *The Global Justice Movement in Cross-National and Transnational Perspective.* Paradigm, Boulder, CO.

– (2008) Eventful protests, global conflicts. *Distinktion. Scandinavian Journal of Social Theory* 17, 27–56.

– (ed.) (2009a) *Democracy in Social Movements.* Palgrave, London.

– (ed.) (2009b) *Another Europe.* Routledge, London.

– (2009c) Another Europe: an introduction. In della Porta, Donatella (ed.) *Another Europe.* London, Routledge, pp. 3–25.

– (2009d) Another Europe: some conclusions. In della Porta, Donatella (ed.) *Another Europe.* London, Routledge, pp. 225–38.

– (2009e) Global Justice Movement organizations: the organizational population. In della Porta, Donatella (ed.) *Democracy in Movements.* Palgrave, London, pp. 16–43.

– (2009f) *I partiti politici,* 3rd edn. Il Mulino, Bologna.

– (2011) Communications in movements: social movement as agents of participatory democracy. *Information, Communication and Society* 14(6), 800–19.

– (2013a) *Can Democracy be Saved?.* Polity, Cambridge.

– (2013b) *Immoral Neoliberalism and Moral Protest.* Keynote Opening Speech at the Annual Conference of the Consejo Generale del Trabajo Social, Malaga, November.

- (2013c) *Bringing capitalism back in? Antiausterity protests in the crisis of late neoliberalism*, paper presented at the ECPR general conference, Bordeaux, September.
- (2013d) *Lo llaman democracia y no lo es. Antiausterity Protests in the Legitimacy Crisis of Late Neoliberalism*. Keynote opening speech at the annual conference of the Spanish Political Science Association, Seville, September.
- (2013e) *Clandestine Political Violence*. Cambridge University Press, Cambridge.
- (2014a) *Mobilizing for Democracy*. Oxford University Press, Oxford.
- (2014b) Democracy is not a spectator sport! Which democracy in the anti-austerity movements. Keynote speech at the Finnish Sociological Association. Rovaniemi, March.
della Porta, Donatella and Andretta, Massimiliano (2013) Protesting for justice and democracy. *Contemporary Italian Politics* 5(1), 23–37.
della Porta, Donatella and Caiani, Manuela (2009) *Europeanization and Social Movements*. Oxford University Press, Oxford.
della Porta, Donatella and Diani, Mario (2006) *Social Movements: An Introduction*. Blackwell, Oxford.
della Porta, Donatella and Giugni, Marco (2009) Democracy from below: activists and institutions. In della Porta, Donatella (ed.) *Another Europe*. Routledge, London, pp. 86–109.
della Porta, Donatella and Mattoni, Alice (2013) *Civil Society Actors Fighting Against Political Corruption in Italy. A Pilot Study on 'Senza la Corruzione … Riparte il Futuro'*, paper presented at the ECPR general conference, Bordeaux, September.
- (eds.) (2014) *Spreading Protest. Social Movements in Times of Crisis*. ECPR Press, Colchester.
della Porta, Donatella and Mosca, Lorenzo (2007) In movimento: 'contamination' in action and the Italian Global Justice Movement. *Global Networks: A journal of transnational affairs* 7(1), 1–28.
- (2009) Searching the net: websites' qualities in the Global Justice Movement. *Information, Communication and Society* 12, 771–192.
della Porta, Donatella and Reiter, Herbert (2012a) Desperately seeking politics. *Mobilization: An International Quarterly* 17(3), 349–61.
- (2012b) Interactive diffusion: the coevolution of police and protest behaviour with an application to transnational contention. *Comparative Political Studies* 45(1), 119–52.
della Porta, Donatella and Rucht, Dieter (1996) Left-libertarian movements in context: comparing Italy and West Germany (1965–1990). In J. Craig Jenkins and Bert Klandermans (eds), *The Politics of Social Protest: Comparative Perspectives on States and Social Movements*. University of Minnesota Press, Minneapolis, pp. 229–72.
- eds. (2013) *Meeting Democracy*. Cambridge University Press, Cambridge.
della Porta, Donatella and Tarrow, Sidney (2012) Interactive diffusion: the coevolution of police and protest behavior with an application to tansnational contention. *Comparative Political Studies* 20, 1–34.

della Porta, Donatella, Andretta, Massimiliano, Mosca, Lorenzo and Reiter, Herbert (2006) *Globalization from Below*. University of Minnesota Press, Minneapolis.

della Porta, Donatella, Andretta, Massimiliano and Bosi, Lorenzo (2013) Critical trust and protest: analysing marches' participant in seven countries. Paper presented at the ECPR General Conference, Bordeaux. September.

della Porta, Donatella, Mosca, Lorenzo and Parks, Louisa (2014) Subaltern politics in Italy. In Kaldor, Mary (ed.) *Subaltern Politics*, forthcoming.

Diani, Mario (1992) The concept of social movement. *The Sociological Review* 40, 1–25.

– (1995) *Green Networks: A Structural Analysis of the Italian Environmental Movement*. Edinburgh University Press, Edinburgh.

– (2005) Cities in the world: local civil society and global issues in Britain. In della Porta, Donatella and Tarrow, Sidney (eds.) *Transnational Protest and Global Activism*. Rowman and Littlefield, Lanham, MD, pp. 45–67.

Donker, Teije H. (2012) *Tunisia amid Surprise, Change and Continuity* http:// cosmos.eui.eu/Documents/Publications/WorkingPapers/2012WP12COSMOS .pdf

Dore, Ronald (2000) *Stock Market Capitalism, Welfare Capitalism: Japan and Germany versus the Anglo-Saxons*. Oxford University Press, New York/ Oxford.

Dryzek, John S. (2000) *Deliberative Democracy and Beyond*. Oxford University Press, New York.

Eder, Klays (2013) Social Class and Social Movements. In Snow, David, della Porta, Donatella, Klandermans, Bert and McAdam, Doug (eds.) *Blackwell Encyclopedia on Social and Political Movements*. Blackwell, Oxford, pp. 1179–82.

Einwohner, Rachel (2013) Identity Work Process. In Snow, David, della Porta, Donatella, Klandermans, Bert and McAdam, Doug (eds.) *Blackwell Encyclopedia on Social and Political Movements*. Blackwell, Oxford, pp. 584–86.

Eisinger, Peter K. (1973) The conditions of protest behavior in American Cities. *American Political Science Review* 67, 11–28.

El Chazli, Youssef (2012) Sur les sentiers de la revolution. *Revue française de science politique* 62(5), 843–65.

El-Ghobashy, Mona (2011) The praxis of the Egyptian revolution. *Middle East Report* 258, 2–13.

– (2012) The praxis of the Egyptian revolution. In Sowers, Jeannie and Toensing, Chris (eds.) *The Journey to Tahrir: Revolution, Protest, and Social Change in Egypt*. Verso, London, pp. 21–40.

Eliasoph, Nina (1998) *Avoiding Politics: How Americans Produce Apathy in Everyday Life*. Cambridge University Press, New York.

Elster, Jon (1998) Deliberation and Constitution Making. In Elster, Jon (ed.) *Deliberative Democracy*. Cambridge University Press, Cambridge, pp. 97–122.

Epstein, Barbara (2000) Not your parents' protest. *Dissent* 47(2), 8–11.

Eurobarometer (2013) *Standard Eurobarometer*. No. 80, Autumn.

Fattori, Tommaso (2013) Commons, social justice and environmental justice. *Redefining and Combating Poverty: Trends in social cohesion* 25, 325–62.

Fillieule, Olivier (2013a) Age and social movements. In Snow, David, della Porta, Donatella, Klandermans, Bert and McAdam, Doug (eds.) *Blackwell Encyclopedia on Social and Political Movements*. Blackwell, Oxford, pp. 12–5.

– (2013b) Political socialization and social movements. In Snow, David, della Porta, Donatella, Klandermans, Bert and McAdam, Doug (eds.) *Blackwell Encyclopedia on Social and Political Movements*. Blackwell, Oxford, pp. 968–74.

Fillieule, Olivier and Blanchard, Philippe (2006) Individual surveys in rallies (INSURA). A new eldorado for comparative social movement research? Paper presented at the conference on Crossing borders: on the road towards transnational social movement analysis, WZB Berlin, 5–7 October.

Fillieule, Olivier, Blanchard, Philippe, Agrikoliansky, Eric, Bandler, M., Passy, Florence and Sommier, Isabelle (2004) L'Altermondialisme en réseaux: trajectoires militantes, multipositionnalité et formes de l'engagement: les participants du contre-sommet du G8 d'Evian (2003). *Politix* 5, 13–48.

Flesher Fominaya, Cristina (2014) *Social Movements and Globalization. How Protests, Occupations and Uprisings are Changing the World*. Palgrave Mcmillan, London.

Fonts, Joan, della Porta, Donatella and Sintomer, Yves (2014) *Participatory Democracy in Southern Europe*. Rowman and Littlefield, London.

Gallino, Luciano (2007) *Il lavoro non è una merce. Contro la flessibilità*. Laterza, Roma.

Gamson, William (2013) Injustice frames. In Snow, David, della Porta, Donatella, Klandermans, Bert and McAdam, Doug (eds.) *Blackwell Encyclopedia on Social and Political Movements*. Blackwell, Oxford, pp. 607–8.

Gamson, William, Fireman, Bruce and Rytina, Steven (1982) *Encounters with Unjust Authority*. Homewood Ill.: Dorsey Press.

Gerbaudo, Paolo (2012) *Tweet and the Street*. Pluto Press, London.

Gerds, Johannes (2013) The European Convention of human rights. *Redefining and Combating Poverty: Trends in social cohesion* 25, 151–73.

Gitlin, Todd (2012) *Occupy Nations: the Roots, the Spirit, and the Promise of Occupy Wall Street*. HarperCollins Publishers, London.

Giugni, Marco (2013) Biographical consequences. In Snow, David, della Porta, Donatella, Klandermans, Bert and McAdam, Doug (eds.) *Blackwell Encyclopedia on Social and Political Movements*. Blackwell, Oxford, pp. 138–44.

Goldstone, Jack (2011) Cross-class coalition and the making of the Arab revolt of 2011. *Swiss Political Science Review* 17, 457–62.

Goldstone, Jack and Tilly, Charles (2001) Threat (and opportunity): popular action and state responses in dynamics of contentious action. In Aminzade, Ronald et al. (eds.) *Silences and Voices in the Study of Contentious Politics*. Cambridge University Press, Cambridge, pp. 179–94.

Goodwin, Jeff, Jasper, James M. and Polletta, Francesca (eds.) (2001) *Passionate Politics. Emotions and Social Movements*. University of Chicago Press, Chicago.

Graeber, David (2012) *The Democracy Project: A History, a Crisis, a Movement*. Allen Lane, London.

Graefe, Peter (2004) Personal services in the post-industrial economy: adding nonprofits to the welfare mix. *Social, Policy and Administration* 38, 456–69.

Gramsci, Antonio (1955) *Note su Machiavelli, sulla politica e sullo stato moderno*. Einaudi, Torino.

Guibal, Claude and Tangi, Salaun (2011) *L'Egypt de Tahrir: Anatomie d'une Revolution*. Seuil, Paris.

Habermas, Jürgen (1976) *Legitimation Crisis*. Polity, Oxford.

– (1981) *Theorie des kommunikativen Handelns*. Suhrkamp, Frankfurt am Main.

– (1987) *The Theory of Communicative Action*. Polity Press, Cambridge.

– (1996) *Between Facts and Norms: Contribution to a Discursive Theory of Law and Democracy*. MIT Press, Cambridge.

Hall, Peter and Soskice, David (eds.) (2001) *Varieties of Capitalism*. Oxford University Press, Oxford.

Halvorsen, Sam (2012) Beyond the network? Occupy London and the Global Movement. *Social Movement Studies* 11(3–4), 427–33.

Hardt, Michael and Negri, Antonio (2000) *Empire*. Harvard University Press, Cambridge MA.

– (2009) *Commonwealth*. Harvard University Press, Cambridge MA.

Haug, Christoph, Haeringer, Nicolas and Mosca, Lorenzo (2009) The ESF organizing process in a diachronic perspective. In della Porta, Donatella (ed.) *Another Europe*. Routledge, London, pp. 26–45.

Hetland, Gabriel and Goodwin, Jeff (2013) The strange disappearance of capitalism from social movement studies. In Barker, Colin, Cox, Laurence, Krinsky, John and Nilsen, Alf Gunvald (eds.) *Marxism and Social Movements*. Brill, Leiden, pp. 83–102.

Holloway, John (2010) *Crack Capitalism*. Pluto Press, London.

Holmes, Amy Austin (2012) There are weeks when decades happen: Structure and strategy in the Egyptian revolution. *Mobilization* 17, 391–410.

Hosoki, Ralph I. (2013) Demography and social movements and revolutions. In Snow, David, della Porta, Donatella, Klandermans, Bert and McAdam, Doug (eds.) *Blackwell Encyclopedia on Social and Political Movements*. Blackwell, Oxford, pp. 344–47.

Hutter, Swen (2012) Congruence, counterweight, or different logics? Comparing electoral and protest politics. In Kriesi, Hanspeter, Grange, Edgard, Dolezal, Martin, Helbling, Marc, Hoglinger, Dominque, Hutter, Swen and Wuest, Bruno *Political Conflict in Western Europe*. Cambridge University Press, Cambridge, pp. 182–204.

– (2014) *Protesting Culture and Economics in Western Europe: New Cleavages in Left and Right Politics*. University of Minnesota Press, Minneapolis.

Ibase (Brazilian Institute of Social and Economic Analyses) (2006) *Study of participants at the 2005 WSF*. Online, available at: www.ibase.org.br/userimages/relatorio_fsm2005_INGLES2.pdf

Idle, Nadia and Nunns, Alex (eds.) (2011) *Tweets from Tahrir: Egypt's Revolution as it Unfolded, in the Words of the People Who Made It*. OR Books, New York.

Iglesias, Oscar (2012) *Retos de la democracia*. Paper presented at the XII Foro sobre tendencias sociales, Madrid, March.

Inglehart, Ronald (1977) *The Silent Revolution. Changing Values and Political Styles among Western Publics*. Princeton University Press, Princeton.

Institute for Research on World-Systems (2006) Alliances and divisions within the 'Movements of Movements'. University of Riverside, paper irow 29.

Jasper, James M. (1997) *The Art of Moral Protest: Culture, Biography and Creativity in Social Movements*. University of Chicago Press, Chicago.

– (2006) *Getting Your Way. Strategic Dilemmas in the Real World*. University of Chicago Press, Chicago.

Juliusson, Arni D. and Helgason, Magnus S. (2013) The roots of the saucepan devolution in Iceland. In Flesher, Christina and Cox, Laurence (eds.) *Understanding European Movements*. Routledge, London, pp. 189–202.

Juris, Jeffrey S. (2004) Networked social movements: the network society. In Castells, Manuel (ed.) *The Network Society*. Edward Elgar, London, pp. 341–62.

– (2005a) Social forums and their margins: networking logics and the cultural politics of autonomous space. *Ephemera* 5(2), 253–72.

– (2005b) The new digital media and activist networking within anti-corporate globalization movements. *The Annals of the American Academy of Political and Social Sciences* 597, 189–208.

– (2012) Reflections on #Occupy Everywhere: social media, public spaces, and emerging logics of aggregation. *American Ethnologist*, 39(2), 259–79.

Juris, Jeffrey S., Ronayne, Michelle, Shokooh-Valle, Firuzeh and Wengronowitz, Robert (2012) Negotiating power and difference within the 99%. *Social Movement Studies* 11(3–4), 434–40.

Kerbo, Harold R. (1982) Movements of 'crisis' and movements of 'affluence': a critique of deprivation and resource mobilization theory. *Journal of Conflict Resolution* 26, 645–63.

Kerton, Sarah (2012) Tahrir, here? The influence of the Arab uprisings on the emergence of Occupy. *Social Movement Studies* 11(3–4), 302–8.

Khamis, Sahar and Vaughn, Katherine (2011) Cyberactivism in the Egyptian revolution: how civic engagement and citizen journalism tilted the balance. *Arab Media and Society* 14. Available at http://www.arabmediasociety.com/index.php?article=769&printarticle

Khosrokhavar, Farhad (2012) *The New Arab Revolutions that Shook the World*. Paradigm Publishers, Boulder, CO.

Klandermans, Bert (2013a) Frustration-aggression. In Snow, David, della Porta, Donatella, Klandermans, Bert and McAdam, Doug (eds.) *Blackwell Encyclopedia on Social and Political Movements*. Blackwell, Oxford, pp. 493–4.

– (2013b) The dynamics of demand. In van Stekelenburg, Jacquelien, Roggeband, Conny and Klandermans, Bert (eds.) *The Future of Social Movement Research. Dynamics, Mechanisms, and Processes.* University of Minnesota Press, Minneapolis, pp. 3–16.

Klandermans, Bert, Kriesi, Hanspeter and Tarrow, Sidney (eds.) (1988) *From Structure to Action: Comparing Social Movement Research Across Cultures. Vol.1 (International Social Movement Research).* JAI Press, Greenwich, CT, pp. 1–38.

Kluever, Heike (2013) *Lobbying in the European Union: Interest groups, lobbying coalitions, and policy change.* Oxford University Press, Oxford.

Kousis, Maria and Tilly, Charles (2005) Introduction. In Kousis, Maria and Tilly, Charles (eds.) *Economic and Political Contention in Comparative Perspective.* Paradigm Publishers, Boulder.

Kriesi, Hanspeter (1993) *Political Mobilization and Social Change: the Dutch Case in Comparative Perspective.* Avebury, Aldershot.

– (1996) The organizational structure of new social movements in a political context. In McAdam, Doug, McCarthy, John D. and Zald, Mayer N. (eds.) *Comparative Perspective on Social Movements. Political Opportunities, Mobilizing Structures, and Cultural Framing.* Cambridge University Press, Cambridge/New York, pp. 152–84.

– (1998) The transformation of cleavage politics. *European Journal of Political Research,* 33, 165–85.

Kriesi, Hanspeter, Koopmans, Ruud, Duyvendak, Jan-Willem and Giugni, Marco (1995) *New Social Movements in Western Europe.* University of Minnesota Press/UCL Press, Minneapolis/London.

Kriesi, Hanspeter, Grange, Edgard, Lachat, Romain, Dolezal, Martin, Bornschier, Simon and Frey, Timotheos (2008) *West European Politics in the Age of Globalization.* Cambridge University Press, Cambridge.

Kriesi, Hanspeter, Grange, Edgard, Dolezal, Martin, Helbling, Marc, Hoglinger, Dominique, Hutter, Swen and Wuest, Bruno (2012) *Political Conflict in Western Europe.* Cambridge University Press, Cambridge.

Laclau, Ernesto (2005) *On Populist Reason.* Verso, London.

Langman, Lauren (2013) Occupy: a new, new social movement. *Current Sociology,* first published on 17 April.

Leach, Darcy K. (2013) Prefigurative politics. In Snow, David, della Porta, Donatella, Klandermans, Bert and McAdam, Doug (eds.) *Blackwell Encyclopedia on Social and Political Movements.* Blackwell, Oxford, pp. 1004–6.

Liboiron, Max (2012) Tactics of waste, dirt and discard in the Occupy Movement. *Social Movement Studies* 11(3–4) 393–401.

Lipset, Seymour M. and Rokkan, Stein (eds.) (1967) *Party Systems and Voter Alignments: Cross-National Perspectives.* Free Press, New York/London.

Llera, Francisco (2012) *Crisis y Malestar Democratico en España.* Paper presented at the XII Foro sobre tendencias sociales, Madrid, March.

Lotan, Gilad, Graeff, Erhardt, Ananny, Mike, Gaffney, Devin, Pearce, Ian and Boyd, Danah (2011) Information flows during the 2011 Tunisian and Egyptian revolutions. *International Journal of Communication* 5, 1375–405.

Mackell, Austin (2012) Weaving Revolution. *Interface: a journal for and about social movements* 4(1), 17–32.

Mair, Peter (2009) *Representative versus Responsible Government.* MPIfG Working Paper 09/8, Cologne.

Marks, Gary (1989) *Union in Politics. Britain, Germany and the United States in the Nineteenth and Early Twentieth Century.* Princeton University Press, Princeton.

Mattoni, Alice (2012) *Media Practice and Protest Politics. How Precarious Workers Mobilize.* Ashgate, Farnham.

McAdam, Doug, Tarrow, Sidney and Tilly, Charles (2001) *Dynamics of Contention.* Cambridge University Press, Cambridge.

McGarry, Aidan and Jasper, James (eds.) (2014) *The Identity Dilemma: Social Movements and Collective Identity.* University of Chicago Press, Chicago.

McRae, Donald (1970) Populism as an ideology. In Ionescu, Ghita and Gellner, Ernest (eds.) *Populism. The Meanings and National Characteristics.* Weidenfeld and Nicolson, London, pp. 153–65.

Melucci, Alberto (1989) *Nomads of the Present.* Hutchinson Radius, London.

– (1996) *Challenging Codes.* Cambridge University Press, Cambridge/New York.

Mersal, Iman (2011) Revolutionary humor. *Globalizations* 8(5), 669–74.

Meltzner, Allan H. (2012) *Why Capitalism?* Oxford University Press, Oxford.

Motta, Sara C. and Nilsen, Alf G. (2011) Social movements and/in the postcolonial: dispossession, development and resistance in the global south. In Motta, Sara C. and Nilsen, Alf G. (eds.) *Social Movements in the Global South.* Palgrave, London, pp. 1–33.

Nez, Héloïse (2011a) No es un botellón, es la revolución! Le mouvement des Indignés à Puerta del Sol, Madrid. *Mouvements.* Available at: http://www.mouvements.info/No-es-unbotellon-es-la-revolucion.html

– (2011b) Le mouvement des Indignés s'ancre dans les quartiers de Madrid. *Métropolitiques.* Available at: http://www.metropolitiques.eu/Le-mouvementdes-indignes-s-ancre.html

– (2012) Délibérer au sein d'un mouvement social: ethnographie des assemblées des Indignés à Madrid. *Participations* 3, 79–101.

Newton, Kenneth (2007) Social and political trust. In Dalton, Russell J. and Klingemann, Hans-Dieter (eds.) *Oxford Handbook of Political Behaviour.* Oxford University Press, Oxford, pp. 342–61.

Nigam, Aditya (2012) The Arab upsurge and the 'viral' revolutions of our times. *Interface: a journal for and about social movements* 4(1), 165–77.

Norris, Pippa (2001) *Digital Divide? Civic Engagement, Information Poverty and the Internet Worldwide.* Cambridge University Press, New York.

Offe, Claus (1985) New Social Movements: Changing Boundaries of the Political. *Social Research* 52, 817–68.

Offe, Claus and Wiesenthal, Helmut (1980) Two logics of collective action: theoretical notes on social class and organizational form. *Political Power and Social Theory* 1, 67–115.

Oikonomakis, Leonidas and Roos, Jerome E. (2013) Que no nos representan: the crisis of representation and the resonance of the Real Democracy Movement from the Indignados to Occupy. Paper presented at the conference 'Street

Politics in the Age of Austerity: From the Indignados to Occupy' of the University of Montreal, Canada, February.

Osa, Maryjane, and Corduneanu-Huci, Cristina (2003) Running Uphill: Political Opportunity in Non-Democracies, *Comparative Sociology* 2: 606–29.

Osterweil, Michal (2004) A cultural-political approach to reinventing the political. *International Social Science Journal* 56(182), 495–506.

Pateman, Carole (1970) *Participation and Democratic Theory*. Cambridge University Press, Cambridge.

Perugorría, Ignacia and Tejerina, Benjamín (2013) Politics of the encounter: cognition, emotions, and networks in the Spanish 15M. *Current Sociology*, first published on 17 April.

Pestaña Moreno, José Luis (2013) Vie et mort des assemblées. *La vie des idées*. Available at: http://www.laviedesidees.fr/Vie-et-mort-des-assemblees.html

Pianta, Mario (2012) *Nove su Dieci*. Laterza, Roma.

Piore, Michael J. and Sabel, Charles F. (1984) *The Second Industrial Divide: Possibilities for Prosperity*. Basic Books, New York.

Pizzorno, Alessandro (ed.) (1993) *Le Radici della Politica Assoluta e Altri Saggi*. Feltrinelli, Milan.

Pleyers, Geoffrey (2005) The social forums as an ideal model of convergence. *International Journal of the Social Sciences* 182, 507–19.

– (2007) *Forums Sociaux Mondiaux et défis de l'altermondialisme: De Porto Alegre à Nairobi*. Bruylant-Academia, Louvain-La-Neuve.

Pleyers, Geoffrey and Glasius, Marlies (2013) The global moment of 2011: democracy, social justice and dignity. *Development and Change* 44, 547–67.

Polanyi, Karl (1957) (orig. 1944) *The Great Transformation: The Political and Economic Origins of Our Time*. Beacon Press, London.

Polletta, Francesca (2002) *Freedom is an Endless Meeting: Democracy in American Social Movements*. University of Chicago Press, Chicago.

– (2013) Participatory democracy in social movements. In Snow, David, della Porta, Donatella, Klandermans, Bert and McAdam, Doug (eds.) *Blackwell Encyclopedia on Social and Political Movements*. Blackwell, Oxford, pp. 907–10.

Polletta, Francesca, Chen, Pang Chin Bobby, Gardner, Beth Gharrity and Motes, Alice (2013) Is the internet creating new reasons to protest? In van Stekelenburg, Jacquelien, Roggeband, Conny and Klandermans, Bert (eds.) *The Future of Social Movement Research. Dynamics, Mechanisms, and Processes*. University of Minnesota Press, Minneapolis, pp. 17–36.

Postill, John (2012) New protest movements and viral media. *Media/anthropology*, 26 March.

Pugliese, Joseph (2013) Permanent revolution: Mohamed Bouazizi's incendiary ethics of revolt. *Law, Culture and the Humanities* (12 June), 1–13.

Putnam, Robert D. (2000) *Bowling Alone*. Princeton University Press, Princeton.

Razsa, Maple and Kurnik, Andrej (2012) The Occupy Movement in Žižek's hometown: direct democracy and a politics of becoming. *American Ethnologist* 39(2), 238–58.

Regini, Marino (2014) Models of capitalism and the crisis. *Stato e Mercato* 100, 21–44.

Ritter, Daniel (2014) Comparative historical analysis. In della Porta, Donatella (ed.) *Methodological Practices in Social Movements Research*. Oxford University Press, Oxford, forthcoming.

Roberts, Kenneth (2008) The mobilization of opposition to economic liberalization. *Annual Review of Political Science* 11, 327–49.

– (2014) Populism and Social Movements. In della Porta, Donatella and Diani, Mario (eds). *Oxford Handbook on Social Movements*. Oxford: Oxford University Press.

Rochon, Thomas R. (1998) *Culture Moves. Ideas, Activism, and Changing Values*. Princeton University Press, Princeton, NJ.

Roggeband, Conny and Duyvendak, Jan Willem (2013) The changing supply side of mobilization: questions for discussion. In van Stekelenburg, Jacquelien, Roggeband, Conny and Klandermans, Bert (eds.) *The Future of Social Movement Research. Dynamics, Mechanisms, and Processes*. University of Minnesota Press, Minneapolis, pp. 95–106.

Rokkan, Stein (1999) *State Formation, Nation Building and Mass Politics in Europe*. Oxford University Press, Oxford.

Romanos, Eduardo (2011) Les indignés et la démocratie des mouvements sociaux. *La Vie des idées*. Available at: http://www.laviedesidees.fr/La-democratie-directe-de-la-Puerta.html

Roos, Jerome and Oikonomakis, Leonidas (2014) They don't represent us! The global resonance of the Real Democracy Movement from Indignados to Occupy. In della Porta, Donatella and Mattoni, Alice (eds.) *Looking for the Transnational Dimension of Protest from the Arab Spring to Occupy Wall Street*, ECPR Press, forthcoming.

Rosanvallon, Pierre (2006) *La contre-démocratie. La politique a l'age de la defiance*. Seuil, Paris.

Rosenau, James (1998) Governance and democracy in a globalizing world. In Archibugi, Daniele, Held, David and Kohler, Martin (eds.) *Re-imagining Political Community: Studies in Cosmopolitan Democracy*. Polity Press, Cambridge, pp. 28–57.

Rosenthal, Naomi and Schwartz, Michael (1989) Spontaneity and Democracy in Social Movements. In Klandermans, Bert (ed.) *Organizing for Change*. University of Minnesota Press, Minneapolis, pp. 33–60.

Rossi, Federico (2013) Picketeros. In Snow, David, della Porta, Donatella, Klandermans, Bert and McAdam, Doug (eds.) *Blackwell Encyclopedia on Social and Political Movements*. Blackwell, Oxford.

Ruedig, Wolfgang and Karyotis, Georgios (2013) Who protests in Greece? Mass opposition to austerity. *British Journal of Political Science*, firstview, 1–27.

Rueschemeyer, Dietrich, Huber Stephens, Evelyne and Stephens, John D. (1992) *Capitalist Development and Democracy*. University of Chicago Press, Chicago.

Sampedro Blanco, Víctor F. and Sánchez Duarte, José M. (2011) La red era la plaza. Available at: www.ciberdemocracia.es/articulos/RedPlaza.pdf

Saraceno, Chiara (2005) Le differenze che contano tra i lavoratori atipici. *Sociologia del lavoro* 97(1), 15–24.

Sassen, Saskia (2006) *Territory, Authority, Rights: From Medieval to Global Assemblage*. Princeton University Press, Princeton.

Savage, Michael (1987) *The Dynamics of Working Class Politics: the Labour Movement in Preston 1880–1940*. Cambridge University Press, Cambridge.

Schaeffer, Robert K. and Weyer, L. Frank (2013) World system and social movements. In Snow, David, della Porta, Donatella, Klandermans, Bert and McAdam, Doug (eds.) *Blackwell Encyclopedia on Social and Political Movements*. Blackwell, Oxford, pp. 1414–17.

Scharpf, Fritz (2011) *Monetary Union, Fiscal Crisis and Pre-emption of Democracy*, ZSE 2, 163–198.

Schoenleitner, Guenther (2003) World Social Forum: making another world possible? In Clark, John (eds.) *Globalizing Civic Engagement. Civil Society and Transnational Action*. Earthscan Publications Ltd., London, pp. 127–49.

Schumpeter, Joseph A. (1976) *Capitalism, Socialism and Democracy*. George Allen and Unwin, London.

Seoane, José and Taddei, Emilio (2002) From Seattle to Porto Alegre: the anti-neoliberal globalization movement. *Current Sociology* 50(1), 99–122.

Sergi, Vittorio and Vogiatzoglou, Markos (2013) Think globally, act locally? Symbolic memory and global repertoires in the Tunisian uprising and the Greek anti-austerity mobilization. In Cox, Laurence and Flesher, Cristina (eds.) *Understanding European Movements*. Routledge, Oxon, New York, pp. 220–35.

Sewell, William H. (1996) Three temporalities: toward an eventful sociology. In McDonald, Terence J. (eds.) *The Historic Turn in the Human Sciences*. University of Michigan Press, Ann Arbor, pp. 245–80.

Schneider, Cathy Lisa (1995) *Shantytown Protest in Pinochet's Chile*. Temple University Press, Philadelphia.

Shokr, Ahmad (2012) The eighteen days of Tahrir. In Sowers, Jeannie and Toensing, Chris (eds.) *The Journey to Tahrir: Revolution, Protest, and Social Change in Egypt*. Verso, London, pp. 41–6.

Silva, Eduardo (2009) *Challenging Neoliberalism in Latin America*. Cambridge University Press, Cambridge/New York.

Smith, Jackie (2004) The World Social Forum and the challenges of global democracy. *Global Networks* 4(4), 413–21.

Smith, Jackie and Wiest, Dawn (2012) *Social movements in the world-system*. Russell Sage Foundation, New York.

Smith, Jackie et al. (2007) *Global Democracy and the World Social Forum*. Paradigm, Boulder CO.

Snow, David (2013a) Grievances, individual and mobilizing. In Snow, David, della Porta, Donatella, Klandermans, Bert and McAdam, Doug (eds.) *Blackwell Encyclopedia on Social and Political Movements*. Blackwell, Oxford, pp. 540–2.

– (2013b) Identity dilemmas, discursive fields, identity work and mobilization: clarifying the identity-movement nexus. In van Stekelenburg, Jacquelien, Roggeband, Conny and Klandermans, Bert (eds.) *The Future of Social Movement Research. Dynamics, Mechanisms, and Processes*. University of Minnesota Press, Minneapolis, pp. 263–80.

Snow, David and Lessor, Roberta G. (2013) Consciousness, conscience, and social movements. In Snow, David, della Porta, Donatella, Klandermans, Bert and McAdam, Doug (eds.) *Blackwell Encyclopedia on Social and Political Movements*. Blackwell, Oxford, pp. 244–49

Snow, David, Cress, Daniel M., Downey, Liam and Jones, Andrew W. (1998) Disrupting the 'quotidian': reconceptualizing the relationship between breakdown and the emergence of collective action. *Mobilization* 3, 1–22.

Sommier, Isabelle (2005) Produire l'événement: logique de cooperation et conflict feutrés. In Sommier, Isabelle and Agrikoliansky, Eric (eds.) *Radiographie des mouvements altermondialistes en Europe*. La Dispute, Paris, pp. 19–43.

Sorge, Arndt and Streeck, Wolfgang (1988) Industrial relations and technical change: the case for an extended perspective. In Hyman, Richard and Streeck, Wolfgang (eds.) *New Technology and Industrial Relations*, Blackwell, Oxford/New York, pp. 19–47.

Sotirakopoulos, Nikos and Sotiropoulos, George (2013) Direct democracy now! The Greek *indignados* and the present cycle of struggles. *Current Sociology*, first published on 17 April.

Soule, Sarah A. (2013) Bringing organizational studies back into social movement scholarship. In van Stekelenburg, Jacquelien, Roggeband, Conny and Klandermans, Bert (eds.) *The Future of Social Movement Research. Dynamics, Mechanisms, and Processes*, University of Minnesota Press, Minneapolis, pp. 107–24.

Standing, Guy (2011) *The Precariat: the New Dangerous Class*. Bloomsbury Academic, London.

Stanley, Jason and Goodwin, Jeff (2013) Political economy and social movements. In Snow, David, della Porta, Donatella, Klandermans, Bert and McAdam, Doug (eds.) *Blackwell Encyclopedia on Social and Political Movements*. Blackwell, Oxford, pp. 946–49.

Starr, Amory, Martinez-Torres, Maria Elena and Rosset, Peter (2011). Participatory democracy in action. Practices of the Zapatistas and the Movimento Sem Terra. *Latin American Perspectives* 30(1): 102–19.

Stepan-Norris, Judith and Zeitlin, Maurice (2003) *Left out. Reds and America's Industrial Union*. Cambridge University Press, Cambridge.

Stewart, Angus (1970) The social roots. In Ionescu, Ghita and Gellner, Ernest (eds.) *Populism. The meanings and national characteristics*. Weidenfeld and Nicolson, London, pp. 180–96.

Stiglitz, Joseph E. (2008) The end of neoliberalism? *Project Syndicate*. Available at http://www.project-syndicate.org/commentary/the-end-of-neo-liberalism

– (2012a) *The Price of Inequality*. Norton and Co., New York.

– (2012b) Introduction: the world wakes. In Schiffrin, Anya and Kircher-Alle, Eamon (eds.) *From Cairo to Wall Street. Voices from the Global Spring*. The New Press, New York, pp. 1–27.

Stork, Joe (2011) Three decades of human rights activism in the Middle East and North Africa. In Benin, Joel and Vairel, Frédéric (eds.) *Social Movements, Mobilization and Contestation in the Middle East and North Africa*. Stanford University Press, Stanford, CA, pp. 83–106.

Streeck, Wolfgang (2010) E pluribus Unum? Varieties and commonalities of capitalism. MPIFG, Discussion Paper 10/12.

- (2011) The Crisis in Contest. Democratic Capitalism and Its Contradictions. MPIFG, Discussion Paper 11/15.
- (2014) Taking crisis seriously: capitalism in its way out. *Stato e Mercato*, no. 100, 45–68.

Streeck, Wolfgang and Mertens, Daniel (2011) Fiscal austerity and public investment. Is the possible the enemy of the necessary? MPIFG, Discussion Paper 11/12.

Svampa, Maristela (2005) *La sociedad excluyente. La Argentina bajo el signo del neoliberalismo*. Tauros, Buenos Aires.

Svampa, Maristella and Pereyra, Sebastiàn (2003) *Entre la ruta y el barrio. La experiencia de las organizaciones piqueteras*. Editorial Biblios, Buenos Aires.

Sztompka, Piotr (1993) *The Sociology of Social Change*. Blackwell, Oxford.

Tarrow, Sidney (1989) *Democracy and Disorder. Protest and Politics in Italy, 1965–1975*. Oxford University Press, Oxford/New York.
- (2011) *Power in Movement*. Cambridge University Press, Cambridge.
- (2012) *Strangers at the Gates. Movements and States in Contentious Politics*. Cambridge University Press, Cambridge.

Taylor, Astra et al. (eds.) (2011) *Occupy! Scenes from Occupied America*. Verso, London.

Taylor, Verta (2013) Social movement participation in global society: identity, networks and emotions. In van Stekelenburg, Jacquelien, Roggeband, Conny and Klandermans, Bert (eds.) *The Future of Social Movement Research. Dynamics, Mechanisms, and Processes*. University of Minnesota Press, Minneapolis, pp. 37–58.

Taylor, Verta and van Dyke, Nella (2004) 'Get up, stand up': tactical repertoires of social movements, In Snow, David A., Soule, Sarah H. and Kriesi, Hanspeter (eds.) *The Blackwell Companion to Social Movements*. Blackwell, Oxford, pp. 262–93.

Teivainen, Tivo (2002) The World Social Forum and global democratisation: learning from Porto Alegre. *Third World Quarterly* 23(4), 621–32.
- (2004) Twenty-two theses on the problems of democracy in the World Social Forum. *Transform!* 1 Available at http://www.transform.it/newsletter/news _transform01.html

Tejerina, Benjamín, Perugorría, Ignacia, Benski, Tova and Langman, Lauren (2013) From indignation to occupation: a new wave of global mobilization. *Current Sociology*, first published on 17 April.

Tezanos, José F. (2012) Tendencias en disegualidad y desvertebracion social y sus efectos politicos y economicos. Paper presented at the XII Foro sobre tendencias sociales, Madrid, UNED, March.

Therborn, Ghoran (2012) *Evolucion global y perspectivas de los diferentes tipos de disegualidad en el mundo*, paper presented at the XII Foro sobre tendencias sociales, Madrid, UNED, March.

Thompson, Edward P. (1971) The moral economy of the English crowds in the eighteenth century. *Past and Present* 50, 76–136.
- (1991) (orig. 1963) *The Making of the English Working Class*. Penguin Books, London.

Tilly, Charles (1978) *From Mobilization to Revolution*. Addison-Wesley, Reading, MA.

– (1984) Social movements and national politics. In Bright, Charles and Harding, Susan (eds.) *State-Making and Social Movements: Essays in History and Theory*. University of Michigan Press, Ann Arbor, pp. 297–317.

– (1986) *The Contentious French*. Harvard University Press, Cambridge MA.

– (1990) *Coercion, Capital and European States. AD 990–1992*. Oxford: Blackwell.

– (2007) *Democracy*. Cambridge University Press, New York.

Tilly, Chris and Tilly, Charles (1998) *Work Under Capitalism*. Westview Press, Boulder, Col.

Tilly, Louise A. and Tilly, Charles (eds.) (1981) *Class Conflict and Collective Action*. London: Sage.

Touraine, Alain (1977) *The Self-Production of Society*. University of Chicago Press, Chicago.

– (1981) *The Voice and the Eye. An Analysis of Social Movements*. Cambridge University Press, Cambridge.

– (1987) *The Workers' Movement*. Cambridge University Press, Cambridge/ New York.

Trevizo, Dolores (2013) Moral economy theory and peasant movements in Latin America. In Snow, David, della Porta, Donatella, Klandermans, Bert and McAdam, Doug (eds.) *Blackwell Encyclopedia on Social and Political Movements*. Blackwell, Oxford, pp. 765–70.

Tucker, Kenneth H. Jr (1996) *French Revolutionary Syndicalism and the Public Sphere*. Cambridge University Press, Cambridge.

van Gelder, Sarah and the staff of YES! magazine (2011) *This Changes Everything: Occupy Wall Street and the 99% Movement*. BK publisher, San Francisco.

van Stekelenburg, Jacquelien (2013) Collective identity. In Snow, David, della Porta, Donatella, Klandermans, Bert and McAdam, Doug (eds.) *Blackwell Encyclopedia on Social and Political Movements*. Blackwell, Oxford, pp. 219–25.

van Stekelenburg, Jacquelien and Boekkooi, Marije (2013) Mobilizing for change in changing societies. In van Stekelenburg, Jacquelien, Roggeband, Conny and Klandermans, Bert (eds.) *The Future of Social Movement Research. Dynamics, Mechanisms, and Processes*, University of Minnesota Press, Minneapolis, pp. 217–34.

van Stekelenburg, Jacquelien, van Leeuwen, Anouk and van Troos, Dunya (2013) Politicized identity. In Snow, David, della Porta, Donatella, Klandermans, Bert and McAdam, Doug (eds.) *Blackwell Encyclopedia on Social and Political Movements*. Blackwell, Oxford, pp. 974–78.

von Hayek, Friedrich A. (1967) (orig. 1950) Full employment, planning and inflation. *Studies in Philosophy, Politics and Economics*. University of Chicago Press, Chicago, pp. 270–9.

Walder, Andrew G. (2009) Political sociology and social movements. *Annual Review of Sociology* 35, 393–412.

Walgrave, Stefaan (2013) Changing mobilization of individual activists? In van Stekelenburg, Jacquelien, Roggeband, Conny and Klandermans, Bert (eds.) *The Future of Social Movement Research. Dynamics, Mechanisms, and Processes*. University of Minnesota Press, Minneapolis, pp. 205–16.

Walgrave, Stefaan, Wouters, Ruud and Ketelaars, Pauline (2012) Sources of bias in the protest survey design: evidence from fifty one protest events in seven countries. Unpublished paper presented at the CCC workshop in Gothenburg.

Wallerstein, Immanuel (1990) Antisystemic movements: history and dilemma. In Amin, Samir, Arrighi, Giovanni, Gunder Frank, Andre and Wallerstein, Immanuel (eds.) *Transforming the Revolution*. Monthly Review Press, New York.

– (2004) *Historical Capitalism with Capitalist Civilization*. Verso, London.

– (2010) Structural Crises. *New Left Review* 62, 133–42.

Walton, John K. (1998) Urban conflicts and social movements. *International Journal of Urban and Regional Research* 22, 460–81.

Walton, John K. and Seddon, David (1994) Food riots past and present. In Walton, John K. and Seddon, David (eds.) *Free Markets and Food Riots: The Politics of Global Adjustment*. Blackwell, Oxford, pp. 23–54.

Walton, John and Ragin, Charles (1990) Global and national sources of political protest: Third World responses to the debt crisis. *American Sociological Review* 55(6), 876–91.

Warkotsch, Jana (2012) Bread, freedom, human dignity: tales of an unfinished revolution in Egypt. http://cosmos.eui.eu/Documents/Publications/Working Papers/2012WP14COSMOS.pdf.

Wiles, Peter (1970) A syndrome, not a doctrine. In Ionescu, Ghita and Gellner, Ernest (eds.) *Populism. The meanings and national characteristics*. Weidenfeld and Nicolson, London, pp. 166–80.

Williams, Heather L. (2001) *Social Movements and Economic Transition: Markets and Distributive Conflict in Mexico*. Cambridge University Press, Cambridge.

Winegard, Jessica (2012) Taking out the trash: youth clean up Egypt after Mubarak. In Sowers, Jeannie and Toensing, Chris (eds.) *The Journey to Tahrir: Revolution, Protest, and Social Change in Egypt*. Verso, London, pp. 64–9.

Wood, Lesley J. (2013) Anti World Bank and IMF riots. In Snow, David, della Porta, Donatella, Klandermans, Bert and McAdam, Doug (eds.) *Blackwell Encyclopedia on Social and Political Movements*. Blackwell, Oxford, pp. 107–8.

World Social Movements (2002a) Porto Alegre 2002 – call of social movements: resistance to neoliberalism, war and militarism: for peace and social justice. August. Available online at: www.forumsocialmundial.org.br/dinamic/eng_portoalegrefinal.asp

– (2002b) Charter of Principles. Online, available at: www.forumsocialmundial.org.br/main.php?id_menu=4&cd_language=2

Yashar, Deborah J. (2005) *Contesting Citizenship in Latin America: the Rise of Indigenous Movements and the Postliberal Challenge*. Cambridge University Press, Cambridge.

Zamponi, Lorenzo (2013) Why don't Italians occupy? Hypotheses on a failed mobilization. *Social Movement Studies* 11(3–4), 416–26.

Žižek, Slavoj (2012) *The Year of Dreaming Dangerously*. Verso, London.

Index